A WRITER'S GUIDE TO MINDFUL READING

Practice and Pedagogy

Series Editor: Mike Palmquist

The Practice & Pedagogy series addresses the teaching, learning, and practice of writing in all its forms. From Joseph Williams' reflections on introductions to Richard E. Young's taxonomy of "small genres" to Adam Mackie's considerations of technology, the books in this occasional series explore issues and ideas of interest to writers and teachers of writing.

The WAC Clearinghouse, Colorado State University Open Press, and University Press of Colorado are collaborating so that these books will be widely available through free digital distribution and low-cost print editions. The publishers and the Series editor are committed to the principle that knowledge should freely circulate. We see the opportunities that new technologies have for further democratizing knowledge. And we see that to share the power of writing is to share the means for all to articulate their needs, interest, and learning into the great experiment of literacy.

Other Books in the Series

Lillian Craton, Renée Love & Sean Barnette (Eds.), *Writing Pathways to Student Success* (2017)
Charles Bazerman, *Involved: Writing for College, Writing for Your Self* (2015)
Adam Mackie, *New Literacies Dictionary: Primer for the Twenty-first Century Learner* (2011)
Patricia A. Dunn, *Learning Re-abled: The Learning Disability Controversy and Composition Studies* (2011)
Richard E. Young, *Toward A Taxonomy of "Small" Genres and Writing Techniques for Writing Across the Curriculum* (2011)
Joseph M. Williams, *Problems into PROBLEMS: A Rhetoric of Motivation* (2011)
Charles Bazerman, *The Informed Writer: Using Sources in the Disciplines* (2011)

A WRITER'S GUIDE TO MINDFUL READING

Ellen C. Carillo
University of Connecticut

The WAC Clearinghouse
wac.colostate.edu
Fort Collins, Colorado

University Press of Colorado
upcolorado.com
Louisville, Colorado

The WAC Clearinghouse, Fort Collins, Colorado 80523-1040

University Press of Colorado, Louisville, Colorado 80027

ISBN 978-1-64215-027-8 (PDF) | 978-1-64215-028-5 (ePub) | 978-1-60732-777-6 (pbk.)

Printed in the United States of America

Library of Congress Cataloging-in-Publication Data

Names: Carillo, Ellen C., author.
Title: A writer's guide to mindful reading / Ellen C. Carillo.
Description: Fort Collins, Colorado : The WAC Clearinghouse ; Boulder, Colorado : University Press of Colorado, [2017]
Identifiers: LCCN 2017039386| ISBN 9781607327776 (pbk.) | ISBN 9781607327783 (ebook)
Subjects: LCSH: Reading (Higher education) | English language—Rhetoric—Study and teaching (Higher) | Academic writing—Study and teaching (Higher) | Reading comprehension—Study and teaching (Higher) | College reading improvement programs.
Classification: LCC LB2395.3 .C36 2017 | DDC 428.40711—dc23
LC record available at https://lccn.loc.gov/2017039386

Copyeditor: Brandy Bippes
Designers: Mike Palmquist and Ashley Freeman
Cover Art: Joseph A. Gerber
Series Editor: Mike Palmquist

The WAC Clearinghouse supports teachers of writing across the disciplines. Hosted by Colorado State University, and supported by the Colorado State Univeristy Open Press, it brings together scholarly journals and book series as well as resources for teachers who use writing in their courses. This book is available in digital formats for free download at wac.colostate.edu.

Contents

Introduction

WHAT IS MINDFUL READING?

Before we get to **mindful reading**, let's answer what at first might seem like the simpler question: What is reading? Reading is something we all do every day—we read books, street signs, text messages, blogs, product labels, billboards—but have you ever stopped to think about what happens when we read? How does your brain process the marks your eyes see? How are these marks understood as letters, words, and sentences that have meaning? Research has shown that when we read, different regions and systems in the brain play different roles. Neuroscientists at Princeton University, Tanja Kassuba and Sabine Kastner, explain that the visual system and language regions of the brain work together to translate the marks we see on a page into words we can understand. Did you know that our eyes hardly move as they do all of this work? We might think that as we read our eyes move smoothly along the words as we read them, but, instead, our eyes remain largely motionless since eyes can only see when they are in this state. Between these motionless periods, our eyes move very rapidly, jumping along the lines, again with little reference to the words before us (Rayner).

Cognitive psychologists, who research the brain, have conducted various experiments to study the power of reading. For example, in his book *Such Stuff as Dreams: The Psychology of Fiction*, Keith Oatley argues that reading fiction (stories) provides such a vivid simulation of real life that the brain processes a detailed description of an experience one may find in a novel in the same way it would process the actual experience. Equally interesting is that Raymond A. Mar and his colleagues, including Oatley, conducted experiments that ultimately showed that people who read fiction are more empathetic than those who do not. Mar and his colleagues argue that this is the case because fiction offers the unique opportunity to identify with characters, something that fiction readers take with them beyond the text and into real life situations.

As these brain studies suggest, reading can be an escape into another world that often seems as real as the one around you. But not all reading is peppered with colorful characters and exciting scenes. While you may end up reading some fiction in your English classes, you will likely read a lot of textbooks in college, too. Of course, this kind of reading is not intended to send you into another world, but meant to inform you or teach you something in a more straightforward manner. Fiction and textbooks won't be the only reading you'll do in college. You may also be asked to read difficult peer-reviewed articles, dense scientific reports, business memoranda, and editorials, among other kinds of texts. You will, therefore, need to figure out how to move among all of the different types of texts you will encounter and how to adjust your approach so you can get the most out of each text.

This is where the "mindful" in "mindful reading" comes in. If you have heard the word "mindful" it may have been in a different context, perhaps in reference to meditation, yoga, or Buddhism. When you are mindful you are "in the moment." You are not distracted or focused on anything else. Being mindful is a pretty tall order when there is so much around to distract us—smartphones ringing, text messages buzzing, screens blinking. Still, practicing mindful reading by being aware of how you read can help you develop as a reader and—by extension—as a writer. Reading mindfully means paying attention not just to the content of the text—what it says—but rather to the process of reading itself by adjusting how you read based on what the piece asks of you. Skimming something—a newspaper, perhaps—may be a perfectly suitable approach in a particular situation. Skimming, however, might not be the best approach when you are expected to answer specific questions about a more complex reading or connect it to other complex readings, as you will likely have to do in your college classes.

Mindful reading acts as a framework that is intended to remind you of the importance of becoming an active reader who makes careful and deliberate decisions about the reading strategies you might use. As you mindfully read, you will be learning about reading and also about yourself as a reader. These experiences can help you become an altogether stronger reader not just in this course but beyond it.

HOW THIS BOOK ENRICHES AND EXPANDS YOUR READING ABILITY

"But," you may say, "I know how to read! I wouldn't have made it this far if I didn't." You are right—to an extent. You certainly know how to decode language in the ways reading is described in the opening to this introduction, and you can understand certain types of texts. But, in college, expectations change, including those associated with reading. You will need to work on your reading for several reasons:

1. You will be faced with more reading.
2. The types of reading you will be assigned will vary drastically depending on the discipline and the course.
3. You will be expected to read more complex texts.
4. You will be asked to complete more complex tasks associated with your reading.

These reasons suggest why it is important that you gain practice in different reading strategies. As you move through your academic career you will likely find (if you haven't already) that texts from different disciplines demand different types of reading. While you may be used to reading literature in a certain way, that reading approach might not lend itself to that dense biological research study you have been assigned to read. Or, you may find that your go-to reading strategy of highlighting with that yellow marker might not cut it when faced with a jargon-ridden historical essay meant only for expert historians or that equally (but for different reasons) difficult psychology textbook. *A Writer's Guide to Mindful Reading* seeks to prepare you for all of these reading experiences by helping you develop a repertoire or toolkit of reading strategies to which you can turn so you are prepared to effectively read a range of texts as you move through the disciplines.

Although you may be using this textbook in an English or writing course, these reading strategies are useful across disciplines. In fact, I taught one student who regularly spoke about how becoming aware of and practicing various reading approaches within the mindful reading framework helped him to understand word problems in math class (math!). In an evaluation of one of my courses, another student described his use of the "Says/Does" approach in a History course. This reading strategy, which you will learn about in Chapter 2, involves going paragraph by paragraph noticing what each paragraph says—its content—and what each does—its function. The student explains, "In American Studies, I decided to try the 'Says/Does' approach when reading the Dred Scott case proved difficult due to its word choice. Breaking it down paragraph by paragraph proved very useful. If I see another cryptic piece in further history classes, I would return to the method."

Further developing your reading abilities is important work as recent studies have shown that college students and young adults, generally, struggle in this area. A study entitled "America's Skills Challenge: Millennials and the Future," published in 2015 by Educational Testing Services (ETS) found that "one half (50%) of America's millennials," defined as those born after 1980 who were 16–34 years of age in 2012 "failed to reach level 3 in literacy" (11), which tests how well respondents "identify, interpret, or evaluate one or more pieces of information, and often require varying levels of inference" (48). In other words, it tests how well one reads. Only 50% of American millennials met this minimum benchmark, highlighting the difficulty young adults have working with "pieces of information," what we might call sources or informational texts, which make up a large part of college-level reading material. Additionally, the SAT Verbal/Critical Reading Portion, as well as the ACT test, which is also often used for admissions and placement have shown declines in students' reading abilities: "In 2015 [the date of the most recent published study], the average score on the SAT verbal test was near historic lows" (par. 3). Based on 1.9 million students who took the ACT test in 2015, 46% of students met ACT's "college ready benchmark" on the Reading section, a decline from the 51% who did so in 2006. Most recently, in late 2016, the Stanford History Education Group at Stanford University published a study entitled "Evaluating Information: The Cornerstone of Civic Online Reasoning," which reports that middle-school through college-age students are "easily duped" when "it comes to evaluating information that flows through social media channels" (4). Accurately reading, understanding, evaluating, and incorporating credible information into one's writing is, of course, an important aspect of college-level writing.

Despite these dismal statistics, and although you still have a lot to learn and practice, your previous reading experiences can be useful to your current, college-level reading assignments. Completing the following exercise will help you reflect on these earlier experiences.

Ponder This

Take a moment to think back to something that you recently chose to read, something easy that posed no problems for you—maybe a blog entry, a novel, a newspaper article. Jot down a few sentences about that experience. You probably didn't think much about how you read it at the time, why you read it, or how you read it, especially if you chose it. The reading process likely never entered your mind. Now, think about something you read recently that you found was difficult—whether because of its vocabulary, its genre (i.e. the type of text it is), or its subject. Jot down a few sentences about that experience. I bet you became more self-conscious about your reading process. You may have decided to give up altogether or you might have used some strategies to help you work through the difficulty. You may have used a dictionary to help you understand some words or maybe you followed a hyperlink to another source hoping that would offer some guidance. These strategies are helpful, and they are ones that you may already have extensive practice using. This textbook will give you additional strategies, additional ways of reading, so that you never have to give up on a text, no matter how difficult, no matter the discipline, no matter the challenges that face you.

WON'T THIS KIND OF READING TAKE LONGER?

Now that you know that this textbook will give you strategies for reading and encourage you to take time to reflect on—think about—your reading, you are probably wondering: "Won't this kind of reading take longer than just reading?" The answer is "not necessarily." Here's why: When you are reading mindfully and in the present moment, you realize immediately when you begin to zone out and you consider what you can do in that moment to refocus. You ask yourself questions about why your mind drifted. Perhaps you need a different reading strategy—one that will make the reading more relevant or comprehensible. And yes, it may take a minute to regroup, shift gears, and put another strategy into play, but you won't lose the time you would have lost had it taken you 15 minutes (and 8 pages!) to realize that you zoned out and have no idea what you just read, an experience we have all had.

At first, being mindful may seem unnatural and even tedious at times. You may wonder, "Why can't I JUST read without doing all of this extra work?" Here's why: Research shows that in order to **transfer**—or apply—what is learned in one course to another, students need to actively think about—or reflect on—what they have learned. In other words, they need to be mindful. If students simply go through the motions and complete assignments and readings without any awareness of them and their uses beyond the present class, students are not likely to draw on those earlier educational experiences when faced with similar experiences later in their academic careers and beyond. So, taking the time to reflect on what you are learning about reading and about yourself as a reader as you move through the selections in this book will save you time later since it will position you to apply all that you learn here to other courses and contexts. This reflective work will allow you to more easily see connections between the activities and assignments included in this book and those you will encounter outside of this course. Plus, the truth is that it is impossible to "just" read. Whether or not you pay close attention to the reading process, you are still unconsciously making decisions when you read. You are choosing to pay closer attention to certain parts of the text, you are slowing down in some moments, speeding up at others, maybe skipping some parts altogether. This textbook is simply asking you to become more aware of those habits and strategies; it's enriching and adding to them; and it's positioning you to consciously bring them with you to courses and contexts beyond this class.

Speaking of how this work can help you beyond your present course and even beyond school altogether, students in my classes regularly mention how what they learn about reading helps them "read" the world around them. One student explained that just as she was expected to read different viewpoints on the same topic, she now "watch[es] both NBC and Fox to get different perspectives." At first glance this example may not seem to have anything to do with reading, but the student is describing how she reads these perspectives in relation to each other, recognizing that each has its own biases. This student will not simply accept what she hears or reads, but will deliberately consider and compare that information to other ideas and perspectives she encounters. That consciousness, that awareness, is what mindful reading seeks to foster.

WHAT IS "ACADEMIC WRITING"?

So far, this book has talked a lot about reading as if forgetting that it is a "writer's" guide to mindful reading. This has probably left you wondering, "What kind of writing will we be doing?" This book engages you in what is often called academic writing. You might think about academic writing as an ongoing scholarly conversation. In fact, it has become common to use philosopher and rhetorician Kenneth Burke's description of a conversation as a metaphor for academic writing:

> Imagine that you enter a parlor. You come late. When you arrive, others have long preceded you, and they are engaged in a heated discussion, a discussion too heated for them to pause and tell you exactly what it is about. In fact, the discussion had already begun long before any of them got there, so that no one present is qualified to retrace for you all the steps that had gone before. You listen for a while, until you decide that you have caught the tenor of the argument; then you put in your oar. Someone answers; you answer him; another comes to your defense; another aligns himself against you, to either the embarrassment or gratification of your opponent, depending upon the quality of your ally's assistance. However, the discussion is interminable. The hour grows late, you must depart. And you do depart, with the discussion still vigorously in progress.

I bet if you take a few minutes you can come up with an instance in which you walked into a room—like the parlor above—to find a conversation already in progress. Maybe this happened to you at work or at lunch with friends. You arrived to see that folks were already well into a discussion. You likely didn't jump right in, but, instead, you took a minute or two to get a sense of the conversation, what they were talking about, and who was saying what. Only then—after listening and evaluating the situation—did you participate. In the "conversation" of academic writing, you will be expected to do precisely that, which you have likely already done many times in your life. You will need to "listen for a while" to what others have said about the subject until you "[catch] the tenor of the argument," to use Burke's words. Ultimately, you will have to contribute something to the discussion; you will have to "put in your oar" so to speak. But it doesn't end there. You will then need to address how others respond to your contribution and you may need to qualify or revise it. Others will likely respond again, you will do the same, and so on. In less metaphorical terms, many of the writing assignments in this book expect you to read (and understand) what others have said about a subject before you can think alongside them and write a response or develop an argument.

THE IMPORTANCE OF ANNOTATION TO ACADEMIC WRITING

Annotation, marking up a text, is a first step toward participating in academic conversations. When you annotate, you write as you read by responding to that reading in the form of notes, comments, and questions in the margins of your text. This may be done digitally or by hand. These marginal notes represent the initial ways in which you are participating in the scholarly conversation with the author of the text. Your initial contributions to the conversation can be expanded to help you develop more detailed responses in the form of longer, more formal writing assignments, which will likely demand that you qualify and revise those responses as you continue to participate in scholarly conversations. Because annotation requires that you write as you read, it might be thought of as a bridge between those two practices. In fact, research has shown that simultaneous practice in reading and writing leads to stronger abilities in both.

DIGITALLY ANNOTATING THE SELECTIONS IN THIS TEXTBOOK

You have several options for digitally annotating them, including the following:

1. You may use the Adobe Acrobat Reader, which is available for free download at https://get.adobe.com/reader. This program will allow you to highlight and add sticky notes to any of the readings printed in the textbook. You can save your documents with the notes and share them.
2. You may download an annotation management system like Diigo for free at https://www.diigo.com. The basic, free service will allow you to annotate up to 100 webpages and PDFs.
3. You may add sticky notes to any webpage with https://www.mystickies.com. You will need to sign up (it's free) and install a Chrome Browser extension.
4. You may download https://web.hypothes.is, an open-source digital annotation management system that allows you to annotate anything on the Web and share those annotations. You will need to register for an account and install a browser extension. The "Education" section of the website includes a "Quick Start Guide for Students" and other useful resources.

READING AND WRITING TO MAKE MEANING

Notice that throughout this introduction, both reading and writing are described as active, creative practices. This textbook imagines reading as an exercise in *creating* meaning, not *finding* it. Take a minute to consider the difference between the acts of creating and finding. Conceiving of reading as *finding* meaning suggests that the text holds the meaning and it is the reader's job to simply locate the meaning therein rather than take part in how the text's meaning is created. When we think about reading as an act of creation, we might imagine a reader who brings her background, previous reading experiences, culture, religion, and worldview with her to the reading. All of this contributes to how that reader creates meaning from the text. Think about it this way: If meaning was located (or hidden) in a text then each time you read that text it would mean the same thing to you. Every reading experience of the text would be exactly the same. This isn't the case, though. Have you ever read a story when you were much younger and returned to it a decade later to find that it means something different to you? The story hasn't changed; it's you who has changed! That change affects how you make or create meaning from the story. Sometimes, unfortunately, that change means that you end up disliking a book you once loved or it could mean the opposite and you end up loving a book you couldn't stand as a youngster. Neuroscientist Richard Restak explains this phenomenon as follows: "As a result of the lifetime plasticity of the brain, we're literally a different person than the person who read the book the first time." No matter the kind of feelings that the act of rereading may evoke, this very scenario—that texts mean differently to us at different times—demonstrates that the reader and the text *create meaning together*.

Along the same lines, you will likely notice that as you participate in class discussions about the reading selections in this book, your classmates may have noticed different elements than you. They may think the piece means something different. They are not wrong. The selection does mean differently to them because their reading experience has been different from yours. Because of qualities they bring to the text—their background, previous reading experiences, culture, religion, worldview, and so on—they paid attention to different aspects of the text and so came away with different understandings of it. That's not to say that anything goes when reading since the text must support all readings, but rather that meaning does not reside in the text alone.

HOW THIS BOOK IS ORGANIZED

By way of conclusion, this section provides an overview of how *A Writer's Guide to Mindful Reading* is organized. The book is divided into two parts with Chapter 5 (in Part Two) serving as a bridge between them. Part One includes the instructional apparatus: it teaches you about the reading strategies, provides writing instruction; and explains multimodal composing. Entitled "Readings on Reading," Chapter 5 is comprised of selections on the subject of reading, which will support your understanding of the very concept of reading and set you on a path toward becoming a more reflective reader. All of the readings in Chapters 6–10 address technology and its relationship to some other idea or concept (e.g. Gender and Technology) and are accompanied by questions and long writing assignments. These assignments will help you understand, respond to, and synthesize the readings, as well as apply ideas and concepts within them. Parts One and Two, however, are not totally distinct. As you are asked to complete the assignments throughout Part Two, you are directed to the chapter in Part One that can help you complete each assignment. For example, if an assignment asks you to complete a rhetorical reading, a link in that assignment provides the chapter number from Part One in which rhetorical reading is described. As you move between the two parts of this book, learning and applying the reading strategies while writing in response to the included readings, you will become that mindful reader who is prepared to engage the range of texts you will encounter as a college student and beyond. To further support your understanding of the terms and concepts associated with mindful reading, a glossary is included at the end of this textbook. Words that appear in boldface throughout this textbook are included in that glossary.

A NOTE ABOUT THE LINKS TO READINGS

In many cases rather than providing you with the full text of a reading you are provided with a link that takes you directly to the reading online. Please note that in many instances you are reading a selection on a website, such as *The New Yorker* or *Wired*, that requires a subscription after you visit a certain number of times. Keep this in mind as you are working from those readings.

A NOTE ABOUT ACCESSIBILITY

This textbook strives to be accessible to a diverse readership by offering a flexible user experience. The textbook is available in different formats, including ePub. In addition, the textbook contains a navigable table of contents, is searchable, and allows viewers to adjust the size of the text and other textual elements using the "zoom" feature while reading. As explained in Chapter 2, the "read aloud and paraphrase" reading strategy can be modified for deaf readers. Please contact the publisher with any additional questions about accessibility.

ACKNOWLEDGMENTS

A textbook project of this kind is only possible with the help of many people. Its first editor, John Sullivan, was a great supporter, and his keen eye and guidance were instrumental in the development of this book. I am grateful to Mike Palmquist, the textbook's ultimate editor, for his belief in this project and his feedback and advice throughout the development and publication processes. I would also like to thank copyeditor Brandy Bippes for taking such care with the project, and for her many insights about its design and layout. For being so generous with her time and expertise on open educational resources, I thank University of Connecticut Librarian Kathy Labadorf. Without Kathy's guidance, I would not have considered publishing a textbook in this format. I would also like to acknowledge my colleagues in First-Year Writing at UConn's Waterbury campus, including Lois Lake Church, Daniela Falco, Kelly Jarvis, and Sam Robinson, whose support is constant and whose excitement about this project has been both affirming and contagious. Also at UConn, I am grateful to Pam Bedore, Lisa Blansett, Brenda Brueggemann, Serkan Gorkemli, Oliver Hiob, and Tom Recchio who took time away from their own projects and teaching to offer guidance and encouragement. I must also thank Edward Neth in the Chemistry Department at UConn for sharing the insights gleaned from developing his own open textbook and for paving the way for other UConn professors to publish in this format.

Beyond my colleagues at UConn, I am grateful to Kirstin Collins Hanley who has been a sounding board on this project and many others, as well as a steadfast friend since graduate school. Finally, I must thank my husband David and the rest of my family for their unwavering support and valuable advice that saw me through the many challenges this project presented.

COPYRIGHT ACKNOWLEDGMENTS

I must thank the writers who have generously allowed me to reprint their excellent work in this textbook. When I first heard Stacey Waite read her poetry, we were both graduate students at the University Pittsburgh, and I was blown away. I am grateful to Stacey and Tupelo Press for granting me permission to reprint "On the Occasion of Being Mistaken for a Man by Security Personnel at Newark International Airport." I must also thank Sarah Davis for her permission to reprint "The 'Blurred Lines' Effect: Popular Music and the Perpetuation of Rape Culture," which she wrote in a research writing course in 2014 at the University of Connecticut. It is an honor to publish her essay in this textbook as it is a wonderful model of engaging, persuasive, and thoughtful writing, and I hope it will be an inspiration to other undergraduates.

I would also like to thank Carrie Stewart at NCTE for helping me secure the rights to reprint the selections in Chapter 6: Readings on Reading; Dan Parker at Oxford UP for granting me permission to reprint blog entries from OUP's Blog; Bryan Troyer at Grist.org for permission to reprint Wendell Berry's "Environmentalists Have Given Up too Much by Not Being Radical Enough" and Amelia Urry's "If you Think Technology Has no Place in the National Parks, Think

Again;" Matthew Smoot at xkcd.com for his guidance in reprinting "The Pace of Modern Life;" and Karen Gagne at *Orion Magazine* for permission to reprint Derrick Jensen's "Forget Shorter Showers."

FOR FURTHER READING

"America's Skills Challenge: Millennials and the Future." ETS, 2015. http://www.ets.org/millennials.

Burke, Kenneth. *The Philosophy of Literary Form*. University of California Press, 1941.

"The Condition of College and Career Readiness," *ACT*, 2015. http://www.act.org/content/dam/act/unsecured/documents/CCCR15-NationalReadinessRpt.pdf.

"Evaluating Information: The Cornerstone of Civic Online Reasoning." https://sheg.stanford.edu/upload/V3LessonPlans/Executive%20Summary%2011.21.16.pdf.

Kassuba, Tanja and Sabine Kastner. "The Reading Brain." *Scientific American*. 12 May 2015.

Mar, Raymond A. et al. "Exploring the Link Between Reading Fiction and Empathy: Ruling Out Individual Differences and Examining Outcomes." *Communications*, vol. 34, 2009.

Oatley, Keith. *Such Stuff as Dreams: The Psychology of Fiction*. Wiley, 2011.

"Performance on SAT Verbal/Critical Reading and Writing Exams." *Humanities Indicators*, American Academy of Arts and Sciences, 2016, http://www.humanitiesindicators.org/content/indicatordoc.aspx?i=23.

Rayner, Keith. "Eye Movements in Reading and Information Processing: 20 Years of Research." *Psychological Bulletin*, vol. 124, no.3, 1998, pp. 372–422.

Restak, Richard. "Empathy and Other Mysteries." *American Scholar*, 1 December 2010, https://theamericanscholar.org/empathy-and-other-mysteries/#.

Part One. Experiencing the Connections between Reading and Writing

Chapter 1. Annotating Your Way into Academic Discourse

WHAT IS ACADEMIC DISCOURSE?

In the simplest terms, **academic discourse** is how scholars—or academics, as they are sometimes called—speak and write. Believe it or not, you already have some experience with academic discourse. Think back to the type of writing you completed in high school. You were probably expected to write in a more formal manner than if you were writing a text message or email to your friends. This formality is one aspect of academic discourse. Think, too, about your participation in class discussions. You probably spoke more formally and precisely during these discussions than if you were simply hanging out and talking with your friends. Academic discourse is not as casual as everyday speaking and writing, but strives to be more formal, complex, and precise. At the college level, you will be expected to further develop your abilities to participate in academic discourse. While each field or discipline (e.g. Biology, English, Psychology) has its own specific ways of writing, all disciplines within the academy encourage more sophisticated forms of communication than those we use every day.

In order to participate in the conversations that go on across disciplines within the academy, you will need to hone your abilities to use academic discourse effectively. This is a goal that should guide you early in your general education courses and all the way through the courses in your major. Inserting your voice into scholarly conversations—rather than just summarizing what other scholars have said—may be new for you. Some previous instructors may have told you not to include your "opinion" or "voice" in your writing. Maybe you have been prohibited from using "I." This was the case for one of my students who described the difficulty this posed for him while writing a research paper: "I had to concentrate most of my efforts on analyzing my sources while trying to make sure my own voice was heard. I will admit that it was tough due to the fact that much of my high school writing career had been focused on keeping my voice out of [my] paper[s]." While it may take some time for you to become comfortable inserting your own voice into scholarly conversations, as a college-level reader and writer it is important that you become a visible and active part of your writing, just as you are expected to be an active reader. As noted in the introduction, annotation—which brings the acts of reading and writing together—can lay the foundation for your productive participation in scholarly conversations.

WHAT IS ANNOTATION?

You have probably been asked by instructors to "mark-up" something you are reading. Maybe you were asked to jot down questions or notes in the margins, highlight the important parts, or circle words you don't know. Maybe you have developed these habits on your own. The act of marking up a text is commonly referred to as annotating. The word "annotate" comes from the Latin word for "to note or mark" or "to note down." To **annotate** is exactly that—it's when you make notes on a text. "What does this have to do with entering scholarly conversations?" you may be wondering. How can marking up a reading help you respond to other scholars in your discipline?

When you annotate you are writing as you read. You make notes, you comment, react, and raise questions in the margins of your text. Reflections of your engagement with the text and its author, annotations represent the initial and preliminary ways you are participating in a scholarly conversation with the author of what you are reading. As such, your annotations can serve as the basis for the more extensive contributions you will be expected to make to scholarly conversations. For example, if you need to write an essay about something you have read, you can return to your annotations—to the questions you posed and comments you made in the margins—because these are moments in which you are already interacting with the text and its author. From there you can develop those preliminary interactions into a more detailed and comprehensive response.

Annotations can be handwritten on a printed text or applied digitally on an electronic text. As noted in the Introduction, annotating digitally will allow you to mark up any text, including those on the Web, access your annotations from any computer, and share your annotations with others. See the Introduction for specific instructions on how to digitally annotate the reading selections in this textbook.

Instead of annotating the readings digitally, some instructors might ask you to print out the readings from this textbook and annotate them by hand as in the sample that follows.

As you read the annotations in the two sample texts, notice the different ways the student uses annotations. The students ask questions, challenge points, define some words, and make personal connections. In these examples, the students are engaging in more general annotation practices that are not governed by a specific reading strategy like those you will be introduced to in Chapter 2.

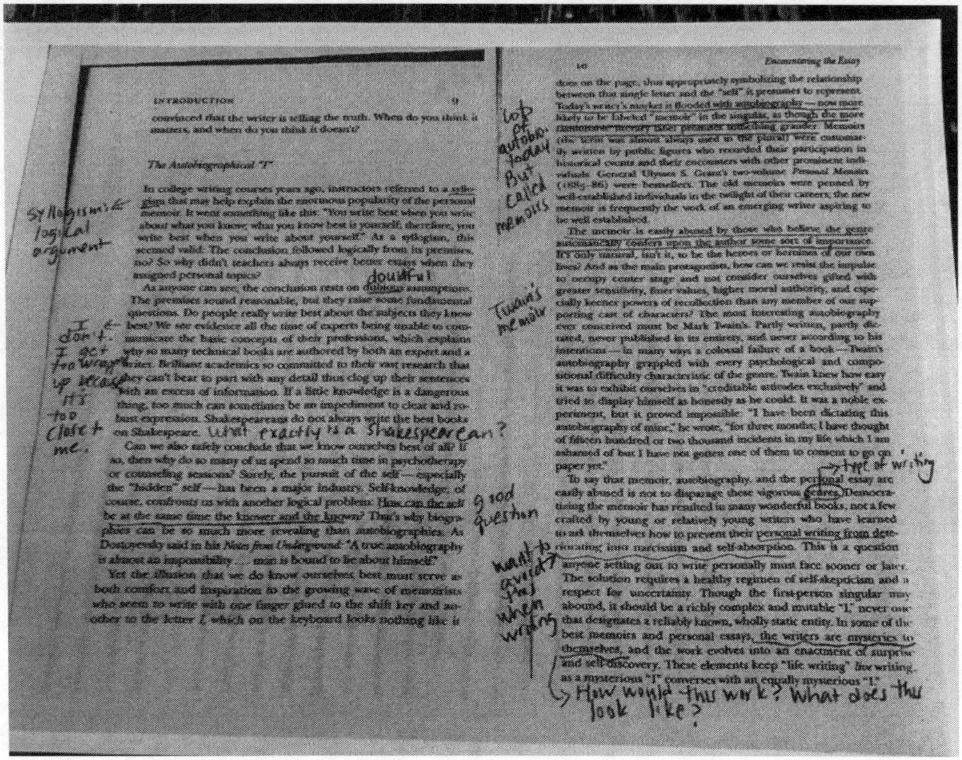

WHAT ARE THE DIFFERENCES BETWEEN ANNOTATING AND HIGHLIGHTING?

It is important to keep in mind that annotating and highlighting often serve different purposes. Highlighting draws your attention to what you deem to be the important parts of a reading. Highlighting can help you recall those moments and the information presented in them. On the other hand, annotating encourages you to mark additional elements of the text—those beyond just "the important parts." You will notice that in the previous samples highlighting is never used on its own. Rather, the yellow highlighting that does appear is accompanied by a comment, question, or some kind of written response. Although highlighting may be an important supplement to annotating, highlighting on its own is usually better preparation for assignments that ask you to memorize concepts and ideas from readings as opposed to those that ask you to write about and respond to what you have read. A record of your reading and your responses to the text and its author, annotations can provide you with the foundation for entering scholarly conversations, which is what you will be asked to do throughout college.

Chapter 2. Developing a Repertoire of Reading Strategies

WHAT IS A REPERTOIRE?

The previous chapter describes the importance of annotating—both as a means to understanding what you read and responding to it. This chapter includes additional strategies for engaging texts. Specifically, this chapter offers you a repertoire of reading strategies. A **repertoire** is like a collection or catalog, and this chapter shares with you a collection of reading strategies that you can begin to practice as you move through the chapters in this textbook. This chapter is intended to serve as a resource because it is the one place where all of the reading strategies are listed and described. In Part Two you will have the opportunity to apply the reading strategies as you answer questions about and complete assignments related to each chapter's readings. The more of these strategies you practice and reflect on as you do so, the better prepared you will be to read the range of texts (broadly defined) you will encounter in this class, your other classes, and beyond school. Remember that these strategies may go by different names in different courses and contexts. More important than their names, though, are how they help you understand and respond to what you read. As the descriptions indicate, these strategies are useful across different genres or kinds of texts, as well as across media.

Ponder This

Think about what you read and how you read. How would you describe the types of texts you read for school, pleasure, your job? Do you find yourself using any strategies for doing so? How would you compare the experiences of reading these different texts?

CHOOSING A READING STRATEGY: THE IMPORTANCE OF PURPOSE

As you think about which strategy suits your particular needs, it would be wise to think about your purpose for reading. This is, perhaps, the most important question you must ask yourself. As you consider that question, consider other, related questions. For example:

- Are you reading to then write a summary of the text?
- Are you reading to compare that text to another one?
- Are you reading to see if the text can serve as a source in a research paper?
- Are you reading to design a multimodal project?
- Are you reading to imitate an author's style?

Determining why you are reading is crucial to choosing the most productive strategy. One strategy might help you understand a text's argument while another might be more useful in helping you determine a text's organization or design. Some strategies might work better when you read poetry while others work better with informational texts.

As you practice each strategy, you also need to reflect on it, to think about it. This is the crux of mindful reading—paying close, deliberate attention to how you are reading and how each strategy works. Tracking how well you are reading is not as easy as tracking your writing progress, which can be rather easily done by revising drafts into more polished pieces of writing. This is where annotation comes in. As you apply the reading strategies introduced in this chapter, you are expected to annotate your texts—digitally or by hand—so you can make the very act of reading visible. This will allow you to track your reading, as well as the connections between the practices of writing and reading. Your written annotations will show you what you were thinking and how you were constructing meaning as you were applying each strategy. You might think of your annotations as written drafts of your readings, evidence of preliminary understandings and responses to what you are reading while you are reading. As you apply different reading strategies to the same texts, your annotations will represent articulations of how you interact with the text across multiple experiences of reading.

Ponder This

Why do you read for school? Why do you read for pleasure? Can you develop a list of the purposes for reading in each situation? How do these purposes compare?

THE READING STRATEGIES—PREVIEWING

Previewing is one strategy you probably already use, although unconsciously, when you approach both online and printed texts. When you preview a text, you quickly scan it and all that surrounds and supports it. You notice its title, its author, its general design and whether there is an accompanying summary or abstract. You get a sense of its structure, including any subject headings, images, and hyperlinks it may contain. And, ultimately, you determine its **genre**, which means you decide what type of text it is. You might ask yourself: Is it an informational text or a literary text? Beyond that more general question, you might consider whether it is a piece of poetry, a play, a newspaper article, a blog entry, or a novel. If you determine that the text is a newspaper article, for example, you are going to read it differently than if it were a piece of poetry. In other words, you wouldn't get very far reading a newspaper article for symbolism and metaphors or reading a piece of poetry simply for information. That is how genre structures your reading.

When you pay attention to genre and these other elements while you are previewing a text, you are paying attention to **schemas**—elements or frameworks that structure or impact how you read. Schemas depend upon readers drawing on prior knowledge and experiences to help understand what and how the text means. For example, if you read a story that begins with "Once upon a time," you will—albeit probably unconsciously—recognize that you may be reading a fairy tale. From there, all of the prior knowledge of and experiences you have with fairy tales will kick in, and you will expect to see the elements of a fairy tale in the piece you are reading: the prince and princess; the castle; perhaps a dragon or some other ominous creature; and a happily-ever-after ending. You do a lot of this work unconsciously when you pick up a text or read online. The point is to become more aware of how reading works so you can use this information to make your reading more productive. Keep in mind, though, that it will likely be necessary to use previewing as a preliminary reading strategy and supplement it later with another one that will allow you to more deeply and comprehensively understand what you have read. You apply this strategy by annotating—by marking—the schemas of texts, the aspects that help you understand it.

Practice Previewing

To experience the power of a schema read the following paragraphs.

> The procedure is actually quite simple. First you arrange things into different groups. Of course, one pile may be sufficient depending on how much there is to do. If you have to go somewhere else due to lack of facilities that is the next step,

> otherwise you are pretty well set. It is important not to overdo things. That is, it is better to do too few things at once than too many. In the short run this may not seem important but complications can easily arise. A mistake can be expensive as well. At first the whole procedure will seem complicated.
>
> Soon, however, it will become just another facet of life. It is difficult to foresee any end to the necessity for this task in the immediate future, but then one never can tell. After the procedure is completed one arranges the materials into different groups again. Then they can be put into their appropriate places. Eventually they will be used once more and the whole cycle will then have to be repeated. However, that is part of life. (Bransford and Johnson 722)

Doesn't make much sense, does it? In the following example, the same paragraphs are inserted, but with a heading.

> **Laundry**
>
> The procedure is actually quite simple. First you arrange things into different groups. Of course, one pile may be sufficient depending on how much there is to do. If you have to go somewhere else due to lack of facilities that is the next step, otherwise you are pretty well set. It is important not to overdo things. That is, it is better to do too few things at once than too many. In the short run this may not seem important bu complications can easily arise. A mistake can be expensive as well. At first the whole procedure will seem complicated.
>
> Soon, however, it will become just another facet of life. It is difficult to foresee any end to the necessity for this task in the immediate future, but then one never can tell, After the procedure is completed one arranges the materials into different groups again. Then they can be put into their appropriate places. Eventually they will be used once more and the whole cycle will then have to be repeated. However, that is part of life. (Bransford and Johnson 722)

That heading, "Laundry," acts as a schema that allows you to understand the paragraphs. These excerpts were used in an experiment conducted by cognitive psychologists John D. Bransford and Marcia K. Johnson who found that without that heading as a schema, readers didn't understand or remember the paragraph. Was that your experience, too?

Practice Working with Schemas

Choose an excerpt from an online source and anticipate which schemas offer the most important clues about how to read and make sense of it; remove them. Share this version with a classmate. To what extent can your classmate make sense of it? Try adding the schemas back one at a time and giving your classmate additional tries at comprehending the excerpt. Which schema(s) ultimately proved the most important?

Skimming

You read right . . . skimming! You might be surprised that you are being encouraged to skim—read quickly—rather than to always read closely or deeply, but skimming is an important reading strategy and is the best reading strategy in some situations. You probably don't need much instruction in skimming as research shows that this is the most common approach to reading online. Skimming is a lot like previewing and is an appropriate reading practice when you do not need to develop (in your mind) or provide (via a writing assignment) a deep and detailed understanding of a text. Skimming can be a particularly useful practice in the early stages of research when you are looking for sources that are relevant to your topic, but you do not yet need to work closely with them. When you are in the later stages of the writing process of a research essay, if you have determined that it is a useful piece of writing for your purposes, you will need to return and re-read the text using a different reading strategy so that you can work more closely with it in an essay. In other instances, you may not need to do more than skim. As you skim, you may want to annotate a piece by noticing the elements in the following list (some of which involve previewing since the practices are closely related) and marking them as they appear in the text.

1. The elements you notice by "previewing" the piece, such as its title; author; introductory material (e.g. an abstract); and general design and structure (e.g. subject headings, graphics, and hyperlinks). See you if you can determine its genre, which means you decide what type of text it is.
2. The introduction since introductions often (although not always) describe the piece as a whole.
3. The first sentence of each paragraph since first sentences are usually topic sentences and can give you an overall sense of the subject of the paragraph.

4. The conclusion or the final paragraph of the piece since conclusions often (although not always) summarize a piece.

Practice Skimming

1. **Choose** a page in one of your books or textbooks to skim. What would you notice if you were skimming it by using the techniques discussed above?
2. **Using the guidelines above, skim** three online movie reviews of films you would like to see (either older or current films). How much do you know about each film after skimming? What questions about the films have not be answered by skimming? Could you describe each film to someone else?

The Says/Does Approach

This approach to reading asks you to pay attention to two different elements of any given text. It asks you to notice what the text *says*—its content—and what the text *does*—how it functions. This approach is useful because it shifts attention away from content, which is often easier to figure out and toward how a text or sections of a text function. Being able to recognize both what a paragraph (or aspect of a multimodal project) says and what it does—and being able to recognize the difference between the two—can help you understand the piece as a whole. For example, a particularly difficult paragraph in a text you are reading may be addressing the mating habits of bees. That's the content, the "says" part. In an effort to figure out what that paragraph is doing, you may realize that it is presenting an opposing view that challenges the claim the author is making. In recognizing this, you have avoided the common mistake of attributing all of the ideas within an article to its author. In this case, by focusing on how that paragraph functions, on what it does, you realized that it is not the author speaking, but rather the author is *using the example to challenge his own claim*. That is what it is doing. This approach can help you determine how the different parts of a text work together to create meaning. When faced with a difficult or especially long text, you can annotate each paragraph by noting what it says and what it does. In the following example, annotations indicate what each paragraph says and does.

Addressing Students' Affective Responses to Conducting Online Research

In recent years, there have been studies that indicate that students are not particularly adept at conducting online research. Students' reliance onWikipedia (Nicholas, Rowlands & Huntington, 2009), as well as Google-based searches, has been documented (Nicholas, Rowlands & Huntington, 2009; Purdy, 2012), as have their difficulties evaluating the credibility of the sources they find online (Ostenson, 2009; Hargittai, Fullerton, Menchen-Trevino & Thomas, 2010). Studies have indicated that students choose sources based on their ease of use as opposed to the relevance to their subject (Purdy, 2012, p. 7) and that students—who quote primarily from the abstracts and first page of sources—may even lack the ability to understand what they are reading (Howard, Serviss & Rodrigue, 2010, p. 189).

Says: Students are not that good at conducting online research.

Does: Introduces the subject of the piece, namely students' online research habits.

Certainly, instructors at all levels and across the disciplines have a significant amount of work to do in order to help students develop stronger information literacy skills and digital research practices. Part of that work must address the affective—or emotional—component of conducting digital research in an age with so much readily-accessible information. Conducting online research is understandably overwhelming for students. While studies of students' research practices often report students' feelings of frustration at various points in the research process (Head, 2007; Head and Eisenberg 2009, 2010; Kuhlthau, 2004) these important findings tend to be overshadowed by findings that provide insight into students' progress toward more intellectually productive research practices.

Says: People who teach students and study their research habits need to take into account the affective/emotional (rather than just the intellectual) aspects of conducting online research.

Does: Describes an otherwise neglected aspect of this research and argues for incorporating attention to it in studies.

Now that you have read the excerpt and its annotations, go back to the annotations to notice the specific verbs used to characterize what each paragraph "does." This is usually what separates the "says" from the "does" since the "does" is active while the "says" is more descriptive. Let's go paragraph by paragraph: The first paragraph *introduces* while the second *describes* and *argues*. These verbs—along with other verbs and verb phrases—such as *summarizes, challenges, argues, elaborates; supports; narrows the subject*; *defines*; *redefines*; *provides historical context*; *presents opposing evidence*; *provides new evidence*—will help you define what paragraphs do.

Practice the Says/Does Approach

1. **Choose** a reading from this textbook and annotate the first ten paragraphs using the says/does approach.
2. **Return** to your says/does annotations from question 1—and particularly to your "does" notes. Either in the form of a paragraph or an outline, develop an overview of the structure of those first 10 paragraphs by describing what each paragraph is doing.

Rhetorical Reading

Rhetorically reading involves reading a text with an eye toward the **rhetoric** of what you are reading. Rhetoric is the available means of persuasion at a writer's disposal. When you read something rhetorically you are paying particular attention to how certain elements of the text influence you as you read. By paying attention to those elements as you read, you become more aware of how a text persuades you or acts upon you. This awareness can also help you as a writer make choices about how you will use rhetoric to influence those who read your work, whether it is something you have written or a multimodal project you have created.

When reading rhetorically, there are at least four rhetorical elements to which you should pay attention by asking yourself the following questions about purpose, audience, claims, evidence, and appeals. As you read rhetorically, annotate a text by marking the parts of the piece that help you determine the following:

1. What is the author's purpose? Is the author arguing a point? Bringing awareness to a problem? Trying to make sense of an experience? Calling people to action?
2. Who is the intended audience? To whom does the author seem to be writing?
3. What are the author's claims? What claims and what kind of claims does the author make?
4. What kinds of evidence are used? Scientific data, anecdotes, personal experience?

Ancient Greek philosopher Aristotle taught his own students that there are three specific types of appeals that orators might make in order to persuade their audiences. These appeals are still taught today as strategies that writers can use to persuade readers and appeals that readers can recognize as ways that texts persuade them. These three persuasive strategies make up the rhetorical triangle.

Ethos: Appeals to credibility. Notice how the author tries to persuade readers by establishing his/her credibility.

Logos: Appeals to logic. Notice how the author uses the logic of his argument or his claims to persuade readers.

Pathos: Appeals to emotions. Notice how the author tries to persuade readers by engaging their emotions.

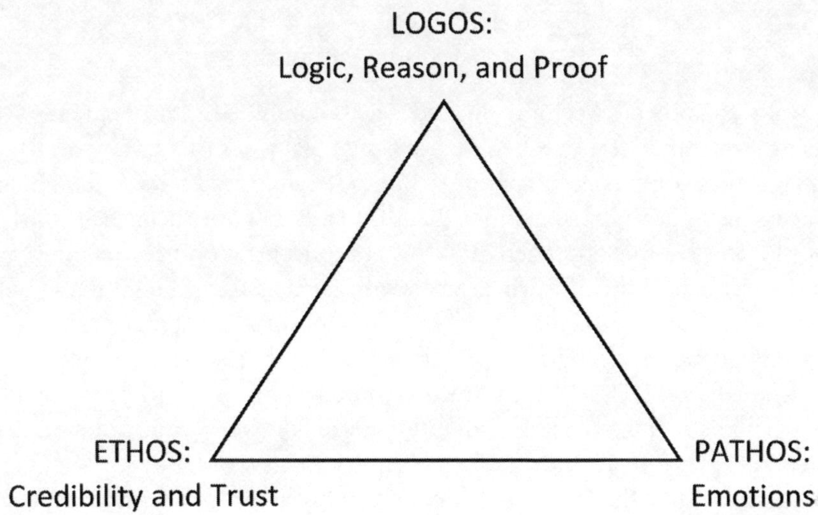

Practice Rhetorical Reading

1. **Choose** any piece of writing—digital or print. You might choose a blog entry, a newspaper, an excerpt from one of your textbooks, or even a piece of your own writing. Rhetorically read it by answering the four questions on the previous page.

2. **Think** of a cause that you believe in (e.g. civil rights; environmental issues; campus issues). Design two flyers advertising the meeting of a campus group that will support the cause. Maybe the cause is something as well-known as global warming or as localized as dorm curfews. The audience for the first flyer is students who have already

signed a petition indicating their commitment to the cause. The audience for the second flyer is new, first-year students who likely don't know about this group on campus. How do these different audiences affect the other rhetorical aspects of your flyers? Look back at the four questions for guidance to determine how the content and the design of the flyers might be impacted by these different audiences.

Reading Aloud to Paraphrase

This strategy really consists of two individual strategies combined into one, namely reading aloud and paraphrasing. You should feel free to separate them if that works better for you. The combination, though, brings together complementary approaches to reading: reading aloud highlights each word as the reader hears it and paraphrase requires that the reader not only hear each word but translate it in her own words. This reading approach, thus, fosters concentration in ways that some others may not, and it may be especially helpful when faced with particularly difficult paragraphs or sections of texts. Unfortunately, many students rarely read aloud beyond elementary school. You may come across a professor who requires you to read poetry aloud, but that is likely the extent of reading aloud in high school and college. Still, if you can recall a time when you heard poetry read aloud (either by yourself or a classmate) it likely made a lot more sense than when you read it on the page. As you read aloud to paraphrase, you need not paraphrase every single word, but you should stop every few sentences or so and annotate the text by writing, in your own words, what you just read.

Practice Reading Aloud to Paraphrase

1. Choose a reading from this textbook. Read it aloud, stopping regularly to paraphrase—in the form of annotations—what you are reading. To what extent do these annotations help you understand what you are reading?
2. Choose a short piece of nonfiction. First, read it to yourself, and when you are finished write a brief summary of what you have read. Now, read it again aloud, paraphrasing—in the form of annotation—as you read. How were the experiences different?
3. If you do not want to read aloud or have difficulty hearing, choose a reading from this textbook and read it to yourself stopping regularly to paraphrase—in the form

of annotations—what you are reading. To what extent do these annotations help you understand what you are reading?

Mapping

Education scholar and optometrist Héctor C. Santiago, among others, have found that "visual tools may help . . . students develop better recall, comprehension and critical thinking skills" (137). Mapping is one of those visual tools that can be adapted to various reading purposes and helps readers visually organize information. When you map a text you present visually what the text says. You might map the text as a whole, you might choose a few pages to map, or you might choose a single element to map such as a text's argument. When you map a text, you become highly aware of the relationships among its different parts, and the visual representation often highlights aspects of the text that aren't otherwise visible.

Maps come in different shapes and sizes, and can be adjusted to suit your needs. Perhaps the most common is the web or radial map in which the main idea or concept is in the center while threads radiate from it to indicate the connections between the central concept/idea and the other, less central ideas. From those threads come other threads and so on from there. Maps can be developed by hand or with digital, text mapping software. The most important element of any map is that it allows you to see how different elements of a text (e.g. its argument, evidence, characters) are related and structured. Often, these visual representations allow you to recognize relationships you hadn't noticed while reading.

Maps also underscore the importance of returning to and revising your reading as you visually represent, rank, and connect the different elements of the text since you will likely need to revise your map as you continue reading and re-reading. Annotating a text can help you map it because your annotations draw your attention to the various elements of a text you will need to represent visually. The radial map on the following page is based on Sarah Davis' "'The Blurred Lines' Effect: Popular Music and the Perpetuation of Rape Culture" (see Chapter 9 for the full text of Sarah Davis' essay). By placing the concept of rape culture at the center and related issues around it, the student can begin to visualize some of the ways that rape culture is perpetuated, as well as the challenges of recognizing these forces. It is worth noting that this is a very basic version of a map that would be added to over time as the student sought to further explore the connections among these ideas and others in the text.

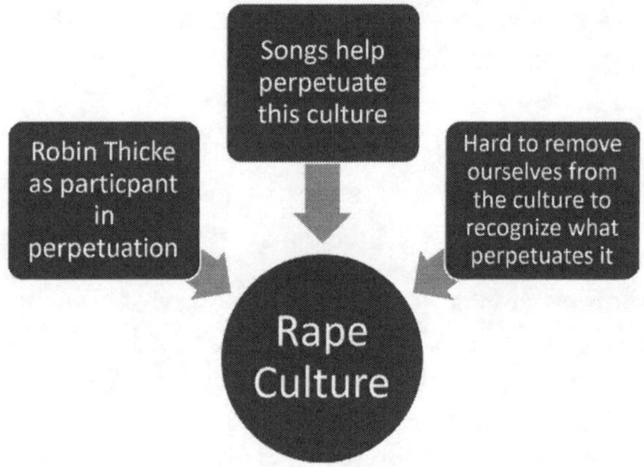

Just as this reader would be expected to go back and revise this map in order to incorporate more details, you should imagine that your maps are open to revisions and additions as you read and reread the text you are mapping. Still, this initial map allows you to see how the reader is working toward figuring out what causes and perpetuates rape culture.

Practice Mapping

1. **Choose** a reading from this textbook and annotate its first two pages using a reading strategy of your choice. Then use your annotations to develop a map.
2. **Read** the next four pages of the same selection you read in question 1. Now that you have read a total of six pages, return to your map and make necessary revisions.

The Believing/Doubting Game

This strategy was developed by scholar and teacher Peter Elbow and encourages you, the reader, to play two roles while reading. First, you read a text or engage a project as though you believe it. You annotate the text by marking the reasons why you (in your role as "believer") would believe these things. You might keep a list in or adjacent to the text and might even add other evidence to the list to further support the writer's position. Then, you take on the role of the "doubter." You go back to the text to cast doubt on it. Again, you annotate the text by keeping a running list of the problems or faults you find in the writer's position. This is an especially useful strategy when you need to figure out where you stand on an issue and what you truly believe in light of what a writer has said. This strategy also helps you understand why others believe what they do since you will have to "believe" a position you may truly doubt.

Practicing the Believing/Doubting Game

1. **Go online** to a website that supports a view of an issue that is opposed to your view. For example, if you support stronger gun control laws go to a website that publishes information on the opposing viewpoint such as the National Rifle Association (NRA) site. Spend some time reading the information on the site. Putting your true viewpoint aside and "believing" what the site says, write a letter to someone associated with the cause (e.g. a government official; an environmentalist; a news reporter) outlining your "beliefs" and their rationale.
2. **Reflect** on the letter completed in #1 by writing a paragraph about any new information you came across as you read the site. To what extent did this information affect where you truly stand on the subject? Have you changed your mind? Explain.

Reading Like a Writer (RLW)

In 1990, English professor Charles Moran published an essay encouraging students to read like writers. More recently, English professor Mike Bunn extended Moran's thinking by developing a series of steps that one can take in order to read like a writer, which he often abbreviates as "RLW." Bunn explains RLW as follows: "When you Read Like a Writer you work to identify some of the choices the author made so that you can better understand how such choices might arise in your own writing. The idea is to carefully examine the things you read, looking at the writerly techniques in the text in order to decide if you might want to adopt similar (or the same) techniques in your writing" (72). Bunn uses the phrase "writerly techniques" to describe the ways that writers present their ideas and make their points. You might think about this as their style. Perhaps the author of the text you are reading has opened her piece with a quotation and concludes with a question. Maybe she switches between formal and informal language throughout. Perhaps she includes dialogue. The key to RLW is noticing these different techniques in order to determine whether you might try them in your own writing. Bunn further explains that this reading approach is not about learning or understanding the content of a reading. Instead, when you adopt this approach you do so to learn about writing. Bunn lists many questions one might ask while using this reading strategy, and he recommends keeping a pen or pencil nearby and marking—or annotating—moments in the text that reveal especially interesting choices that the writer has made. Bunn suggests answering the following central questions about each moment:

- What is the technique the author is using here?
- Is this technique effective?
- What would be the advantages and disadvantages if I tried this same technique in my writing? (81)

Note that these three questions are equally relevant to "reading" multimodal projects, although Bunn's focus is on print-based work. Keep in mind that while you may not be able to use the technical names all of the different techniques the writer is using, this strategy makes these techniques visible, and, therefore, they can still be imitated. This reading strategy might be especially useful if you are expected to use writing techniques or design techniques similar to those used by another author, as well as if you are looking for new techniques to try out in your own work.

Practice Reading Like a Writer

1. **Choose** a reading from this textbook and answer the three questions above.
2. **Look up** reviews of movies, books, or products on amazon.com or another site that publishes reviews. **Choose** one review and answer the three questions above. Then choose a book, movie, or product of your own to review, imitating the author's approach. How closely does your version resemble the model you were imitating?

Reading and Evaluating Online Sources

Reading online often involves using search engines and other tools on the internet to search for texts. Because there is so much information—so much to read—online and none of it is regulated in any way, reading online means being especially vigilant about the quality of what you encounter. This reading strategy, then, is not about helping you understand a text's content, but rather "reading" its credibility—determining whether it is worthy of being believed—so that you can make informed decisions about whether it is a text that will serve your purposes. When faced with online texts—whether digital texts that may have a printed, hardcopy counterpart or websites—evaluate the text by keeping the following questions in mind to gain insight into whether it is an appropriate source for your needs. You may use annotation as a tool for recording your answers.

1. Consider the differences among these domains. What kind of website does the text appear on? Is it a .com, .org, .gov, .edu?
2. Know the author. Who is the author, organization, or company that sponsors the website? Search for more information once you have this information. If there is no author, try looking up the website at WHOIS, which provides this information: https://whois.icann.org/en.
3. Try to determine if the piece is peer-reviewed, which means that it goes through an evaluation by other scholars in the field. If you are looking at a journal article, for example, notice the press that publishes the journal. Then search that press to find information about it.
4. Look to see if the text has a bibliography at the end. If so, what kinds of texts are cited?
5. Consider if any sources are cited in the piece. If so, what kinds?

Practice Reading and Evaluating Online Sources

1. **Choose** an online article or essay and annotate it by answering the five questions above.
2. **Look back** at the annotations you made in #1 and notice any gaps or questions that remain about your sources. Develop a plan for answering those questions and filling in those gaps.

FOR FURTHER READING

Bransford, John D. and Marcia K. Johnson. "Contextual Prerequisites for Understanding: Some Investigations of Comprehension and Recall." *Journal of Verbal Learning and Verbal Behavior,* vol. 11, 1972, pp. 717–726.

Bunn, Mike. "How to Read Like a Writer." *Writing Spaces: Readings on Writing*, Volume 2, Parlor Press, 2011, pp. 71–86. http://www.parlorpress.com/pdf/bunn--how-to-read.pdf.

Moran, Charles. "Reading Like a Writer." *Vital Signs 1*, edited by James L. Collins, Boynton/Cook, 1990, pp. 60–69.

Santiago, Héctor C. "Visual Mapping to Enhance Learning and Critical Thinking Skills." *Optometric Education*, vol. 36, no. 3, 2011, pp. 125–195.

Chapter 3. Further Strategies That Make Reading Visible

This chapter details assignments that your instructor may ask you to complete throughout the course. Although writing assignments, these activities are focused on reading and, therefore, allow you to experience the connections between the two practices, while simultaneously developing your reading and writing abilities. Some of these activities are also assigned in Part Two of this textbook.

THE READING JOURNAL: DEVELOPING AND RECORDING YOUR KNOWLEDGE ABOUT READING

A reading journal, which may be an electronic document on your computer or the more traditional bound notebook, gives you the opportunity to reflect on your reading and learn about yourself as a reader, which can be helpful as you read in this class, other classes, and beyond school. The journal is a space in which you record your experiences reading. You might return to your journal periodically to look at your notes to better understand how you can be a more productive reader. While you may use the journal to document your personal and emotional responses to each reading, please regularly also answer the following questions:

1. Which reading strategy did I employ first and why? (see Chapter 2 on reading strategies)
2. How far did this reading strategy take me?
3. What did this reading strategy allow me to notice in the text?
4. What must I ignore because of this strategy's limits?
5. At which point in the reading (and why) did I need to abandon my initial strategy?
6. What does this tell me about the strategy, as well as about me as a reader?
7. Which other strategy do I need to introduce in order to construct a meaning that achieves the goals associated with my reading/writing assignment?
8. How might this reading experience be useful as I read texts in my other courses?

Notice how this excerpt from a student's reading journal reflects her use of different reading strategies as she moves toward writing an essay for her geography class:

> For my geography class today, I had to read Jamaica Kincaid's book called *A Small Place*, which is about Antigua, a Caribbean island. She talks about the divide there

between the fancy, wealthy white tourists on vacation and the poverty-stricken people who live there. I'm supposed to write a similar kind of essay to Kincaid's with the same sort of aggressive tone but about a different geographic place that has meaning to me and also has some sort of problem or tension I want to expose about that place.

I decided to reread *A Small Place* using the RLW strategy so I could really see what Kincaid is doing and why her writing comes off really aggressive. I noticed that she uses the word "you" a lot, which makes the reader feel attacked. I think this is something I can try in my own piece to get that same effect.

But, RLW didn't really help me think about the audience for Kincaid's book, which will be important for my essay, too. So I went back and reread using the rhetorical reading strategy and I realized that it seems as though she thinks her audience are those fancy, white tourists. This seems important because she is calling attention to a problem that the audience is causing and so that's why she is so aggressive. Her audience is to blame and so she writes in a really aggressive way because she is angry at them. I will need to keep this in mind as I write my essay and think about the audience's relationship to my subject.

Practice Writing a Reading Journal Entry

Now that you have read the excerpt from the reading journal, try your hand at your own reading journal entry. Pick something to read—either from this book or elsewhere—and write a few paragraphs answering some of the questions on the previous page.

DIFFICULTY INVENTORY: TRACKING AND OVERCOMING READING DIFFICULTIES

You may have had teachers develop reading guides for you to help support your reading, particularly of difficult texts. Perhaps these guides contained definitions of difficult vocabulary words, some historical context useful in understanding the reading, and some questions to direct your attention to the most important aspects of the reading. These can be enormously helpful resources, but when a teacher creates reading guides for students, it is the teacher who comes to recognize and work with the difficulties that the readings pose. When students develop these, however, *they* learn to recognize the sources of their difficulties, which is a first step toward working through them. Developing a list of the difficulties you are facing as you read a text makes you aware of why you are having trouble and gives you the opportunity to address those difficulties. The following list contains elements that may cause you difficulty. As you read, create your own list, drawing from this list, and adding to it as necessary. Then, next to each "difficulty" indicate where you might go (e.g. a dictionary) to work through it. You may be asked to share your list with a peer from your class so that you can work through some of the difficulties together, or your instructor might wish to make a master list of these difficulties and support students while they work through these difficulties. No matter what you end up doing with your list, the very act of developing it and imagining which resources can support you will help you feel less overwhelmed when reading difficult texts and give you the confidence to address these difficulties.

Some Potential Difficulties You May Face When You Read

- You aren't the intended audience for the piece
- You don't understand certain words or concepts
- You don't have necessary background knowledge
- You don't understand the historical context
- You don't recognize the genre
- The visuals or graphics are confusing
- You are distracted by advertisements on the screen
- The website on which the reading appears is not user-friendly
- The print or type-face of the piece is off-putting
- The piece's organization is hard to follow

Here is a sample difficulty inventory in the form of a chart:

DIFFICULTY	RESOURCE
The unfamiliar word "consciousness"	A dictionary. If a word isn't in a dictionary, I can look at all of the places in the text where the word is used. Looking at all of those moments together can help me figure out what the word means and how it is used.
References to the importance of the Korean War.	A reliable website that explains this War. A website that is a .org or .edu is probably best.
I can't follow the text's organization	The says/does strategy to help me figure out what each paragraph is doing.

Practice Developing a Difficulty Inventory

Choose one of the readings in this book and, as you read, keep a difficulty inventory—whether in the form of a chart or any other format you like—that lists both the source of the difficulty as well as potential resources that would help you overcome that difficulty.

THE PASSAGE-BASED PAPER

By asking you to choose a single passage from a longer reading, this assignment demands that you slow down and pay attention to how you make sense of the passage, how you read it. Passage-based papers offer you the opportunity to experience the connections between the interpretive practices of reading and writing as you make your reading visible through the act of writing. Here is how you would do this:

1. Choose a short passage (3-5 sentences) from the text you are reading and write a 1-2 page passage-based paper on this excerpt.
2. Transcribe the passage onto the top of the page (including the page number from which the passage is taken) and then "unpack" the passage, paying close attention to the textual elements including the passage's language, tone, and construction.
3. Once you have examined the passage closely, conclude your paper by connecting this passage to the rest of the work. In other words, once you have completed a close, textual analysis of your passage, contemplate the meaning of the passage and its place in or contribution to the meaning(s) of the text as a whole.

The following sample from a passage-based is taken from a paper that discusses a passage from Sven Birkerts' essay "MahVuhHuhPuh" from his book *The Gutenberg Elegies*. The passage-based paper has been annotated to highlight its elements.

> The magnet that pulled them into shape was Woolf's classic essay, *A Room of One's Own*. Not the what of it, but the how. Reading the prose, I confronted a paradox that pulled me upright in my chair. Woolf's ideas are, in fact, few and fairly obvious—at least from our historical vantage. Yet the thinking, the presence of animate thought on the page, is striking. How do we sort that? How can a piece of writing

have simple ideas and still infect the reader with the excitement of its thinking? (Birkerts 11)

In this passage, Birkerts is discussing how it is that he was able to think through and pull together some of the ideas he had been concerned with for a while. It proved to be Woolf's *A Room of One's Own* that helped him to do this.

This paragraph sets the context and provides some background for the discussion of the passage.

Throughout this passage, Birkerts creates a distinction—one that Woolf helped him to discover—between "what" and "how." This is a distinction he repeats throughout the passage. He even italicizes those words to show they are important. But, even if the words themselves weren't italicized it would still be clear because of the repetition of both words. For example, he writes that it was not the "what" of Woolf's essay but the "how" that helped him. Toward the end of the passage he asks about the relationship between "what" and "how" by posing the question: "How can a piece of writing have simple ideas and still infect the reader with the excitement of its thinking?" In all of these instances and in other moments in the passage, Birkerts is trying to figure out how a piece of writing—like Woolf's *A Room of One's Own*—can be lacking in sophistication when it comes to ideas but still make readers take notice. In other words, he wasn't blown away by the topic of her essay, but by how she wrote about the topic. He seems drawn to how she says what she says rather than what she says so much so that it "pulled [him] upright in his chair." The question then becomes how did Woolf say what she said? In the passage above, Birkerts describes her style as "animate thought on the page" and it is this that he found "striking." So, he was impressed by her style because it seemed as though she was actually thinking onto the page.

The reader chooses two textual elements to focus on. She notices a pattern in the passage and two key words. The reader begins to describe the many instances in which Birkerts seems interested in the differences between the concepts of "what" and "how."

In the last section of this paragraph, the reader asks So What that Birkerts repeats these words? The reader comes to some tentative conclusions about the importance of the concept of "how" to Birkerts. The reader notes that Birkerts values how Woolf makes her points, how she shows her thinking in her writing. The reader says that this seems more important than Woolf's ideas.

This passage seems important to the rest of Birkerts' essay because it sets up or introduces what he will go on to do in his essay. He spends not just this passage—but the first few pages—talking about Woolf's *A Room of One's Own* and how much he is impressed by the way she writes. Based on his description of her writing in this passage and in

This final paragraph connects the pattern and the key terms that the reader has noticed in this passage to the rest of the text. The reader points out that Birkerts mimics Woolf's style throughout his essay as he explores the subject of reading and meaning. Taking this point even further, the reader concludes by noting that just as Woolf's method of thinking inspired Birkerts he seems to want to inspire readers to think in complex ways, as well.

the next few pages it seems as though Birkerts tries to mirror her style by thinking onto the pages of his essay. In other words, he takes the same approach in his essay that she took in hers. This suggests that Birkerts believes that his ideas are not necessarily groundbreaking and that the way he will present them is just as—if not more important—than the ideas themselves. By introducing his essay in this way he lets his readers know that the topic he will be discussing—reading and meaning—is not new, but that the way he will discuss it is important, which is how Woolf presented her ideas—by thinking on the page. Therefore, thinking itself becomes very important. Just as Woolf inspired Birkerts' thinking it seems he's trying to inspire his readers' thinking by using the same style. This is a key element to what Birkerts seems to be doing overall in the essay, which is emphasizing the importance of continuing to think (by reading) rather than just giving into technology, computers, and movies and allowing them to think for you.

Practice Writing a Passage-Based Paper

Choose a passage from one of the readings from this book and write a passage-based paper on it.

SOURCE SYNTHESIS

As you read in previous chapters, it is important that you hone your reading and writing abilities so you can effectively participate in scholarly conversations in the academy. This assignment asks that you do just that as you **synthesize**, or bring together, sources that are on the same subject in order to orchestrate a scholarly conversation, of which you are also a part.

In order to enter this conversation, you will need to understand what each participant is saying individually. In other words, you should be able to **summarize**—restate and condense—it. You have likely written a summary in other academic contexts, and you should feel free to draw on those experiences as you complete the summary assignments throughout this textbook. A summary can be a useful step in understanding what you read as summaries compel you to restate and condense the most important elements of a text. In certain instances you will be asked not to summarize a text in its entirety, but to focus your summary on specific elements. Summaries are particularly useful when texts are dense and include multiple perspectives on a subject. They are also a first step toward more complex academic moves such as those you are expected to make in source syntheses and other assignments.

Once you are sure you can summarize the ideas belonging to each participant in the "conversation," you will need to synthesize their ideas to help you see how they relate to each other. Source syntheses are usually shorter versions of the typical source-driven, longer essays you will be assigned in many of your classes. Their compact nature helps you really focus on refining your abilities to mindfully read and respond to other scholars.

Although sometimes the term "response" is associated with emotions, you want to be sure that you are responding in what we might call an intellectual manner. An **intellectual response** is one that depends upon ideas rather than emotions (e.g. I feel X or Y or about the subject). You want to participate in a scholarly conversation by contributing your ideas. In other words, what would you say to those who have already written on the subject, participated in the conversation? Some intellectual ways to respond—that go beyond the more simplistic modes of agreeing and disagreeing—include the following:

1. Taking a point further
2. Redefining the context of the discussion
3. Exploring different implications for the findings
4. Complicating an argument
5. Locating a fault (an unfounded assumption, for example) and remedying it
6. Exploring why a particular approach is limiting and applying an alternative approach
7. Redefining some of the terms or ideas offered
8. Raising unexplored questions and their significance

As you develop your source synthesis, look back at your annotations for insights into how you are already interacting with the ideas presented in the texts, how you are already participating in the conversation. For example, perhaps one of the questions you pose in the margins can serve as your focus. Here are some additional guidelines:

- Be sure to **focus** the conversation on a specific issue or idea that you can explore in depth by offering the writers' different perspectives rather than very quickly and superficially touching upon a bunch of different issues or ideas in your piece.

- You will need to **quote** your sources throughout since you cannot orchestrate and then participate in a conversation unless you give each source a voice. As you quote your sources, make sure that at the level of form the piece reads like a conversation. This means that, on the whole, each paragraph should contain more than one voice. One page devoted to one voice and a second page devoted to another voice does not represent the give-and-take of a conversation.

The following source synthesis is based on two readings, Sven Birkerts' "MahVuhHuhPuh," an essay from his collection entitled *The Gutenberg Elegies* and Dennis Baron's blog entry entitled "Should We Read a World Without Books?" from his website *The Web of Language*. The student's work has been annotated to show the elements of the assignment:

In this paragraph, the student lays out the two different perspectives she will put into conversation with each other.

In Birkerts' essay "MahVuhHuhPuh," he talks about technology and argues that it is to blame for what he believes will lead to the loss of the written word. Not just fearing the loss of the words themselves, he describes the potential loss of all of the associated activities that seem to be under threat, including the ability to verbally communicate and mental passion. Dennis Baron's "Should We Fear A World Without Books?," on the other hand, tries to show how advances in technology are inevitable and not necessarily detrimental.

This paragraph explores where each writer stands on technology's relationship to deep thinking and inquiry.

Birkerts believes that the encroaching reliance on technologies diminishes an interest in exploring language. Computers and other technologies encourage speed rather than the importance of focus or thinking in depth about something. Birkerts explains that a dependence on technology could lead to a "reduced attention span and general impatience with sustained inquiry" (27). Writing about the ebook, one of the most recent technological advances in book publishing, Baron argues that "There's nothing about the printed book that shouts, 'Attention must be paid.' Even when we're wide awake and concentrating, the mind does wander, and whether it's a best-selling page-turner or an assigned textbook, every reader knows the experience of getting five pages further along, with no recollection of reading the intervening words, or even turning the pages." In other words, Baron complicates the rather common argument, which Birkerts makes, that technology is likely to blame for our reduced attention spans. He points out that we have all been equally distracted while reading printed texts as when we have been reading ebooks. Simply put, Baron's point is that minds wander. He's not convinced that technology itself has caused this or has caused our reduced attention span.

Related to this loss of depth when it comes to language and thinking is Birkerts' concern over the potential loss of in-depth relationships between people. He blames our "interaction[s] with new modes" (31) for this. "We all feel a desire for connection" writes Birkerts "and we are utterly at sea about our place as individuals with the world at large" (20) because of all of these advances in technology with which we cannot keep up. Where is the place for individuals and individuality in this new world?, Birkerts wonders. Finally, according to Birkerts, technology leaves our lives devoid of any reason to reach outside our electronic scope to interact with others. We become "solipsistic," according to Birkerts, engaged in our own little worlds. With the loss of the written word, which Birkerts thinks is around the corner, we lose even the opportunity to live in the literary world of books or escape through them. Baron agrees with Birkerts that "writing earned an honored place in human communication," (9) however, he also points out that "the briefest network crash makes us feel cut off from the world" (12). Baron is suggesting, in other words, that our digital lives actually bring us closer, more connected, to the world around us. While he doesn't cite social media sites specifically, one could imagine that these would be on the list of ways our digital lives connect us. Ultimately, Baron would call Birkerts a "defender of the printed word" and while finding some truth in Birkerts' arguments—such as the impact of reading and writing on all human behavior—Baron ultimately finds the technological evolution to be unavoidable and thus something to which we must adapt.

Further developing the discussion about technology's relationship to depth, this paragraph considers what both writers say about how technology affects how people connect with each other.

The sentence beginning with "While he doesn't cite social media . . ." is an idea that the student contributes to the conversation. She take Baron's ideas further by including an example that supports his position.

This issue of adapting seems crucial and demands additional exploration. Writing several years after Birkerts, Baron raises the issue of needing to adapt, but he doesn't take it much further than that. Taking into consideration Birkerts' concerns about new technologies making everything so easy that there is no longer any investment in sustained inquiry, I would argue that integral to our adapting—which Baron points out as inevitable—is the need to reflect on how we adapt. We must be aware of the choices we have and the choices we make in the face of the new technologies. In other words, while Baron describes the importance of adapting, he does not address how particular ways of adapting might be better than others. Whereas Birkerts is concerned that we are all just passively accepting these new technologies, he does not address that there are, in fact, ways to adapt that are not passive. We can consider our choices and the consequences of those choices. We can make informed decisions about which technologies to embrace and which to reject. Birkerts seems all too quick to assume that the masses are just sheep who are willing to simply go along with every new advance in technology. Instead, we can reflect more deliberately on how and when we embrace technology in our lives. If we remain conscious throughout this process and consistently analyze and inquire into these technologies rather than simply accepting them we will be adapting in responsible ways rather than just following the crowd.

This final paragraph draws on the two writers' perspectives in order to lay the foundation for the student's greatest contribution to the conversation. The student complicates Birkerts' argument that people are sheep and offers an alternative way of thinking about the issue.

Practice Writing a Source Synthesis

Choose three readings either from this book or from one of your other courses. Develop a source synthesis by putting these into a scholarly conversation and entering that conversation.

FOR FURTHER READING

Baron, Dennis. "Should We Fear a World Without Books?" *Web of Language*, 26 Jan. 2009, https://illinois.edu/blog/view/25/5800.

Birkerts, Sven. "MahVuhHuhPuh." The Gutenberg Elegies: The Fate of Reading in an Electronic Age, Farrar, Strauss & Giroux, 2006, pp. 11–32.

Chapter 4. Writing and Revising Academic Projects

Ponder This

What do you already know about writing and revision? How would you define these practices?

What have you learned in high school or elsewhere about writing academic essays?

Have you been taught the five-paragraph essay?

COLLEGE-LEVEL ACADEMIC WRITING: MOVING BEYOND THE FIVE-PARAGRAPH ESSAY

Just as reading is defined as the process of creating meaning (rather than hunting for it in a text), this book defines writing as an active enterprise wherein you, the writer, make inquiries into a subject. You raise questions, discover, and develop ideas rather than report ideas or knowledge you already have. This work will allow you to play a role in the academic "conversation."

You may have learned to write in the five-paragraph form wherein you choose a subject, develop a three-part thesis about it, and then devote each of the following three paragraphs to one of those ideas. Once you are expected to engage in more sophisticated thinking and writing—as you are in college—a few problems with this approach begin to emerge.

First, the one-paragraph-per-point format prohibits the writer from going into much depth about each point. Not only is there no room to develop each point, but the points keep getting repeated. In the five-paragraph format, each point gets repeated (but not developed!) several times. The points are introduced in the introduction, dealt with in a paragraph, and then repeated again in the conclusion. Instead of promoting the *development* of the idea, the five-paragraph essay format promotes the *repetition* of it. It is worth noting that nothing is inherently wrong with the five-paragraph format, and, in fact, some standardized tests score these kinds of essays the highest. But, its strict rules—such as one paragraph per idea—prohibit more in-depth explorations of subjects. In college, you will be expected to develop more complex ideas and to elaborate on them. The five-paragraph essay format does not allow for this. Instead of letting a particular format determine what you can say about your subject, this textbook suggests that you let your subject determine how you will format your essay, including how many paragraphs you will allot to each idea.

Now that you are writing at the college level, the five-paragraph format will no longer suffice since it necessarily restricts what you can say and how you say it. In its place, this textbook encourages you to consider and reflect on which kinds of forms suit your needs as a writer and how to make decisions about form based on the context of the writing and the purpose of each writing assignment.

Ponder This

How much of what you read in your classes and for pleasure adheres to the five-paragraph format, which many instructors require students to use? See if you can locate one or more published texts that are written in the five-paragraph form. If you find an example consider why it is written in this form. If you cannot find any examples consider why not.

MOVING TOWARD A WORKING ACADEMIC ARGUMENT

As you know by now, to be a strong writer you need to be a strong reader. This chapter moves into more specifics about writing, and academic writing, in particular. You have probably heard teachers talk about writing as a process. In fact, you have likely already experienced this process in some form. You may have developed an outline or taken some notes on readings before writing an essay. You may have spent some time brainstorming ideas or you may have just sat down at your computer and started writing a few body paragraphs. Everyone's writing process is different and so this textbook will not provide a formula for you to follow. Instead, it will provide steps, which are intended to be flexible, toward writing a final, polished essay.

One place to begin is to think about the three key terms in the phrase "working academic argument," the title of this chapter. Let's start with "working." The term "working" is crucial here because it reminds you that you are not committed to this argument; you are simply *working* with it for now.

In fact, you will likely need to return to it and revise it as you develop your first draft. By the final draft, you may not even recognize your working argument. For now, though, that working academic argument provides some focus.

Next is the term "academic." Think of an academic argument as one that involves joining the conversation—the academic discourse—about a subject, as is described throughout this book. Your contribution to that conversation is your argument, it's your position on the subject, and it usually comes on the first page of your piece of writing. Often it is the final sentence of the introductory paragraph, but its successful placement will, of course, depend on a range of other factors, including how much background information you need to offer in order for your argument to make sense. The most successful academic arguments are like extended syntheses (see Chapter 3 for more on writing syntheses) in which you develop your argument as you work, think, and write alongside what others have said about the subject.

British novelist E. M. Forster once said "How do I know what I think until I see what I say?" In order to know what you think, you can look at what you have already said in the form of the annotations you made on your readings. Remember that your annotations serve as the bridge between your reading and writing, are a rich resource that represent your initial contribution to the academic conversation, and can ultimately help you develop a more comprehensive academic argument.

The final term, *argument* is often misunderstood because in everyday discourse it suggests a confrontation wherein there is a winner and a loser. When qualified by the term *academic*, though, argument takes on a different meaning. When you develop an *academic argument*, you are not seeking to win a debate by shooting down your opponent. In fact, academic arguments value exploration and open-endedness. How could there be a winner or loser if you are writing to explore rather than writing to prove something or resolve it?

You will want to use your argument to take a *position* in response to others who have written on the subject. You are situating yourself in terms of what others have said and exploring the subject in a particular way, from a specific perspective. But remember that it's not about proving them wrong or winning, but rather about entering the conversation that is already in progress about the subject, and creating a space for yourself and your views by indicating where you stand—your position—on the subject.

The Role of Reading in Developing and Refining a Working Academic Argument

It is important to keep in mind that reading and re-reading play important roles in your writing process. As you seek to refine your working academic argument, and as you write your essays, you will want to return to whatever text you are writing about and re-read it, applying different reading strategies depending on the purpose of the assignment (see Chapter 2 for more on the importance of purpose). As you do so, annotate it appropriately. When all is said and done you will have multiple layers of annotations on your text. Re-read those, too. Use those annotations to help you develop and refine your working academic argument and begin writing your essay. Ask yourself the following related questions: What initial contributions do your annotations make to the "conversation?" How can you develop those now that you have more space to do so in your essay?

Elements of an Academic Essay

Once you have a working academic argument, which will bring some focus to your writing even if you end up **editing** or totally **revising** it, you need to develop the various aspects of the argument. Academic arguments largely depend on logical appeals, which include claims that are supported by evidence and reason. Still, that does not mean that there is not a place for ethos and pathos in academic writing. In order to determine the extent to which you will use these appeals in your academic writing you will need to think about the purpose for your writing and how important it is to establish your credibility (ethos) and to emotionally affect (pathos) your reader. First and foremost, though, your academic arguments will need to be supported by and developed through claims. Those claims will need to be supported by evidence and reasons.

The So What? question

In addition to exploring and supporting your academic arguments, you will need to indicate to your readers why your argument is important, why it matters. This is where the *So What?* question comes in. At first glance, this question may sound a little flip to you, and students have been taken aback when I write *So What*? in the margins of their paper, as if I am trying to demean their ideas. Asking writers *So What?,* though, pushes them to consider the **implications** of their arguments, or the implied effects or results of the argument. When writers become aware of the implications of their arguments they become aware of why their argument matters and for whom. Indicating the implications of your argument is an important step toward connecting to your readers who will likely want to know why they should care about what you have written. Consider the following revision of a working academic argument.

> This essay will argue that climate change and beach erosion are negatively affecting the beaches in Connecticut.

Revision

Many proposals outline steps to address the effects of erosion and climate change on beaches. This essay aims to uncover the aspects of these proposals that are most relevant to Connecticut beaches and considers to what extent these steps are plausible within this context. Without such considerations, Connecticut beaches are at serious risk of major damage, which will have larger ecological impacts, as well.

Notice that in the second example the student answers the following question: "*So What* that climate change and erosion are affecting Connecticut beaches?" The answer is that final sentence, which outlines why this matters: Without such considerations, Connecticut beaches are at serious risk of major damage, which will have larger ecological impacts, as well. This is an important aspect of the writer's argument because it clarifies for readers why this matters and why they should care.

Additional Examples of Revised Working Academic Arguments

Instructors should teach novels that students can relate to.

Revision

Although it seems to be a good idea for instructors to only teach novels that students can relate to, this essay addresses the false assumption on which this idea depends—namely that all students have the same interests and that all students in any given class will be able to relate to the same novels. If instructors believe that they can find novels that all students can relate to they are missing the opportunity to recognize the individuality of students and their interests.

Notice that in the second example the student answers the following question: "*So What* that instructors are making a mistake by trying to find novels that all students can relate to?" The answer is that final sentence, which outlines why this matters: If instructors believe that they can find novels that all students can relate to they are missing the opportunity to recognize the individuality of students and their interests.

Globalism is a positive force in our world.

Revision

Although globalism is generally thought of as a positive force, when looked at closely it becomes clear that globalism may not be working for everyone. It is important to

> understand precisely who is benefiting most from globalism in order to find ways to address these inequities.

Notice that in the second example the student answers the following question: "*So What* that globalism may not be working for everyone?" The answer is that final sentence, which outlines why this matters: It is important to understand precisely who is benefiting most from globalism in order to find ways to address these inequities.

As all of the revised examples indicate, asking the *So What*? question as you lay out your argument lets readers know right away why your argument is important and why they should keep reading.

ANTICIPATING AND ADDRESSING DISAGREEMENTS: INSERTING THE NAYSAYER

Sometimes we can't imagine why someone would disagree with us. But the most sophisticated writers not only imagine that some readers will disagree, they also 1) anticipate those disagreements 2) address them and 3) use them to make their own arguments stronger and more nuanced. In college-level writing you'll be expected to do the same. While it's sometimes tempting to pretend that you never came across someone who challenges your argument or that such challenges or disagreements may not exist, addressing these "naysayers" in your essays will make your arguments even stronger because you have already anticipated objections and have adjusted your argument accordingly. In other words, you won't appear close-minded since you are willing to address arguments that oppose yours.

It is best to address challenges to your argument once you have taken the time to develop your argument and offer evidence for your claims. Beginning with or concluding by addressing those who might challenge your argument might confuse your reader. You can address *naysayers* in various ways.

You may address a general naysayer with a sentence such as the following:

> "Some readers may disagree that . . . ."

You may address a more specific naysayer (in this case, environmentalists) with a sentence such as the following:

> "Environmentalists would likely challenge . . . ."

You may pose questions that are intended to represent the doubts a naysayer may have about your argument:

> "Is this really possible?" the reader may wonder.

The point is that addressing naysayers should be seen as an opportunity to further develop and refine your argument so that it anticipates and addresses those who may challenge it. Pushing opposing arguments under the rug, so to speak, will make you seem short-sighted and incapable of considering and addressing other viewpoints. This, in turn, harms your credibility as a writer and thinker. Finally, keep in mind that you should not just insert the naysayer for the sake of doing so, but you should use other points of view, like the naysayer, to help you refine your own ideas and arguments.

Practice Playing the Naysayer

One of the best ways to anticipate how someone might challenge your argument is to either find people who actually disagree and incorporate their viewpoints into your writing or to pose questions that start with "But what about . . . ." Read the following arguments and respond to them by completing the question "But what about . . . " to see how a naysayer may respond to these arguments.

> Obesity puts a great strain on healthcare costs because it costs so much more to conduct tests on obese patients; therefore obese patients should not be entitled to the same insurance coverage as other patients.

**Play the naysayer: "But what about . . . ."*

> Olympic athletes should be held to especially high standards of conduct because they represent their country and are role models for young children.

*Play the naysayer: "But what about . . . ."

MULTIMODAL COMPOSING

Up until this point, this chapter has largely assumed that you will be composing your essays in the more traditional way by using alphabetic text or words. But, there are other forms of composition in which your instructor may expect you to engage. The word "multimodal" means more than one mode. As such, multimodal composing invites you to use various forms—beyond typographic essays—to develop and communicate your ideas. Print-based multimodal texts include comics, graphic novels, posters, and brochures. Digital multimodal texts include webpages, blogs, films, videos, animation, and social media. As you can tell by these lists of some familiar kinds of multimodal texts, you engage multimodality on a daily basis. As a student, you may be encouraged to use all of these modes. Multimodal composing allows *you* to create these texts rather than just consume them. As you do so, you will need to consider all of the elements you consider as you compose a more traditional typographic essay, but multimodal projects also give you the freedom to bring in other modes to help you develop and communicate your arguments. Additionally, multimodal projects give you opportunities to explore different rhetorical considerations than those you consider when composing strictly printed texts. For example, although the rhetorical appeals described in this book remain relevant, issues of design are often more important when composing multimodal projects than when writing a traditional print-based essay.

Because the expectations of multimodal projects vary so much, this section will not attempt to teach you how to complete every multimodal project you may be assigned. It is impossible to anticipate such a thing. Instead, the remainder of this chapter will address those considerations worth keeping in mind as you complete the multimodal assignments included in Part Two of this textbook, which are representative of different kinds of multimodal projects you may encounter in your classes.

Considerations for Multimodal Composing

Choose mode(s). If it is up to you to choose which modes you will use to compose, choose modes that lend themselves to the goals of the assignment, as well as to your specific goals for your project. You will also need to be able to justify your choice in an accompanying reflective piece, which many multimodal assignments require. For example, if you are asked to develop a project about a specific geographic location intended for potential tourists, don't just rush to compose a podcast wherein you lecture about the place. A photographic essay, brochure, or webpage could make a more persuasive argument as to why people should visit this location. Seeing pictures of the beaches of Bermuda, pictures of the local seafood, or exploring links to local boat tours, for example, may be more compelling for a potential tourist than simply hearing about these in a podcast.

Develop a plan. Once you know which modes you will use, develop a plan for producing your project. You might brainstorm ideas, develop an outline, or construct a working argument. You need to imagine how you are going to execute your project including what you want to communicate, as well as how you are going to do so. For example, make sure you have access to and feel comfortable with whatever technology you would like to use. You may not totally stick to your plan, but you should have one in place to get you heading in the direction of the goals of the assignment.

Consider the rhetorical elements of your project. If you are trying to make a particular kind of rhetorical appeal (see Chapter 2 for more on rhetorical appeals) consider whether this appeal will be effective for the intended audience for your piece. Think about whether the design and the arrangement of the elements of your project underscore and support your central idea or argument. Be sure that the purpose of your project is clear.

Compose ethically. Just as you must abide by the rules of academic integrity when you write a traditional essay, you need to do the same when developing multimodal projects. Many images, videos, and other elements you may want to include in your projects are under copyright law and you can't simply use them. That said, if you look a little harder, you will be able to find items that are under what is called creative commons licensing, which means that you can reproduce these as long as you are not doing so for commercial purposes (i.e. to make money). Just as you are expected to avoid plagiarizing when composing in the traditional sense, you will want to avoid infringing on copyright laws when you engage in multimodal composition.

Reflect Regularly. Many multimodal projects are accompanied by a reflection in which you have the opportunity to describe your process for composing the project and the rationale for the choices you made while doing so. This is important work to complete once you have finished your project because you become more aware of what you have learned while composing, how well you accomplished your personal goals for the project, and how well you have met the goals of the assignment. It is also helpful to reflect along the way, though. Waiting until you are totally finished your project in order to reflect on it means that if you have not met your personal goals or those of the assignment you won't know until it's too late. That's why it is important to check-in with yourself, so to speak, during the composing process to make sure that you are meeting these goals and that the decisions you are making are having a positive effect on your vision for your project.

MINDFULLY READING TO REVISE YOUR WRITING AND MULTIMODAL PROJECTS

Once you have completed your project (or think you have!)—you may be asked to revise it. Revising is different from editing. Think of revising as re-vising or re-seeing, which is much more involved than simply editing for grammar, word choice, or spelling. Those things are important, but revising is an altogether different process that involves re-viewing the larger, conceptual issues that affect your project such as its argument, focus, design, and organization.

You may be asked to revise something on your own or you may have the benefit of readers, including your peers, a tutor in the writing center on your campus, or your professor. Revising on your own without feedback is perhaps more difficult because you need to be able to separate yourself from the piece so you can see where it needs work. That's why it is important to wait as long as you can before returning to your project in order to revise it. That time will give you a fresh way of seeing the piece and will help you more objectively determine the aspects that need additional work.

When you return to your project, use some of the reading strategies you have been applying to published texts to help you re-see your project (see Chapter 2 for the reading strategies). Two strategies that will help you think more deeply about the strength of your argument, the piece's organization, and its focus are the Says/Does Approach and the Mapping Strategy. These strategies, in particular, make visible the connections among the various parts of a project. In addition to relying on the reading strategies and your annotations, you can ask yourself the following questions:

1. How strong is the argument I'm advancing in my project? Is it supported by claims and are those claims supported by reasons and evidence?
2. How well is my project organized? Do paragraphs and/or other elements, for example, transition smoothly and logically?
3. How focused is my project? Do I digress into irrelevant points and ideas? Are my ideas and arguments developed throughout rather than just repeated?

Two Ways to Test the Strength of your Argument

1. Check it for binary thinking
2. Review the relationship between your evidence/reasons and claims

Potential Pitfall: Binary Thinking

It is easy to fall into the trap of binary thinking. We all do it now and then, but it does not have a place in complex, academic thought and writing. Binary thinking is a type of thinking wherein you believe that there are only two sides to every issue. For example, someone who participates in binary thinking would think that either you are for or against video games; for or against animal rights; for or against stem-cell research. The problem with this type of thinking is that it oversimplifies complicated issues. In other words, you might not be for *violent* video games but you might support the use of video games in classrooms to encourage certain types of learning. You might not believe that people should wear fur or test cosmetics on animals, but you might believe that testing *medication* on animals is okay. Or maybe you believe that testing medication on *certain* animals is okay. Or that testing *certain medications* on *certain animals* is okay. See how potentially complex issues can be? This point, however, often raises the question: Is finding the middle ground an appropriate intellectual response? The short answer is no. While it may be tempting to take on a position such as "playing video games in moderation is okay" or "using technology in moderation is okay" consider how vague those responses are. We could say anything in moderation is ok—everything from alcohol use to humor or everything from video games to animal testing. Your intellectual contribution—whether in writing or in the form of a multimodal project—should be more specific by drawing on what you have read in order to help you develop your own ideas through writing. Compare the following arguments.

> Testing on animals is wrong.
>
> The practice of testing certain medications on dogs, like those medications that speed up dogs' heart rates and put them in danger of dying, needs to be reexamined and ultimately rethought in order to protect against unnecessary deaths in animals who cannot protect themselves.

You probably noticed that *argument #1* is vague and general. It leaves so much unexplained like which kind of testing? Which kind of animals? "Wrong" according to whose morals? *Argument #2* collapses the binary implied by *argument #1,* namely that testing on animals is either right or wrong by being far more specific and answering the questions the first version doesn't. Moreover, rather than offering a judgment (sometimes the result of binary thinking), the second version takes a more inquiry-driven approach by calling for a reexamination and rethinking of the testing of certain medications on certain animals.

Practice Avoiding Binary Thinking by Revising the Following Arguments So They Are More Complex and Nuanced.

1. Reading books is better than watching television.
2. The literature of today is not original; it just recycles Shakespeare's own writing.
3. You are either anti-capital punishment or you are for criminals.

Potential Pitfall: Your Evidence Doesn't Support Your Claims

It may sound a bit silly that your evidence wouldn't support your claims, but this gap occurs both in students' writing and published writing more than you might think. The first step to ensuring that your evidence supports your claims is to separate them from each other as is done with the examples that follow:

Author John Gafe notes, "Technology is creating an environment in which people are so distracted from what is going on around them that they don't even realize they have become consumed by these technological advances, and they remain unaware of how they are changing as human beings." This quote proves that because of technology everyone just goes ahead with their lives without an awareness of what is happening around them.

> Claim: This quote proves that because of technology everyone just goes ahead with their lives without an awareness of what is happening around them.
>
> Evidence: Author John Gafe notes, "Technology is creating an environment in which people are so distracted from what is going on around them that they don't even realize they have become consumed by these advances and they remain unaware of how they are changing as human beings."

In this case, the claim is that the quote from author John Gafe *proves* that people are oblivious to what is happening around them. One quote from one source cannot prove anything. As such, the evidence does not support the claim because the claim goes too far based on the evidence. It overstates the case. Revising the claim so that it doesn't describe the quote as proving anything will be important for this student.

Practice Separating Claims from Evidence and Revising Accordingly:

Technology has overtaken our minds. We are surrounded by new computers, phones, and all kinds of fancy gadgets.

1. Which sentence is the claim?
2. Which sentence is the evidence?
3. How might you revise the claim so that it is better reflects the evidence provided?

REVISING BASED ON FEEDBACK

You may have the opportunity to receive feedback from your peers, your instructor, or even a writing center tutor prior to revising. Consider yourself lucky! Their feedback will give you insight into how others respond to your writing and multimodal projects. These people will (perhaps more objectively than you are able to) let you know what needs work. They may address aspects of your argument that need to be explained, developed, or even re-thought. They may suggest that you use different images or technologies, an alternate design, or organize the piece differently.

You may even receive more than one set of responses to each project, which can be confusing. Whose advice do you follow? Your peer's or your instructor's? Your instructor's or the peer tutor's? While your instructor's comments may ultimately take precedence, it is up to you to weigh those responses and determine which you will address and which you will ignore. Remember that you ultimately make the decisions. Generally speaking, when more than one person has made the same comment it is probably worth addressing. Some comments are simply idiosyncratic, though, and may not offer productive routes. As you go through each comment, think about what is at stake—both the potential positive and negative consequences of revising according to the feedback you received. The following questions can help guide you through the feedback you receive. If you make the suggested changes:

- Might you sacrifice the focus of the project?
- Might you confuse other readers/viewers?
- Might you create a more complex argument?
- Might you open up a productive space for analysis in addition to summary?

Ask yourself these and other questions as you consider making the revisions suggested by those who have engaged with your project.

Chapter 5. Working with Sources

CONSISTENCIES (AND DIFFERENCES) BETWEEN SOURCE-BASED WRITING AND ACADEMIC ESSAYS

Research writing—or source-based writing—is often afforded its own chapter in textbooks like this, and sometimes even its own classes in colleges and universities. This is because research writing is often defined as its own genre or type of writing. While research writing certainly has features that may distinguish it from other kinds of academic writing, it is not all that different from the type of academic writing described in this textbook. Nor are the elements you would consider while engaged in source-based writing all that different from those you would consider while developing a multimodal project. Perhaps the greatest similarity among all of this kind of work—as it is defined in this textbook—is that it all requires mindful reading. While nowhere in the phrases *research writing* and *source-based writing* does *reading* come up, one cannot develop a research essay or project without reading the sources that will inform it. Moreover, reading these sources mindfully by applying the most relevant reading strategies is an important element of writing strong source-based papers. Because of this (and other) important similarities between source-based writing and what is called academic writing in the previous chapter, this chapter on research writing will mark the consistencies between these kinds of writing, as well as a few important differences worth addressing. Let's start with the similarities. Here is a list of ways that research writing is just like academic writing as it is described in the previous chapter:

1. Research writing is about inquiry. In source-based writing, the writer uses several sources to explore and discover ideas and subjects.
2. Research writing is about entering a scholarly conversation. The writer reads sources in order to position herself, via an argument, in relation to those authors (i.e. sources) who are involved in a conversation on a particular subject.
3. Sources that you find while conducting research may support but also challenge your argument; use those that challenge your argument to address naysayers and refine your thinking.
4. Research writing involves synthesizing your sources; academic arguments are like extended synthesis papers (see Chapter 3 and Chapter 4 for more on synthesis papers and academic arguments).

5. Research writing demands mindful reading. In order to use the sources in the ways mentioned in this chapter, a writer needs to mindfully read the sources by choosing the appropriate strategies and annotation practices to support the particular research project.

Some differences that separate source-based writing from academic writing include the following:

1. While all of the reading strategies listed in Chapter 2 are potentially useful in academic writing, the final strategy "Reading and Evaluating Online Sources" is of particular use to source-based writing because it demands that the reader evaluate the kinds of sources and the credibility of the sources she is considering.
2. Skimming (see Chapter 2 for more on skimming) can be an especially important reading strategy initially when determining whether a source is going to be useful.
3. Research-based writing might involve field research in which you are expected to conduct interviews or observe situations. These activities are less likely to be part of academic writing.
4. Avoiding plagiarism becomes especially important when working with sources.

This rest of this chapter will address the four differences, listed just above, to help prepare you for source-based writing.

Reading Online Sources for Credibility

Although many of the reading strategies introduced in Chapter 2 can help you understand the content of online sources, the final reading strategy in that chapter outlines ways of reading online sources for their credibility, which means reading them to determine whether the sources can be trusted. The following questions (also included in Chapter 2) can help you determine whether the source meets your needs. Remember that you may use annotation as a tool for recording your answers to these questions directly on the text.

1. *Consider* the differences among these domains. What kind of website does the text appear on? Is it a .com, .org, .gov, .edu?
2. *Know*. Who is the author, organization, or company that sponsors the website? Search for more information once you have this information. If there is no author, try looking up the website at WHOIS, which provides this information: https://whois.icann.org/en.
3. *Determine*, if you can, whether the piece is peer-reviewed, which means that it goes through an evaluation by other scholars in the field. If you are looking at a journal article, for example, notice the press that publishes the journal. Then search that press to find information about it.

4. *Look* to see if the text has a bibliography at the end. If so, what kinds of texts are cited?
5. *Consider* whether any sources are cited in the piece. If so, what kinds?

THE ROLE OF SKIMMING IN SOURCE-BASED WRITING

Skimming, the second reading strategy described in Chapter 2, is rarely useful on its own and usually requires that the reader return for a closer, second reading. That's not necessarily the case when it comes to skimming sources for research writing. The exciting and also overwhelming aspect of research writing is that there are so many sources out there to read. The internet, your library's specialized databases, and print books offer so much information. When you are in the early stages of developing an argument for a source-based project or paper, you will need to determine which sources will be most useful. At this point in the process, it's not necessary to closely read each source and annotate it. You could end up wasting valuable time on many sources that will be of no use to you. Instead, you can start by skimming and annotating the sources in the ways described in Chapter 2. The following steps (which also appear on Chapter 2) can help you productively skim potential sources and make informed decisions about their uses to you. As you skim, you may want to annotate a piece by noting the elements in the following list and marking them as they appear in the text.

1. The elements you notice by "previewing" the piece, such as its title; author; introductory material (e.g. an abstract); and general design and structure (e.g. subject headings, graphics, and hyperlinks). See you if you can determine its genre, which means you decide what type of text it is.
2. The introduction since introductions often (although not always) describe the piece as a whole.
3. The first sentence of each paragraph since first sentences are usually topic sentences and can give you an overall sense of the subject of the paragraph.
4. The conclusion or the final paragraph of the piece since conclusions often (although not always) summarize a piece.

FIELD RESEARCH IN SOURCE-BASED WRITING

Field research is research that takes the writer into the subject's field to conduct first-hand research as opposed to simply relying on research that others have completed. Field research often includes observations and interviews. For example, if you are writing about daycare centers, you might visit a few centers and observe what goes on. If you are writing about how fast-food restaurants treat their employees, you might develop questionnaires for employees to complete and/or set up interviews with them. This sort of first-hand research may be done in conjunction with research that other scholars have conducted and published or it may be done on its own.

Although they may not seem relevant at first, the reading strategies in Chapter 2 are helpful with field research, too. For example, the same way you may read online sources for their credibility you should think about the credibility of the participants in the research you are conducting. How trustworthy are their perspectives? Are some more trustworthy than others? You may also consider the best reading strategies to use while reading over participants' answers to interview questions and questionnaires, as well as any transcripts you may have from your field research.

AVOIDING PLAGIARISM

You plagiarize when you use someone else's ideas, words, or visuals (e.g. graphs, cartoons, images, maps) but do not give them credit. **Plagiarism** may be intentional or unintentional, meaning that you may be aware you are plagiarizing (but still trying to get away with it) or be unaware that a summary you have written, for example, resembles the original too closely without proper citation.

There really is no reason to plagiarize ever, but particularly not when writing is defined as entering a conversation with others who have thought and written about a subject, as it is in this textbook. You are expected, in other words, to consult and to use what other scholars have said about a subject; there is no reason to hide the fact that you have consulted others. Conceiving of writing as entering a conversation *depends* upon your using what others have said to help you develop your own ideas. This is precisely what professional scholars do. They engage, respond, and think alongside other scholars and use each other's ideas to develop their own. Examples of this kind of work come more easily when we think about the sciences: certain discoveries could not have been made if earlier scientists didn't lay the groundwork. But, the same is true in the humanities. Look at any piece of writing from a humanities scholar and you will see that they consistently quote other scholars in order to give those scholars credit for helping them develop their own ideas and think more complexly about a subject. By quoting these other scholars, they have avoided plagiarizing.

Avoiding plagiarism is crucial in all of your writing, but in source-based writing it can be a bit more difficult to avoid since you are juggling a bunch of different sources. You may have trouble keeping track of who said what or you may not know how to cite your sources correctly. There are online resources to help you with both, and your instructor will likely have other resources, as well, to help you avoid plagiarizing. Refworks, EasyBib, and other online bibliographic management programs provide an online space to both save your references and develop correctly formatted citations for them. Of course, you will always want to compare the citations generated by these programs to the most up-to-date handbooks (e.g. the *MLA Handbook*) and online sources (The Purdue OWL) to be sure they are correct.

Your institution has a statement or code that describes how students are expected to conduct themselves, and these often include expectations about academic integrity. Take some time to research your own institution's statement about academic integrity so you understand the intricacies of how issues related to academic integrity, including plagiarism, are addressed on your specific campus.

Part Two. Readings

Chapter 6. Readings on Reading

This chapter serves as a bridge between Part One of this textbook, which includes the instruction, and Part Two, which includes the readings on technology and related assignments. You'll find selections on the subject of reading written by scholar-teachers within the fields of composition, rhetoric, literacy studies, and education. These are peer-reviewed scholarly essays that have been published in some of the most prestigious scholarly journals. In these essays, scholars address a range of issues surrounding reading. Some essays describe research on how well students read and what motivates students to read. Others explore the most effective ways of defining and teaching reading in writing classes, and others, still, address the difficulties students have transitioning from the expectations of high-school-level reading to those of college-level reading. Although you may have some difficulty reading these dense pieces—and are encouraged to use the reading strategies outlined in Chapter 2—the subjects these essays address should be rather familiar to you. After all, students, and particularly first-year students, figure prominently in these pieces. At the end of this chapter you will find general questions about the reading selections that will help you understand, respond, and apply what you have learned from these pieces. These essays will support your understanding of the very concept of reading and set you on a path toward becoming a more reflective reader.

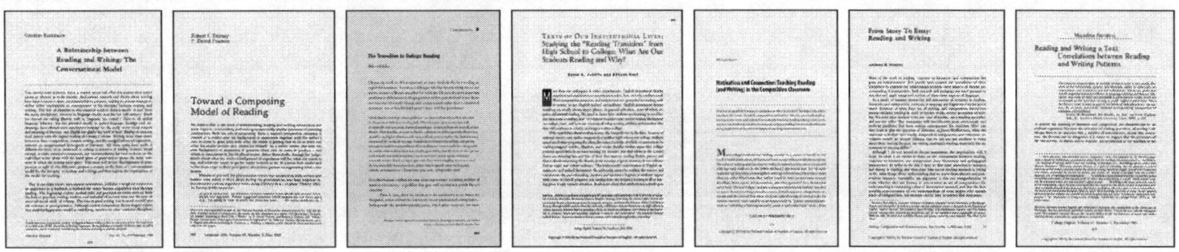

PRIOR TO READING EACH SELECTION IN THIS CHAPTER

Look at the questions at the end of the chapter. What are you expected to do after reading the selections? In other words, what are your purposes for reading? Although you will be asked to apply particular reading strategies in order to complete some of the tasks, other questions will leave the choice of strategy up to you. Refer to the descriptions of the reading strategies in Chapter 2 and decide which will be most useful in helping you accomplish those tasks.

College English Volume 41, Number 6, February 1980

A Relationship between Reading and Writing: The Conversational Model[1]

Charles Bazerman[2]

The connection between what a person reads and what that person then writes seems so obvious as to be truistic. And current research and theory about writing have been content to leave the relationship as a truism, making no serious attempt to define either mechanisms or consequences of the interplay between reading and writing. The lack of attention to this essential bond of literacy results in part from the many disciplinary divorces in language studies over the last half century: *Speech* has moved out taking *Rhetoric* with it; *Linguistics* has staked a claim to all skilled language behavior, but has attended mostly to spoken language; *Sociology* and *Anthropology* have offered more satisfactory lodgings for the study of the social context and meaning of literacy; and *English* has gladly rid itself of basic *Reading* to concern itself purely with the higher reading of *Literary Criticism.* Writing in its three incarnations as basic composition, creative writing, and the vestigial advanced exposition, remains an unappreciated houseguest of *Literature.* All these splits have made it difficult for those of us interested in writing to conceive of writing in terms broad enough to make essential connections: our accommodation has been to focus on the individual writer alone with the blank piece of paper and to ignore the many contexts in which the writing takes place. This essay will review developments in composition in light of this difficulty, propose a remedy in the form of a conversational model for the interplay of reading and writing, and then explore the implications of the model for teaching.

One of the older views, with ancient antecedents, held that a neophyte writer was an apprentice to a tradition, a tradition the writer became acquainted with through reading. The beginning student studied rules and practiced set forms derived from the best of previous writing; analysis and imitation of revered texts was the core of more advanced study of writing. The way to good writing was to mold oneself into the contours of prior greatness. Although current composition theory largely rejects this tradition/apprentice model as stultifying, teachers of other academic disciplines still find the model attractive, because writing in content disciplines requires mastery of disciplinary

1 **Citation:** Bazerman, Charles. "A Relationship between Reading and Writing: The Conversation Model." *College English*, vol. 41, no. 6, 1980, pp. 656–661.

2 Charles Bazerman is an associate professor of English at Baruch College of the City University of New York and serves as co-chair of the CUNY Association of Writing Supervisors. He has published on a number of literary topics as well as composition, and he is currently investigating the character of writing in academic disciplines.

literature. The accumulated knowledge and accepted forms of writing circumscribe what and how a student may write in disciplines such as history, biology, and philosophy.

Recent work in composition has chosen instead to emphasize the writer's original voice, which has its source in an independent self. The model of the individual writer shaping thought through language informs recent investigations into the composing process, growth of syntactic maturity, and the source of error. We have aided the student in the struggle to express the self by revealing the logic of syntax, by asking for experiential and personal writing, and by offering techniques for pre-writing and invention to help the student get closer to the wellsprings of thought that lie inside. Even traditional rhetoric finds its new justification in the reflection of organic psychological realities. By establishing the importance of the voice of the writer and the authority of personal perception, we have learned to give weight to what the student wants to say, to be patient with the complex process of writing, to offer sympathetic advice on *how to* rather than *what not to,* and to help the student discover the personal motivations to learn to write.

Yet the close observation of the plight of the individual writer has led us to remember that writing is not contained entirely in the envelope of experience, native thought, and personal motivation to communicate. Communication presupposes an audience, and deference to that audience has led to a revived concern for the forms of what is now called Standard Written English. E. D. Hirsch, in *The Philosophy of Composition* (Chicago: University of Chicago Press, 1977), locates the entire philosophy in readability; that is, concern for the audience. We have also noticed that most writing our students do during college is in the context of their academic studies; interest in writing across the curriculum has been the result. In the most thoughtful study coming out of this approach, *The Development of Writing Abilities (11–18)* (London: Macmillan, 1975), James Britton and his colleagues begin to notice that students use readings, but in personal and original ways, in order to write for their academic courses. "Source-book material may be used in various ways involving different levels of activity by the writer" (p. 23).

We may begin to understand those "various ways" and "different levels of activity" Britton refers to if we consider each piece of writing as a contribution to an on-going, written conversation. Conversation requires absorption of what prior speakers have said, consideration of how earlier comments relate to the responder's thoughts, and a response framed to the situation and the responder's purposes. Until a final statement is made or participants disengage themselves, the process of response continues. The immediacy of spoken conversation does, I must admit, differ significantly from the reflectiveness of written conversation, but the differences more illuminate the special character of writing than diminish the force of the model. Speech melody, gestural communication, rapidly shifting dynamics, and immediate validation on one side are set against explicitness, development, complexity, contemplation, and revision on the other. The written conversation also may bring together a more diffuse range of participants than the spoken one, although the example of an exchange of office memos or the closed circle represented in professional journals indicates that such is not always the case. Further, in spoken conversation the makers of previous comments are more likely to be the auditors of the response. But again the counter-examples of the teacher who turns one student's question into the occasion for a lecture to the entire class, or the printed back and forth of a literary war, suggest that this distinction should not be oversimplified.

The conversational model points up the fact that writing occurs within the context of previous writing and advances the total sum of the discourse. Earlier comments provide subjects at issue, factual content, ideas to work with, and models of discourse appropriate to the subject. Later comments build on what came before and may, therefore, go farther. Later comments also define themselves against the earlier even as they dispute particulars, redefine issues, add new material, or otherwise shift the discussion.

If as teachers of writing we want to prepare our students to enter into the written interchanges of their chosen disciplines and the various discussions of personal and public interest, we must cultivate various techniques of absorbing, reformulating, commenting on, and using reading. In the tradition/apprentice model such skills were fostered only implicitly under the umbrella assignment of the research paper, but they were not given explicit, careful attention. Only access to the tradition (information gathering) and acknowledgement of the tradition (documentation) were the foci of instruction. In the newer model of the voice of the individual self, assignments such as the research paper are superfluous, remaining only as vestiges of former syllabi or as the penance imposed on a service department. The model of the conversation, however, suggests a full curriculum of skills and stages in the process of relating new comments to previously written materials. The following partial catalogue of stages, skills, and assignments points toward the kinds of issues that might be addressed in writing courses. The suggestions are in the form of a framework rather than of specific lessons in order to leave each teacher free to interpret the consequences of the model through the matrix of individual thoughts, experiences, and teaching styles. Similarly the teacher will need to interpret the model through those conversations that are most familiar and important to students. Given the diversity of existing written conversations and the variety of individual responses, it is not profitable to prescribe a single course for everyone.

Intelligent response begins with *accurate understanding of prior comments,* not just of the facts and ideas stated, but of what the other writer was trying to achieve. A potential respondent needs to know not just the claims a writer was making, but also whether the writer was trying to call established beliefs into question or simply add some detail to generally agreed upon ideas. The respondent needs to be able to tell whether a prior statement was attempting to arouse emotions or to call forth dispassionate judgment. The more we understand of the dynamics as well as the content of a conversation, the more we have to respond to. Vague understanding is more than careless; it is soporific. Particular writing assignments can help students become more perceptive readers and can help break down the tendency toward vague inarticulateness resulting from purely private reading. Paraphrase encourages precise understanding of individual terms and statements; the act of translating thoughts from one set of words to another makes the student consider exactly what was said and what was not. Summary reveals the structure of arguments and the continuity of thought; the student must ferret out the important claims and those elements that unify the entire piece of writing. Both paraphrase and summary will also be useful skills when in the course of making original arguments the student will have to refer to the thoughts of others with some accuracy and efficiency. Finally, having students analyze the technique of writing in relation to the writing's apparent purpose will make students sensitive to the ways writing can create effects that go beyond the overt content. Analysis of propaganda and advertising will provide the extreme and easy cases, but analysis of more subtle designs, such as that of legal arguments or of reports of biological research, will more fully reveal the purposive nature of writing.

The next stage, *reacting to reading,* gives students a sense of their own opinions and identity defined against the reading material. As they try to reconcile what they read with what they already think, students begin to explore their assumptions and frameworks of thought. At first their responses may be uninformed, either fending off the new material or acquiescing totally to what appears to be the indisputable authority of the printed word. But with time and opportunities to articulate their changing responses, students can become more comfortable with the questions raised by their reading; they enter into a more dialectical relationship with those who have written before. Prior assimilated reading becomes grist for processing new reading. Three kinds of exercise encourage the development of more extensive and thoughtful reactions: marginal comments on reading, reading journals, and informal reaction essays. From early in the semester teachers should encourage students to record their thoughts about the reading in marginal notes. The teacher must be careful to distinguish this kind of reaction annotation from the more familiar study skills kind of content annotation, perhaps by suggesting that content annotations go on the inside margin and reactions go on the wider outside margins. This reaction in the margins increases the student's awareness of moment-by-moment responses to individual statements and examples. Reading journals written after each day's reading give the student additional room to explore the immediate responses at greater length and to develop larger themes. Again the teacher must insist on the distinction between content summaries and reactions, no matter how tentative the latter may at first be. Finally, the informal response essay allows the student to develop a single reaction at length, perhaps drawing on a number of related, more immediate responses. Here the teacher should make sure that the response maintains contact with issues growing out of the reading and does not become purely a rhapsody on a personal theme unrelated to the reading. For all three types of assignment the teacher can refer the student to previously held opinions, experiences, observations, and other readings as starting points for reactions. As students become more sensitive to their responses to reading, they will spontaneously recognize likely starting points.

Developing reactions leads to more formal *evaluation of reading*, measuring what a book or article actually accomplishes compared to its apparent ambitions, compared to reality, and compared to other books. The evaluative review, if treated as more than just a notice covered with a thin wash of reaction, is an effective exercise, for it requires the student both to represent and to assess the claims of the book or article. The reader's reaction to the book is also significant to the evaluation, for if the reader finds herself laughing when she should be nodding in assent, the book has failed to meet at least some of its purposes. Another kind of evaluative essay measures the claims of the reading against observable reality. The data the student compares to the book's claims may be from prior experience, new observations, formal data-gathering using social science techniques, or technical experiments. Here the teacher may discuss the variety of purposes, criteria, and techniques of data gathering in different academic disciplines as well as other human endeavors. Finally the student may be asked to compare the claims and evidence of a number of different sources. In this kind of exercise the students have to judge whether there is agreement, disagreement, or merely discussion of different ideas; then the student must identify on what level the agreement or disagreement occurs, whether of simple fact, interpretation, idea, or underlying approach; and finally he must determine how the agreements can be fitted together and the disagreements reconciled or adjudicated. Conflicts cannot, of course, always be resolved, but students become aware of the difficulties of evaluation. Comparison of matched selections, reports requiring synthesis, reviews of literature, and annotated bibliographies are all assignments compatible with this last purpose. Reviews of literature and annotated bibliographies also give the student a coherent picture of how previous comments add up in pursuit of common issues.

Students can then begin to define those *issues* they wish to pursue and to develop *informed views* on those issues. Two kinds of exercise, definitions of problem areas and research proposals, require the student to identify some issue he or she would like to know more about, to assemble the prior statements relevant to the issue, and to indicate the limitations of those sources. The proposal requires the further task of planning how the gap of knowledge in the literature can be overcome. Problem definitions and proposals are early stages of the familiar assignment of the research paper. Also familiar is the teacher's disappointment upon receiving a derivative research report instead of an original, informed view in the form of a research essay. The use of preparatory assignments—not just the proposal, but also progress reports, reflections on the evidence, hypothesis testing and idea sketches—will help remind the student of the original goal of the work while encouraging creative and detailed use of the source material. Prior instruction in the skills discussed above will also insure that the student knows how to use reading to form independent attitudes toward the sources and so facilitate the development of original theses. Other, more specific exercises that set the conditions for the development of informed views involve setting factual and theoretical sources against each other. Three case studies can be compared to elicit general patterns, or one writer's theories can be measured against another's factual material. These two assignments are, in fact, forms of critical analysis using a coherent set of categories derived from a theoretical standpoint to sort out specifics. Such exercises show the student the many uses of source material beyond simple citation of authority in support of predetermined opinion.

The independent, critical standpoint the student develops with respect to reading other people's works can also help the student frame and revise his or her own writing to be a purposeful and appropriate contribution to an on-going conversation. Consideration of the relationship to previous statements will help the student decide what techniques are likely to serve new purposes. Will a redefinition of basic concepts, the introduction of a new concept, or the close analysis of a case study best resolve confusion? Or perhaps only a head-on persuasive argument will serve. Further, knowledge of the literature likely to have been read by an audience helps a writer determine what needs to be explained at length and what issues need to be addressed.

The model of written conversation even transforms the technical skills of reference and citation. The variety of uses to be made of quotation, the options for referring to others' ideas and information (e.g., quotation, paraphrase, summary, name only), and the techniques of introducing and discussing source materials are the tools which allow the accurate but pointed connection of one's argument to earlier statements. The mechanics of documentation, more than being an exercise in intellectual etiquette, become the means of indicating the full range of comments to which the new essay is responding.

When we ask students to write purely from their selves, we may tap only those prior conversations that they are still engaged in and so limit the extent and variety of their thinking and writing. We can use reading to present new conversational opportunities that draw the students into wider public, professional, and academic communities. Thus the students will learn to write within the heavily literate contexts they will meet in college and later life. Whether writing tasks are explicitly embedded in prior written material—a review of literature, a research paper, or a legal brief—or whether they are only implicitly related to the thought and writing of others, as in critical analyses or matters of public debate, if students are not taught the skills of creating new statements through evaluating, assimilating, and responding to the prior statements of the written conversation, we offer them the meager choice of being parrots of authority or raconteurs stocked with anecdotes for every occasion. Only a fortunate few will learn to enter the community of the literate on their own.

Language Arts, Volume 60, Number 5, May 1983

Toward a Composing Model of Reading[1]

Robert J. Tierney and P. David Pearson[2]

We believe that at the heart of understanding reading and writing connections one must begin to view reading and writing as essentially similar processes of meaning construction. Both are acts of composing.[3] From a reader's perspective, meaning is created as a reader uses his background of experience together with the author's cues to come to grips both with what the writer is getting him to do or think and what the reader decides and creates for himself. As a writer writes, she uses her own background of experience to generate ideas and, in order to produce a test which is considerate to her idealized reader, filters these drafts through her judgments about what her reader's background of experiences will be, what she wants to say, and what she wants to get the reader to think or do. In a sense both reader and writers must adapt to their perceptions about their partner in negotiating what a text means.

Witness if you will the phenomenon which was apparent as both writers and readers were asked to think aloud during the generation of, and later response to, directions for putting together a water pump (Tierney at al., in press; Tierney 1983). As Tierney (1983) reported:

> At points in the text, the mismatch between readers' think-alouds and writers' think-alouds was apparent: Writers suggested concerns which readers did not focus upon (e.g., I'm going to have to watch my pronouns here. . . . It's rather stubborn—so I better tell how to push it hard . . . he should see that it looks very much like a syringe), and readers expressed concerns which writers did not appear to consider (I'm wondering why I should do this . . . what function does it serve). As writers thought aloud, generated text, and moved to the next set of sub-assembly directions, they would often comment about the *writers' craft* as readers might (e.g., no confusion there. . . . That's a fairly clear descriptor

1 **Citation:** Tierney, Robert J. and P. David Pearson. "Toward a Composing Model of Reading." *Language Arts*, vol. 60, no. 5, May 1983 pp. 568–580.

2 Robert J. Tierney and P. David Pearson are associated with the Center for the Study of Reading at the University of Illinois at Urbana-Champaign.

3 This work was supported in part by the National Institute of Education under Contract No. NIE 400–81–0030. Selected aspects of relevance to the model are also discussed in a paper "On Becoming a Thoughtful Reader: Learning to Read Like a Writer" by P. David Pearson and Robert J. Tierney and "Writer Reader Interactions: Defining the Dimensions of Negotiation" by Robert J. Tierney. Special Thanks go to T. Rogers and others, including A. Crismore, L. Fielding, J. Hansen, and J. Harste for their reactions and help with the paper.

> . . . and we've already defined what that is). There was also a sense in which writers marked their compositions with an "okay" as if the "okay" marked a movement from a turn as reader to a turn as writer. Analyses of the readers' *think alouds* suggested that the readers often felt frustrated by the writers' failure to explain why they were doing what they were doing. Also the readers were often critical of *the writer's craft,* including writers' choice of words, clarity, and accuracy. There was a sense in which the readers' *think alouds* assumed a reflexive character as if the readers were rewriting the texts. If one perceived the readers as craftpersons, unwilling to blame their tools for an ineffective product, then one might view the readers as unwilling to let the text provided stand in the way of their successful achievement of their goals or pursuit of understanding. (p. 150)

These data and other descriptions of the reading act (e.g., Bruce 1981; Collins, Brown and Larkin 1970; Rosenblatt 1976, 1980; Tompkins 1980) are consistent with the view that texts are written and read in a tug of war between authors and readers. These think-alouds highlight the kinds of internal struggles that we all face (whether consciously or unconsciously) as we compose the meaning of a text in front of us.

Few would disagree that writers compose meaning. In this paper we argue that readers also compose meaning (that there is no meaning on the page until a reader decides there is). We will develop this position by describing some aspects of the composing process held in parallel by reading and writing. In particular, we will address the essential characteristics of effective composing: planning, drafting, aligning, revising and monitoring.

Planning

As a writer initially plans her writing, so a reader plans his reading. Planning involves two complementary processes: goal-setting and knowledge mobilization. Taken together, they reflect some commonly accepted behaviors, such as setting purposes, evaluating one's current state of knowledge about a topic, focusing or narrowing topics and goals, and self-questioning.

Flower and Hayes (1981) have suggested that a writer's goals may be procedural (e.g., how do I approach this topic), substantive (e.g., I want to say something about how rockets work), or intentional (e.g., I want to convince people of the problem). So may a reader's goals be procedural (e.g., I want to get a sense of this topic overall), substantive (e.g., I need to find out about the relationship between England and France), or intentional (e.g., I wonder what this author is trying to say) or some combination of all three. These goals can be embedded in one another or addressed concurrently; they may be conflicting or complementary. As a reader reads (just as when a writer writes) goals may emerge, be discovered, or change. For example, a reader or writer may broaden, fine tune, redefine, delete, or replace goals. A fourth grade writer whom we interviewed about a project he had completed on American Indians illustrates these notions well: As he stated his changing goals, " . . . I began with the topic of Indians but that was too broad, I decided to narrow my focus on Hopis, but that was not what I was really interested in. Finally, I decided that what I really wanted to learn about was medicine men . . . I really found some interesting things to write about." In coming to grips with his goals our writer suggested both procedural and substantive goals. Note also that he refined his goals prior to drafting. In preparation for reading or writing a draft, goals usually change; mostly they become focused at a level of specificity sufficient to allow the reading or writing to continue. Consider how a novel might be read. We begin reading a novel to discover the plot, yet find ourselves asking specific questions about events and attending to the author's craft—how she uses the language to create certain effects.

The goals that readers or writers set have a symbiotic relationship with the knowledge they mobilize, and together they influence what is produced or understood in a text (Anderson, Reynolds, Schallert and Goetz 1977; Anderson, Pichert and Shirey 1979; Hays and Tierney 1981; Tierney and Mosenthal 1981). A writer plans what she wants to say with the knowledge resources at her disposal. Our fourth grade writer changed his goals as a function of the specificity of the knowledge domain to which he successively switched. Likewise readers, depending on their level of topic knowledge and what they want to learn from their reading, vary the goals they initiate and pursue. As an example of this symbiosis in a reader, consider the following statement from a reader of *Psychology Today.*

> I picked up an issue of *Psychology Today.* One particular article dealing with women in movies caught my attention. I guess it was the photos of Streep, Fonda, Lange, that interested me. As I had seen most of their recent movies I felt as if I knew something about the topic. As I started reading, the author had me recalling my reactions to these movies (Streep in "Sophie's Choice," Lange in "Tootsie," Fonda in "Julia"). At first I intended to glance at the article. But as I read on, recalling various scenes, I became more and more interested in the author's perspective. Now that my reactions were nicely mobilized, this author (definitely a feminist) was able to convince me of her case for stereotyping. I had not realized the extent to which women are either portrayed as the victim, cast with men, or not developed at all as a character in their own right. This author carried me back through these movies and revealed things I had not realized. It was as if I had my own purposes in mind but I saw things through her eyes.

What is interesting in this example is how the reader's knowledge about films and feminism was mobilized at the same time as his purposes became gradually welded to those of the author's. The reader went *from* almost free association, *to* reflection, *to* directed study of what he knew. It is this directed study of what one knows that is so important in knowledge mobilization. A writer does not just throw out ideas randomly; she carefully plans the placement of ideas in text so that each idea acquires just the right degree of emphasis in text. A successful reader uses his knowledge just as carefully; at just the right moment he accesses just the right knowledge structures necessary to interpret the text at hand in a way consistent with his goals. Note also how the goals a reader sets can determine the knowledge he calls up; at the same time, that knowledge, especially as it is modified in conjunction with the reader's engagement of the text, causes him to alter his goals. Initially, a reader might "brainstorm" his store of knowledge and maybe organize some of it (e.g., clustering ideas using general questions such as who, what, when, where, or why *or* developing outlines). Some readers might make notes; others might merely think about what they know, how this information clusters, and what they want to pursue. Or, just as a writer sometimes uses a first draft to explore what she knows and what she wants to say, so a reader might scan the text as a way of fine tuning the range of knowledge and goals to engage, creating a kind of a "draft" reading of the text. It is to this topic of drafting that we now turn your attention.

Drafting

We define drafting as the refinement of meaning which occurs as readers and writers deal directly with the print on the page. All of us who have had to write something (be it an article, a novel, a memo, a letter, or a theme), know just how difficult getting started can be. Many of us feel that if we could only get a draft on paper, we could rework and revise our way to completion. We want to argue that getting started is just as important a step in reading. What every reader needs, like every writer, is a first draft. And the first step in producing that draft is finding the right "lead." Murray (1982) describes the importance of finding the lead:

> The lead is the beginning of the beginning, those few lines the reader may glance at in deciding to read or pass on. These few words—fifty, forty, thirty, twenty, ten—establish the tone, the point of view, the order, the dimensions of the article. In a sense, the entire article is coiled in the first few words waiting to be released.
>
> An article, perhaps even a book, can only say one thing and when the lead is found, the writer knows what is included in the article and what is left out, what must be left out. As one word is chosen for the lead another rejected, as a comma is put in and another taken away, the lead begins to feel right and the pressure builds up until it is almost impossible not to write. (p. 99)

From a reader's perspective, the key points to note from Murray's description are these: 1) "the entire article is coiled in these first few words waiting to be released," and 2) "the lead begins to feel right. . . ." The reader, as he reads, has that same feeling as he begins to draft his understanding of a text.

The whole point of hypothesis testing models of reading like those of Goodman (1967) and Smith (1971) is that the current hypothesis one holds about what a text means creates strong expectations about what succeeding text ought to address. So strong are these hypotheses, these "coilings," these drafts of meaning a reader creates that incoming text failing to cohere with them may be ignored or rejected.

Follow us as we describe a hypothetical reader and writer beginning their initial drafts.

A reader opens his or her textbook, magazine or novel; a writer reaches for his pen. The reader scans the pages for a place to begin; the writer holds the pen poised. The reader looks over the first few lines of the article or story in search of a sense of what the general scenario is. (This occurs whether the reader is reading a murder mystery, a newspaper account of unemployment, or a magazine article on underwater life.) Our writer searches for the lead statement or introduction to her text. For the reader, knowing the scenario may involve knowing that the story is about women engaged in career advancement from a feminist perspective, knowing the murder mystery involves the death of a wealthy husband vacationing abroad. For the writer, establishing the scenario involves prescribing those few ideas which introduce or define the topic. Once established, the reader proceeds through the text, refining and building upon his sense of what is going on; the writer does likewise. Once the writer has found the "right" lead, she proceeds to develop the plot, expositions, or descriptions. As the need to change scenarios occurs, so the process is repeated. From a schema-theoretic perspective, coming to grips with a lead statement or, if you are a reader, gleaning an initial scenario, can be viewed as schema selection (which is somewhat equivalent to choosing a script for a play); filling in the slots or refining the scenario is equivalent to schema instantiation.

As our descriptions of a hypothetical reader suggest, what drives reading and writing is this desire to make sense of what is happening—to make things cohere. A writer, achieves that fit by deciding what information to include and what to withhold. The reader accomplishes that fit by filling in gaps (it must be early in the morning) or making uncued connections (he must have become angry because they lost the game). All readers, like all writers, ought to strive for this fit between the whole and the parts and among the parts. Unfortunately, some readers and writers are satisfied with a piecemeal experience (dealing with each part separately), or, alternatively, a sense of the whole without a sense of how the parts relate to it. Other readers and writers become "bogged down" in their desire to achieve a perfect text or "fit" on the first draft. For language educators our task is to help readers and writers to achieve the best fit among the whole and the parts. It is with this concern in mind that we now consider the role of alignment and then revision.

Aligning

In conjunction with the planning and drafting initiated, we believe that the alignment a reader or writer adopts can have an overriding influence on a composer's ability to achieve coherence. We see alignment as having two facets: stances a reader or writer assumes in collaboration with their author or audience, and roles within which the reader or writer immerse themselves as they proceed with the topic. In other words, as readers and writers approach a text they vary the nature of their stance or collaboration with their author (if they are a reader) or audience (if they are a writer) and, in conjunction with this collaboration, immerse themselves in a variety of roles. A writer's stance toward her readers might be intimate, challenging or quite neutral. And, within the contexts of these collaborations she might share what she wants to say through characters or as an observer of events. Likewise, a reader can adopt a stance toward the writer which is sympathetic, critical or passive. And, within the context of these collaborations, he can immerse himself in the text as an observer or eye witness, participant or character.

As we have suggested, alignment results in certain benefits. Indeed, direct and indirect support for the facilitative benefits of adopting alignments comes from research on a variety of fronts. For example, schema theoretic studies involving an analysis of the influence of a reader's perspective have shown that if readers are given different alignments prior to or after reading a selection, they will vary in what and how much they will recall (Pichert 1979; Spiro 1977). For example, readers told to read a description of a house from the perspective of a homebuyer or burglar tend to recall more information and are more apt to include in their recollections information consistent with their perspective. Furthermore, when asked to consider an alternative perspective these same readers were able to generate information which they previously had not retrieved and which was important to the new perspective. Researchers interested in the effects of imaging have examined the effects of visualizing—a form of alignment which we would argue is equivalent to eye witnessing. Across a number of studies it has been shown that readers who are encouraged to visualize usually perform better on comprehension tasks (e.g., Sodoski, in press). The work on children's development of the ability to recognize point of view (Hay and Brewer 1982; Applebee 1978) suggests that facility with alignment develops with comprehension maturity. From our own interviews with young readers and writers we have found that the identification with characters and immersion in a story reported by our interviewees accounts for much of the vibrancy, sense of control and fulfillment experienced during reading and writing. Likewise, some of the research analyzing proficient writing suggests that proficient writers are those writers who, when they read over what they have written, comment on the extent to which their story and characters are engaging (Birnbaum 1982). A number of studies in both psychotherapy and creativity provide support for the importance of alignment. For purposes of generating solutions to problems, psychotherapists have found it useful to encourage individuals to exchange roles (e.g., mother with daughter). In an attempt to generate discoveries, researchers have had experts identify with the experiences of inanimate objects (e.g., paint on metal) as a means of considering previously inaccessible solutions (e.g., a paint which does not peel).

Based upon these findings and our own observations, we hypothesize that adopting an alignment is akin to achieving a foothold from which meaning can be more readily negotiated. Just as a filmmaker can adopt and vary the angle from which a scene is depicted in order to maximize the richness of a filmgoer's experience, so too can a reader and writer adopt and vary the angle from which language meanings are negotiated. This suggests, for language educators, support for those questions or activities which help readers or writers take a stance on a topic and immerse themselves in the ideas or story. This might entail having students read or write with a definite point of view or attitude. It might suggest having students project themselves into a scene as a character, eye witness or object (imagine you are Churchill, a reporter, the sea). This might occur at the hands of questioning, dramatization, or simply role playing. In line with our hypothesis, we believe that in these contexts students almost spontaneously acquire a sense of the whole as well as the parts.

To illustrate how the notion of alignment might manifest itself for different readers, consider the following statement offered by a professor describing the stances he takes while reading an academic paper:

> When I read something for the first time, I read it argumentatively. I also find later that I made marginal notations that were quite nasty like, "You're crazy!" or "Why do you want to say that?" Sometimes they are not really fair and that's why I really think to read philosophy you have to read it twice. . . . The second time you read it over you should read it as sympathetically as possible. This time you read it trying to defend the person against the very criticisms that you made the first time through. You read every sentence and if there is an issue that bothers you, you say to yourself, "This guy who wrote this is really very smart. It sounds like what he is saying is wrong; I must be misunderstanding him. What could he really want to be saying?" (Freeman 1981, p. 11)

Also, consider Eleanor Gibson's description of how she approaches the work of Jane Austen:

> Her novels are not for airport reading. They are for reading over and over, savoring every phrase, memorizing the best of them, and getting an even deeper understanding of Jane's "sense of human comedy . . . ." As I read the book for perhaps the twenty fifth time, I consider what point she is trying to make in the similarities and differences between the characters. . . . I want to discover for myself what this sensitive and perceptive individual is trying to tell me. Sometimes I only want to sink back and enjoy it and laugh myself. (Gibson and Levin 1975, pp. 458–460)

Our professor adjusted his stance from critic to sympathetic coauthor across different readings. Our reader of Austen was, at times, a highly active and sympathetic collaborator and, at other times, more neutral and passive.

Obviously, the text itself prompts certain alignments. For example, consider how an author's choice of words, arguments, or selection of genre may invite a reader to assume different stances and, in the context of these collaborations, different roles.[4] The opening paragraph of Wolfe's *Electric Kool-Aid Acid Test* (1977) illustrates how the use of first person along with the descriptive power of words (e.g., cramped . . . metal bottom . . . rising . . . rolling . . . bouncing) compels the reader to engage in a sympathetic collaboration with an author and be immersed as an active participant in a truck ride across the hills of San Francisco.

> That's good thinking there, Cool Breeze. Cool Breeze is a kid with 3 or 4 days' beard sitting next to me on the cramped metal bottom of the open back part of the pickup truck. Bouncing along. Dipping and rising and rolling on these rotten springs like a boat. Out the back of the truck the city of San Francisco is bouncing down the hill, all those endless staggers of bay windows, slums with a view, bouncing and streaming down the hill. One after another, electric signs with neon martini glasses lit up on them, the San Francisco symbol of "bar"—thousands of neon-magenta martini glasses bouncing and streaming down the hill, and beneath them thousands of people wheeling around to look at this freaking crazed truck we're in, their white faces erupting from their lapels like marshmallows—streaming and bouncing down the hill—and God knows they've got plenty to look at. (p. 1)

Also, consider the differences in collaboration and role taking the following text segments invite. While both texts deal with the same information, in one text, the information is presented through a conversation between two children, and in the other text, the information is presented in a more "straight forward" expository style.

> FLY
>
> Lisa and Mike were bored. It was Saturday and they did not know what to do until Lisa had an idea. "I know a game we can play that they play in some countries . . . .

> FLY
>
> All over the world children like to play different games. In some countries, children enjoy playing a game called "Fly."

---

4 It is not within the scope of this paper to characterize the various mechanisms by which writers engage readers. We would encourage readers to examine different texts for themselves and some of the analytic schemes generated by Bruce (1981) and Gibson (1975), among others.

We have found that readers of the first text usually assume a sympathetic collaboration with the writer and identify with the characters. They view the game through the eyes of the children and remain rather neutral with respect to the author. Our readers of the second text tend to have difficulty understanding the game at the same time as they are critical of the author. They adopt a role more akin to an observer who, lacking a specific angle, catches glimpses of the game without acquiring an overall understanding. Some of us have experienced a similar phenomenon as viewers of an overseas telecast of an unfamiliar sport (e.g., the game of cricket on British television). The camera angles provided by the British sportscasters are disorienting for the native viewer.

Clearly a number of factors may influence the nature of a reader's alignment and the extent to which his resulting interpretation is viable. A reader, as our last example illustrated, might adopt an alignment which interferes with how well he will be able to negotiate an understanding. Sometimes a reader might adopt an alignment which overindulges certain biases, predispositions, and personal experiences. Doris Lessing (1973) described this phenomenon in a discussion of readers' responses to her *The Golden Notebook:*

> Ten years after I wrote [it], I can get, in one week, three letters about it. . . . One letter is entirely about the sex war, about man's inhumanity to woman, and woman's inhumanity to man, and the writer has produced pages and pages all about nothing else, for she—but not always a she—can't see anything else in the book.
>
> The second is about politics, probably from an old Red like myself, and he or she writes many pages about politics, and never mentions any other theme.
>
> These two letters used, when the book was—as it were—young, to be the most common.
>
> The third letter, once rare but now catching up on the others, is written by a man or a woman who can see nothing in it but the theme of mental illness.
>
> But it is the same book.
>
> And naturally these incidents bring up again questions of what people see when they read a book, and why one person sees one pattern and nothing at all of another pattern, and how odd it is to have, as author, such a clear picture of a book, that is seen so very differently by its readers. (p. xi)

Such occurrences should not be regarded as novel. It is this phenomenon of reader-author engagement and idiosyncratic response which has been at the center of a debate among literary theorists, some of whom (e.g., Jakobson and Levi Strauss 1962) would suggest that a "true" reading experience has been instantiated only when readers assume an alignment which involves close collaboration with authors. Others would argue that readers can assume a variety of alignments, whether these alignments are constrained by the author (Iser 1974) or initiated freely by the reader (Fish 1970). They would rarely go so far as to suggest the destruction of the text, but instead, as Tompkins (1980) suggested, they might begin to view reading and writing as joining hands, changing places, "and finally becoming distinguishable only as two names for the same activity" (p. ii). We do not wish to debate the distinctions represented by these and other theorists, but to suggest that there appears to be at least some consensus that effective reading involves a form of alignment which emerges in conjunction with a working relationship between readers and writers. In our opinion, this does not necessitate bridling readers and writers to one another. Indeed, we would hypothesize that new insights are more likely discovered and appreciations derived when readers and writers try out different alignments as they read and write their texts. This suggests spending time rethinking, reexamining, reviewing and rereading. For this type of experience does not occur on a single reading; rather it emerges only after several rereadings, reexaminations, and drafts. It is to this notion of reexamination and revision that we now turn.

Revising

While it is common to think of a writer as a reviser it is *not* common to think of a reader as someone who revises unless perhaps he has a job involving some editorial functions. We believe that this is unfortunate. We would like to suggest that revising should be considered as integral to reading as it is to writing. If readers are to develop some control over and a sense of discovery with the models of meaning they build, they must approach text with the same deliberation, time, and reflection that a writer employs as she revises a text. They must examine their developing interpretations and view the models they build as draft-like in quality—subject to revision. We would like to see students engage in behaviors such as rereading (especially with different alignments), annotating the text on the page with reactions, and questioning whether the model they have built is what they really want. With this in mind let us tum our attention to revising in writing.

We have emphasized that writing is not merely taking ideas from one's head and placing them onto the page. A writer must choose words which best represent these ideas; that is, she must choose words which have the desired impact. Sometimes this demands knowing what she wants to say and how to say it. At other times, it warrants examining what is written or read to discover and clarify one's ideas. Thus a writer will repeatedly reread, reexamine, delete, shape, and correct what she is writing. She will consider whether and how her ideas fit together, how well her words represent the ideas to be shared and how her text can be fine tuned. For some writers this development and redevelopment will appear to be happening effortlessly. For others, revision demands hard labor and sometimes several painful drafts. Some rework the drafts in their head before they rewrite; others slowly rework pages as they go. From analyses of the revision strategies of experienced writers, it appears that the driving force behind revision is a sense of emphasis and proportion. As Sommers (1980) suggested, one of the questions most experienced writers ask themselves is "what does my essay as a *whole* need for form, balance, rhythm, and communication?" (p. 386). In trying to answer this question, writers proceed through revision cycles with sometimes overlapping and sometimes novel concerns. Initial revision cycles might be directed predominately at topical development; later cycles might be directed at stylistic concerns.

For most readers, revision is an unheard-of experience. Observations of secondary students reveal that most readers view reading competency as the ability to read rapidly a single text once with maximum recall (Schallert and Tierney 1982). It seems that students rarely pause to reflect on their ideas or to judge the quality of their developing interpretations. Nor do they often reread a text either from the same or a different perspective. In fact, to suggest that a reader should approach text as a writer who crafts an understanding across several drafts—who pauses, rethinks, and revises—is almost contrary to some well-established goals readers proclaim for themselves (e.g., that efficient reading is equivalent to maximum recall based upon a single fast reading).

Suppose we could convince students that they ought to revise their readings of a text; would they be able to do it? We should not assume that merely allowing time for pausing, reflecting, and reexamining will guarantee that students will revise their readings. Students need to be given support and feedback at so doing. Students need to be aware of strategies they can pursue to accomplish revisions, to get things restarted when they stall, and to compare one draft or reading with another. The pursuit of a second draft of a reading should have a purpose. Sometimes this purpose can emerge from discussing a text with the teacher and peers; sometimes it may come from within; sometimes it will not occur unless the student has a reason or functional context for revision as well as help from a thoughtful teacher.

Monitoring

Hand in hand with planning, aligning, drafting, and revising, readers and writers must be able to distance themselves from the texts they have created to evaluate what they have developed. We call this executive function monitoring. Monitoring usually occurs tacitly, but it can be under conscious control. The monitor in us keeps track of and control over our other functions. Our monitor decides whether we have planned, aligned, drafted, and/or revised properly. It decides when one activity should dominate over the others. Our monitor tells us when we have done a good job and when we have not. It tells us when to go back to the drawing board and when we can relax.

The complexity of the type of juggling which the monitor is capable of has been captured aptly in an analogy of a switchboard operator, used by Flower and Hayes (1980) to describe how writers juggle constraints:

> She has two important calls on hold. (Don't forget that idea.)
>
> Four lights just started flashing. (They demand immediate attention or they'll be lost.) A party of five wants to be hooked up together. (They need to be connected somehow.) A party of two thinks they've been incorrectly connected. (Where do they go?)
>
> And throughout this complicated process of remembering, retrieving, and connecting, the operator's voice must project calmness, confidence, and complete control. (p. 33)

The monitor has one final task—to engage in a dialogue with the inner reader.

When writers and readers compose text they negotiate its meaning with what Murray (1982) calls the other self—that inner reader (the author's first reader) who continually reacts to what the writer has written, is writing and will write or what the reader has read, is reading and will read. It is this other self which is the reader's or writer's counsel, and judge, and prompter. This other self oversees what the reader and writer is trying to do, defines the nature of collaboration between reader and author, and decides how well the reader as writer or writer as reader is achieving his or her goals.

A Summary and Discussion

To reiterate, we view both reading and writing as acts of composing. We see these acts of composing as involving continuous, recurring, and recursive transactions among readers and writers, their respective inner selves, and their perceptions of each other's goals and desires. Consider the reader's role as we envision it. At the same time as the reader considers what he perceives to be the author's intentions (or what the reader perceives to be what the author is trying to get the reader to do or think), he negotiates goals with his inner self (or what he would like to achieve). With these goals being continuously negotiated (sometimes embedded within each other) the reader proceeds to take different alignments (critic, co-author, editor, character, reporter, eye witness, etc.) as he uses features from his own experiential arrays and what he perceives to be arrayed by the author in order to create a model of meaning for the text. These models of meaning must assume a coherent, holistic quality in which everything fits together. The development of these models of meaning occurs from the vantage point of different alignments which the reader adopts with respect to these arrays. It is from these vantage points that the various arrays are perceived, and their position adjusted such that the reader's goals and desire for a sense of completeness are achieved. Our diagrammatic representation of the major components of these processes is given in Figure 1.

Such an account of reading distinguishes itself from previous descriptions of reading and reading-writing relationships in several notable ways:

1. Most accounts of reading versus writing (as well as accounts of how readers develop a model of meaning) tend to emphasize reading as a receptive rather than productive activity. Some, in fact, regard reading as the mirror image of writing.

2. Most language accounts suggest that reading and writing are interrelated. They do not address the suggestion that reading and writing are multidimensional, multi-modal processes—both acts of composing.

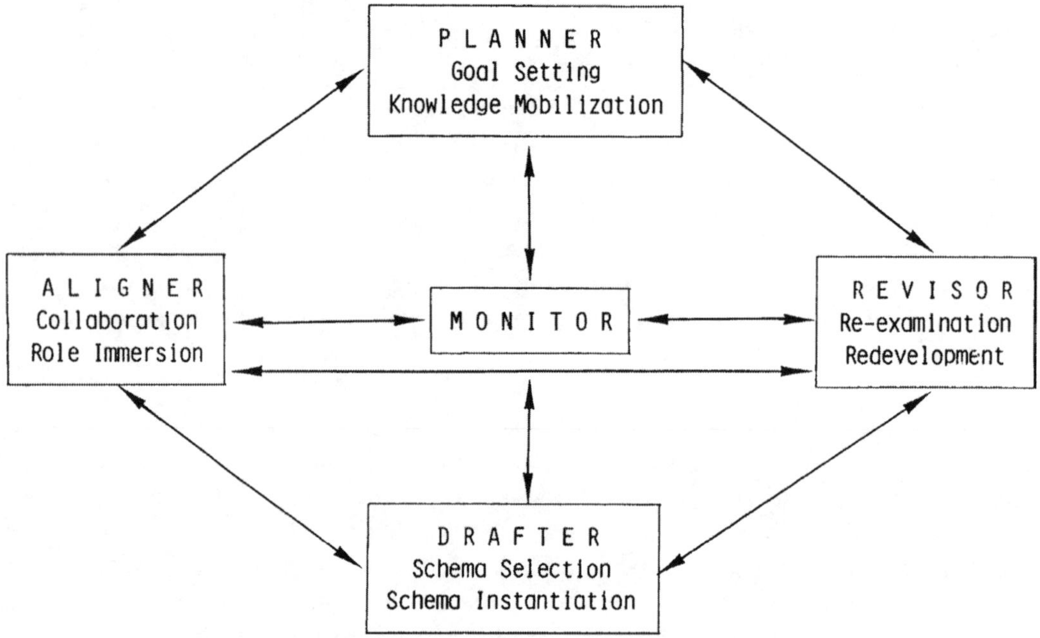

Figure 1. Some Components of the Composing Model of Reading

3. The phenomenon of alignment as integral to composing has rarely been explored.
4. Most descriptions of how readers build models of meaning fail to consider how the processes of planning, drafting, aligning, and revising are manifested.
5. Previous interactional and transactional accounts of reading (Rosenblatt 1978; Rumelhart 1980) give little consideration to the transaction which occurs among the inner selves of the reader and writer.

What our account fails to do is thoroughly differentiate how these composing behaviors manifest themselves in the various contexts of reading and writing. Nor does it address the pattern of interactions among these behaviors across moments during any reading and writing experience. For example, we give the impression of sequential stages even though we believe in simultaneous processes. We hope to clarify and extend these notions in subsequent writings.

References

Anderson, R. C.; Pichert, J. W.; and Shirey, L. L. *Effects of the Reader's Schema at Different Points in Time.* Technical Report No. 119. Urbana, IL: Center for the Study of Reading, University of Illinois, April 1979. (ERIC Document Reproduction Service No. ED 169 523)

Anderson, R. C.; Reynolds, R. E.; Schallert, D. L.; and Goetz, E. T. "Frameworks for Comprehending Discourse." *American Educational Research Journal* 14 (1977): 367–382.

Applebee, A. N. *The Child's Concept of Story.* Chicago: University of Chicago Press, 1978. Birnbaum, J. C. "The Reading and Composing Behavior of Selected Fourth and Seventh Grade Students." *Research in the Teaching of English* 16 (1982): 241–260.

Bruce, B. "A Social Interaction Model of Reading." *Discourse Processes* 4 (1981): 273–311.

Collins, A.; Brown, J. S.; and Larkin, K. M. "Inference in Text Understanding." In *Theoretical Issues in Reading Comprehension,* edited by R. J. Spiro, 8. C. Bruce, and W. F. Brewer. Hillsdale, NJ: Erlbaum, 1980.

Fish, S. "Literature in the Reader: Affective Stylistics." *New Literary History* 2 (1970): 123–162. Flower, L. and Hayes, J. R. "A Cognitive Process Theory of Writing." *College Composition and Communication* 32 (1981): 365–387.

Freeman, M. "How to Read a Philosophical Text." Unpublished paper, Harvard University, 1982.

Gibson, E. J. and Levin, H. *The Psychology of Reading.* Cambridge: M.I.T. Press, 1975. Gibson, W. *Persona.* New York: Random House, 1969.

Goodman, K. S. "Reading: A Psycholinguistic Guessing Game." *Journal of the Reading Specialist* 6 (1967): 126–135.

Hay, A. and Brewer, W. F. *Children's Understanding of the Narrator's Point of View in Prose.* Urbana, IL: Center for the Study of Reading, University of Illinois, 1982.

Hayes, D. and Tierney, R. "Developing Readers' Knowledge Through Analogy." *Reading Research Quarterly* 17 (1982): 256–280.

Iser, W. *The Implied Reader: Patterns in Communication in Prose Fiction from Bunyan to Beckett.* Baltimore: John Hopkins University Press, 1974.

Jakobson, R. and Levi-Strauss, C. "Les Chats de Charles Baudelave." *L'Homme* 2 (1962): 5–21.

Lessing, D. *Introduction to The Golden Notebook.* New York: Bantam Books, 1973.

Murray, D. *Learning by Teaching.* Montclair, NJ: Boynton/Cook Publishers, Inc., 1982. Murray, D. "Teaching the Other Self: The Writer's First Reader." *College Composition and Communication* 33 (1982): 140–147.

Pichert, J. W. *Sensitivity to What Is Important in Prose.* Technical Report No. 149. Urbana, IL: Center for the Study of Reading, University of Illinois, November 1979. (ERIC Document Reproduction Service No. ED 179 946)

Rosenblatt, L. M. *Literature As Exploration,* 3rd edition. New York: Noble and Noble, 1976 (originally published 1939).

Rosenblatt, L. *The Reader, the Text, the Poem: The Transactional Theory of the Literary Work.* Carbondale, IL: Southern Illinois University Press, 1978.

Rumelhart, D. "Schemata: The Building Blocks of Cognition." In *Theoretical Issues in Reading Comprehension,* edited by R. J. Spiro, B. Bruce, and W. Brewer. Hillsdale, NJ: Erlbaum, 1980.

Sadoski, M. "An Exploratory Study of the Relationships Between Reported Imagery and the Comprehension and Recall of a Story." *Reading Research Quarterly,* in press.

Schallert, D. and Tierney, R. J. *Learning from Expository Text: The Interaction of Text Structure with Reader Characteristics.* Final report. National Institute of Education, 1982.

Smith, F. *Understanding Reading.* New York: Holt, Rinehart & Winston, 1971.

Sommers, N. I. "Revision Strategies of Student Writers and Experienced Adult Writers." *College Composition and Communication* 31 (1980): 378–388.

Spiro, R. J. "Remembering Information from Text: The 'State of Schema' Approach." In *Schooling and the Acquisition of Knowledge,* edited by R. C. Anderson, R. J. Spiro, and W. E. Montague. Hillsdale, NJ: Erlbaum, 1977.

Tierney, R. J. "Writer-Reader Transactions: Defining the Dimensions of Negotiation." In *Forum: Essays on Theory and Practice in the Teaching of Writing,* edited by P. Stock. Montclair, NJ: Boynton/Cook, 1983.

Tierney, R. J.; LaZansky, J.; Raphael, T.; and Cohen, P. "Author's Intentions and Reader's Interpretation." In *Understanding Readers Understanding,* edited by R. J. Tierney, P. Anders, and J. Mitchell. Hillsdale, NJ: Erlbaum, in press.

Tierney, R. J. and Mosenthal, J. *The Cohesion Concept's Relationship to the Coherence of Text.* Technical Report No. 221. Urbana, IL: Center for the Study of Reading, University of Illinois, October 1981. (ERIC Document Reproduction Service No. ED 212 991)

Tompkins, J. P. *Reader-Response Criticism.* Baltimore: John Hopkins University Press, 1980. Wolfe, T. *Electric Kool-Aid Acid Test.* New York: Bantam, 1977.

Pedagogy: Critical Approaches to Teaching Literature, Language, Composition, and Culture, Volume 2, Number 2, © 2002 Duke University Press

Commentary

The Transition to College Reading[1]

Robert Scholes

I began my work on this assignment, as many students do, by e-mailing an expert for assistance. I wrote to a colleague who has been teaching one of our survey courses at Brown and asked her what she felt were the most important problems or deficiencies in the preparation of first-year students in her literature courses. Her reply, though only a hasty e-mail rather than a considered statement, was so helpful that I quote it here, with her permission:

> I think that the new high school graduates I see (and sophomores with no previous lit classes) most lack close reading skills. Often they have generic concepts and occasionally they have some historical knowledge, though perhaps not as much as they should. I find that they are most inclined to substitute what they generally think a text should be saying for what it actually says, and lack a way to explore the intricacies and interests of the words on the page. Sometimes the historical knowledge and generic concepts actually become problems when students use them as tools for making texts say and do what students think they should, generalizing that all novels do X or poems do Y. Usually the result is that they want to read every text as saying something extremely familiar that they might agree with. I see them struggling the most to read the way texts differ from their views, to find what is specific about the language, address, assumptions etc. (Tamar Katz, pers. com., 17 September 2001)

Her observations confirm my own sense that we have a reading problem of massive dimensions—a problem that goes well beyond any purely literary concerns.

This, in turn, drew my attention to the asymmetry in our topics for this panel, which mirrors the asymmetry in our professional arrangements.[i] Setting aside the institutional differences, which affect everyone, the other two topics were divided into writing and literature. The natural reciprocal of writing—which, of course, is reading—had somehow disappeared, apparently subsumed under the topic of literature. (I have taken the liberty of compensating for this asymmetry in my own title for this piece by replacing the word *literature* with the word *reading.*) But this division of the English

1 **Citation:** Scholes, Robert. "The Transition to College Reading." *Pedagogy*, vol. 2, no. 2, 2002, pp. 165–172.

project is not just an aberration in the thought of this session's organizer. It is the way that most English departments at college and secondary levels think of their enterprise. This, as I have argued for some time, is an unfortunate error that we need to correct.

Why is it an error? I shall spend the rest of this essay counting the ways. We normally acknowledge, however grudgingly, that writing must be taught and continue to be taught from high school to college and perhaps beyond. We accept it, I believe, because we can see writing, and we know that much of the writing we see is not good enough. But we do not see reading. We see some writing about reading, to be sure, but we do not see reading. I am certain, though, that if we could see it, we would be appalled. My colleague Tamar Katz, like many perceptive teachers, has caught a glimpse of the real problem, which she puts this way: "They want to read every text as saying something extremely familiar that they might agree with." The problem emerges as one of difference, or otherness—a difficulty in moving from the words of the text to some set of intentions that are different from one's own, some values or presuppositions different from one's own and possibly opposed to them.[ii] This problem, as I see it, has two closely related parts. One is a failure to focus sharply on the language of the text. The other is a failure to imagine the otherness of the text's author.

One of the great ironies in this situation is that the study of literature, especially as conceived by the New Critics, whose thought still shapes much of our literary education, was supposed to develop the student's ability to focus on the language of texts. If we nonetheless fail to teach close reading—and many of us would agree with Katz and with Arlene Wilner (in this issue) that we do—then the problem may lie not so much in the words themselves as in the otherness of their authors. That is, if the words belong to the reader, they are likely to express the reader's thoughts. What we actually mean by "close" reading may be distant reading—reading as if the words belonged to a person at some distance from ourselves in thought or feeling. Perhaps they must be seen as the words of someone else before they can be seen as words at all—or, more particularly, as words that need to be read with close attention. It is no secret, of course, that the New Critics defined as a fallacy any attempt to read a text for its author's intention. Since then we have had the death of the author, reader-response criticism, the self-deconstructing text, and the symptomatic readings of cultural studies, all of which, in various ways, undermine the notion of authorial intention as a feature of the reading process. And all of them, in various degrees and respects, are right and useful, but only if reading for authorial intention precedes them. The author must live before the author can die. We teachers must help our students bring the author to life.

The reading problems of our students can themselves be read as a symptom of a larger cultural problem. We are not good, as a culture, at imagining the other. After 11 September 2001 we have begun to learn, perhaps, that this deficiency is serious, though I am afraid that much of our response has been to shout our own words louder and to try to suppress those that differ from ours. On the present occasion, however, we must focus on this problem at the level of schooling. I mention the larger picture not to aggrandize the topic but to indicate the depth of the problem, which is as much a matter of ideology as of methodology. English teachers must solve it at the level of the curriculum and the classroom. We must make some changes both in what we teach and in how we teach it, starting in secondary schools.

First, the past. Consider the following advice from a textbook on reading:

> The great object to be accomplished in reading as a rhetorical exercise is to convey to the *hearer*, fully and clearly, the ideas and feelings of the writer.
>
> In order to do this, it is necessary that a selection should be carefully studied by the pupil before he attempts to read it. In accordance with this view, a preliminary rule of importance is the following:
>
> Rule I.—Before attempting to read a lesson, the learner should make himself fully acquainted with the subject as treated of in that lesson, and endeavor to make the thought, and feeling, and sentiments of the writer his own.

I linger over the word *hearer*, which I have emphasized in this quotation. What has a hearer to do with reading? This unexpected word alerts me to the fact that I am facing a text that I must read carefully, attending to presuppositions different from my own. This advice about the teaching of reading comes immediately after the table of contents in McGuffey's (1879: 9) *Fifth Eclectic Reader*. It applies to what the text calls "reading as a rhetorical exercise," that is, reading aloud—and also reading to express "the thought, and feeling, and sentiments of the writer." That is where the hearer comes in. Odd, isn't it, that attending to "the thought, and feeling, and sentiments of the writer" is exactly what our students now find difficult? The older pedagogy saw it as a problem, too, but had a solution for it. The solution was "elocution," or reading aloud. That is one thing we can learn from our predecessors, for reading aloud makes the reading process evident to the ear in tone and rhythm and to the eye in bodily posture and facial expression, just as writing makes the composing process evident in written signs. In this older dispensation, failure to "get" the author's thought, feeling, and sentiments would emerge during an elocutionary performance. I am not certain how close we can come to the McGuffey method in our classrooms, but I think that we should try to bridge the gap. [iii] I know that we can come very close to it in teaching drama, where the move to oral interpretation requires no explanation or apology—which is an argument for getting more drama into our courses.

It should follow that we need to consider including in our courses texts that are difficult for students to read as "saying something extremely familiar that they might agree with"—texts that say things that many students will not, in fact, agree with and that we may not agree with, either. For some years Gerald Graff has urged us to "teach the conflicts." Insofar as our intradepartmental conflicts are concerned, I have never been persuaded that students would care enough about them to make the enterprise worthwhile, but Graff (forthcoming) is clearly broadening his notion of conflicts in *Clueless in Academe*, and I am happy to agree with him about the need to teach texts that express conflicting positions. There has been concern, since Quintilian at least, and probably since the Sophists, about whether a good rhetorician was necessarily a good person. Without rushing in where angels like Richard Lanham have trod warily, I want to say that a good person, in our time, needs to have the rhetorical capacity to imagine the other's thought, feeling, and sentiments. That is, though not all rhetoricians are good people, all good citizens must be rhetoricians to the extent that they can imagine themselves in the place of another and understand views different from their own. It is our responsibility as English teachers to help our students develop this form of textual power, in which strength comes, paradoxically, from subordinating one's own thoughts temporarily to the views and values of another person.

This is one reason that I think it is a bad idea for the Bush administration to tell television networks to censor the words of our enemies in the videos they broadcast. We Americans are seen as arrogant by a large part of the world—and not just the Islamic part—precisely because we do not listen to other points of view, but we have never made it a national policy not to listen to them until now. Nor can our government plead the fact that other parts of the world do not listen to us or understand us as an excuse for refusing to allow us to listen to them. Our form of government and our sort of society depend on the freedom of individuals to interpret texts for themselves. Our roots, as a culture, are deeply embedded in a Protestant tradition of individual interpretation of sacred texts, which rests on access to those texts for all. People died for the right to translate and circulate these crucial texts, taking them out of the hands of a priestly caste. This tradition has also allowed the publication and discussion of profane texts, on the grounds that truth will prevail. It is disheartening, at a time of national crisis, for our government to seek to suppress the words that may enable us to understand our enemies' motives. It is, writ large, the same problem we encounter in students who cannot understand a point of view different from their own.

Katz points out one form of the problem: students simply assimilate the thought and feeling in a text to their own thoughts and feelings. Wilner points out another: students recognize a different position and simply refuse to read it or think about it. These two responses to otherness constitute the American way, I am afraid, and it is a way of responding to texts that we, as teachers, have a duty to counteract. If rhetoric is a schooling in textual virtue as well as in textual power, as I believe it is, this virtue consists largely in our being able to assume another person's point of view before criticizing it and resuming our own. We, and our students, must learn to put ourselves into a text before taking ourselves out of it. Even in these difficult times we must remain open to otherness.

If we accept this rhetorical goal as a part of our teaching mission, it follows that we must organize a curriculum to support it. Our present emphasis on literature, however, is at cross-purposes to this goal because of the way we have defined the term *literature* and because of the methods we employ. In our educational tradition "literature," and its predecessor, "belles lettres," once included powerful speeches and essays along with poems, plays, and stories. But over the past two centuries an opposition between the aesthetic text and the rhetorical text has developed, so that the term *literature* now excludes texts intended to persuade, whether they be essays or orations, advertising or propaganda, in print or in other media. The process through which this has happened is too long and complex for treatment here, but it assuredly did happen, and we are dealing with the results. The insistence that literary texts "should not mean, but be," as Archibald MacLeish put it in his well-known poem "Ars Poetica," contributed mightily. (MacLeish, we should note, was making an argument in a poem that argued against making arguments in poems.) In any case, literature became defined as texts that do not speak to us except with a forked tongue. Paraphrase became a heresy, intentionality a fallacy, the author a mute corpse, and the literary text a self-deconstructing artifact or ideological symptom.

We need to change our definitions as well as our curriculum. First, we need to include more overtly persuasive or argumentative texts in our curricula. We can do it in virtually every kind of course now in the literary curriculum. In the American literature survey, for instance, we can include not only more speeches and documents but texts in traditional literary forms that take strong positions, like Edna St. Vincent Millay's poem "Justice Denied in Massachusetts," about the execution of Sacco and Vanzetti. We can also include critical interpretations of such texts, for example, Allen Tate's attack on Millay's poem in his essay "Tension in Literature" (see Scholes 2001: 17–21, 64–75, for Tate's and Millay's texts).

We can and should do this, in both secondary school and college. The objections to including criticism in literature courses are mainly made on behalf of greater coverage of literature itself, since critical texts must displace some literary texts if they are included. The primary answer to these objections is that, if we are teaching reading, we must give some examples of how it is done, but there is a secondary answer as well. Critical texts, if properly chosen, will differ with one another, so that reading them will lead students to recognize difference itself as they situate their own readings in relation to those of the critics. The purpose of this approach is not to make literary critics more important. They have become too important already. It is to bring criticism out into the open so that every student can be a critical reader. It is to bring criticism back to earth.

Second, newer technologies also offer possibilities for the teaching of reading that we are only beginning to explore. There is a lot of writing on the Web that takes positions and makes arguments, well or badly. There are ongoing arguments, on all sorts of topics, that can be traced through particular threads on Web sites. Part of the problem we face in classrooms, especially in the general-education classrooms of colleges and in the English courses of secondary schools, is that debates about literary interpretation simply do not engage many of our students. These same students, however, may go right from our classrooms to their terminals, where they engage in serious debate about issues that are important to them.

Let me give a trivial example. For my sins, no doubt, I frequently follow discussions on a Web site devoted to the New England Patriots football team. On these pages I have found, and find regularly, debates conducted with a high degree of seriousness and skill over matters related directly to football, including coaching strategies, personnel, media coverage, and training methods. Despite the occasional flame war, these debates typically involve the presentation of evidence (often statistical), the drawing of conclusions, the consideration of opposing views, the eloquent expression of attitudes—in short, all the things that go into persuasive and argumentative writing. One can also find examples of exposition and explanation, such as a clear and cogent description of the differences between one-gap and two-gap defensive-line play. There are hundreds if not thousands of comparable sites dealing with everything from motorcycles to religion. We need to see the Web as a constantly replenished source of textual materials for study. We should be asking students to bring back examples from sites of interest to them and to discuss the positions taken, the quality of various presentations, and their own views of the matters at hand.

We need, in short, to connect the development of reading and writing skills to the real world around us and to the virtual world in which that actual world becomes available to us in the form of texts. Without education, as Thomas Jefferson well understood, participatory democracy cannot function. The basis of an education for the citizens of a democracy lies in that apparently simple but actually difficult act of reading so as to grasp and evaluate the thoughts and feelings of that mysterious other person: the writer. The primary pedagogical responsibility of English teachers is to help students develop those skills. We need to give this humble task more attention, and we need to do a better job of it, too. We can start by recognizing it as a crucial object of our discipline—as more fundamental and more important than "covering" any canon of literary works.

Notes

i. This commentary is a revised version of a talk delivered during a session at the National Council of Teachers of English Conference in Baltimore in November 2001. The session, organized by David Laurence, national director of the Association of Departments of English, focused on the transition from high school to college. Each panelist addressed a specific problem: Sandy Stephan, institutional differences; Tom Jehn, college writing; and Robert Scholes, college literature.

ii. See Arlene Wilner's discussion of this problem in "Confronting Resistance: Sonny's Blues—and Mine" in this issue.

iii. In " 'Reading Fiction/Teaching Fiction': A Pedagogical Experiment," Jerome McGann (2001: 147) makes a similar argument for what he calls "recitation": "Over some years I have observed the (perhaps increasing) disability that students have in negotiating language in an articulate way. This weakness seems to propagate others, most especially an inclination to 'read' texts at relatively high levels of textual abstraction. With diminished skills in perceiving words as such comes, it seems, a weakened ability to notice other close details of language—semantic, grammatical, rhetorical. Recitation—I am talking about oral recitation of the fictional text—forces students to return to elementary levels of linguistic attention. To be effective as a pedagogical tool, however, it must be performed regularly and explicitly discussed and reflected upon. These exercises form the basis for developing higher-level acts of linguistic attention."

Works Cited

Graff, Gerald. Forthcoming. *Clueless in Academe*. New Haven, Conn.: Yale University Press. McGann, Jerome. 2001. "'Reading Fiction/Teaching Fiction': A Pedagogical Experiment." *Pedagogy* 1: 143–65.

McGuffey, William H. 1879. *Fifth Eclectic Reader*. Rev. ed. New York: American Book. Scholes, Robert. 2001. *The Crafty Reader*. New Haven, Conn.: Yale University Press.

College English, Volume 70, Number 6, July 2008

Texts of Our Institutional Lives : Studying the "Reading Transition" from High School to College: What Are Our Students Reading and Why?[1]

David A. Jolliffe and Allison Harl[2]

More than our colleagues in other departments, English department faculty members and administrators need to know what, how, and why students read. Most composition programs and assignments are grounded in reading, and, of course, so are English majors' curriculums. English department faculty members are nearly always major players in general education, most of which requires substantial reading. We need to know how students are learning to read before they come to college, how we continue to foster close, critical reading throughout the college years, and how our students develop reading abilities and practices that they will continue to inhabit and improve after college.

If the scuttlebutt about reading is true, the Visigoths are at the door. An array of national surveys and studies suggests that neither high school nor college students spend much time preparing for class, the central activity of which we presume to be reading assigned articles, chapters, and books. Similar studies argue that college students spend little to no time reading for pleasure and that adults in the United States are devoting less and less of their free time to reading fiction, poetry, and drama. Books lamenting the decline in the reading of great literature in our culture[i] find an eager and ardent audience. The water-cooler conversation in English departments and indeed throughout the university seems to confirm the reports and corroborate the end-of-reading treatises and memoirs: legions of students apparently come to class ill prepared, not having done the assigned reading at all or having given it only cursory attention. Professors admit that students can actually pass exams if they come to the lectures and take (or buy) good notes, whether or not they

1 **Citation:** Jolliffe, David A. and Allison Harl. "Studying the 'Reading Transition' from High School to College: What Are Our Students Reading and Why?" *College English*, vol. 70, no. 6, 2008, pp. 599-617.

2 **David A. Jolliffe** is professor of English and of Curriculum and Instruction at the University of Arkansas, where he also holds the Brown Chair in English Literacy. Currently, he directs a pilot version of a community literacy advocacy program in Augusta, Arkansas, and leads the Arkansas Delta Oral History Project, through which mentors from his university collaborate with students from ten high schools in eastern Arkansas. **Allison Harl** is pursuing a Ph.D. in American Literature and Culture at the University of Arkansas, where her secondary emphasis is rhetoric and composition. Her scholarly interests include frontier American literature, literacy studies, and writing through active citizenship.

have read the assigned material. In short, careful reading seems have become a smaller blip on the higher educational radar screen or dropped off it altogether.

Despite the attention paid to student reading in the national surveys, relatively little scholarship has examined empirically what, how, and whether college students actually do read and how reading thus figures in the transition from high school to college. We set out to address this knowledge gap in a local way during a recent fall semester at our institution, the University of Arkansas. We wanted to know how our first-year students taking college composition, a course in which students mostly write about their reading, perceived and effected the transition from high school to college as readers. Therefore, we studied the reading habits and practices of twentyone first-year composition students during the first two weeks of October, at which time they were in their sixth and seventh weeks of a fifteen-week semester. In some ways, our study provides a remarkably accurate local representation of the data about student reading as reported in the national surveys: first-year students at the University of Arkansas spend just about the same amount of time reading and preparing for class as students at other research universities—probably not as much time as their instructors and institutional administrators think they should. In other ways, however, our study offers insights into the reading environments of first-year college students that neither the national surveys nor the status-quo chatter hints at. We found students who were actively involved in their own programs of reading aimed at values clarification, personal enrichment, and career preparation. In short, we discovered students who were extremely engaged with their reading, but not with the reading that their classes required.

We offer our study as an example of local institutional research, aimed at helping our faculty understand salient aspects of our students' reading experiences and develop key strategies for addressing our students' reading histories. We hope, however, that what we found might help other institutions' faculty members and administrators think more carefully about how they meet and understand their students as readers.

What Do We Know about Reading?: High School, College, and the Transition

Any faculty member who wonders how and whether students prepare for class can probably find sources of consternation and concern in two national surveys. Since its inception in 1999, the National Survey of Student Engagement (NSSE), directed by George Kuh at Indiana University, has provided valuable data to college and university administrators and faculties about first-year and senior-year students' practices and beliefs as related to the survey organization's five "national benchmarks of effective educational practice": "level of academic challenge, active and collaborative learning, student-faculty interaction, enriching educational experiences, and supportive campus environments" (12). Although the answers to questions engendered by each of the benchmark categories might interest faculty members who want to understand their students better, we believe that the questions generated under the rubric of "levels of academic challenge" are most germane to anyone concerned about student reading. The eleven questions in this category ask students about the number of textbooks, books, and book-length packs of course readings that they were required to read; the number and length of the papers that they were required to write; their perceptions of course emphases (for example, analyzing, synthesizing, making judgments, and applying theories or concepts); and the amount of time that they spent preparing for class.

Under the traditional rule of thumb of two hours' preparation time for every one hour in class, this average full-time student should be devoting 24 hours per week to studying, reading, writing, and so on. However, in the 2005 NSSE, taken by about 130,000 first-year students and a similar number of seniors from 523 colleges and universities, 66 percent of first-year students and 64 percent of seniors at all participating colleges and universities reported spending fewer than sixteen hours during a typical seven-day week preparing for class—"studying, reading, writing, doing homework or lab work, analyzing data, rehearsing, and other academic activities."[ii]

If one concludes that college students are spending too little time preparing for class, one would also have to deduce that the situation in high school is even more dire. In 2004, five years after NSSE's debut, the High School Survey of Student Engagement (HSSSE) emerged from the same organization. In the inaugural HSSSE, over 90,000 high school students from grades 9 through 12 completed the survey, providing information about who is planning to go to college and how well students are prepared for college ("Getting Students Ready for College" 3). Among the seniors completing the survey, 94 percent of all respondents and 90 percent of respondents taking "college credit/prep/honors" courses reported spending six hours or fewer per week on "assigned reading." These data notwithstanding, a large majority of all of the respondents agreed with the statement, "I have the skills and abilities to complete my work." ("What We Can Learn from High School Students" 12). In other words, although the large majority of high school students spend less than one hour a day on assigned reading, they feel as though they are good enough readers to get by—perhaps because their schoolwork does not challenge them very much.

The NSSE and HSSSE data find an ominous counterpart in a study reported by Alvin Sanoff in 2006. Nearly 800 high school teachers and about 1,100 college faculty members were surveyed to determine their perceptions of how well students were prepared for college in reading, writing, science, mathematics, and oral communication, as well as in more attitudinal domains such as "motivation to work hard," "study habits," and "ability to seek and use support services." Only one-quarter of high school teachers and one-tenth of college faculty members thought that entering first-year students were "very well prepared" to read and understand difficult materials.

Consider the NSSE, HSSSE, and Sanoff data alongside two widely hailed studies of adult reading in the United States and the situation seems even more portentous. The 2004 report *Reading at Risk* from the National Endowment for the Arts found that literary reading among adult readers in the United States declined by ten percentage points between 1982 and 2002, representing a loss of 20 million readers, a decline mirrored, somewhat less precipitously, in the diminishing numbers of adults who read books of any kind (ix).[iii] More recently, the NEA's 2007 report, *To Read or Not to Read*, maintained that "Americans are spending less time reading, reading comprehension skills are eroding," and "[t]hese declines have serious civic, social, cultural, and economic implications" (5).

Although the NSSE, the HSSSE, and NEA studies provide fodder for the perception that college-bound and college students can't and/or don't read extensively, critically, or even sufficiently, the surveys and reports did not provide us with a rich enough perspective as we planned how to engage in conversations with our institution's faculty members about designing, adjusting, and delivering reading-based composition and general-education curricula to our students. Very few scholars have actually investigated the quality or quantity of college students' reading.[iv] We wanted to know more about the reading lives of our students.

How We Studied Student Reading

In that semester, we randomly selected twenty-one full-time freshmen from a volunteer pool of about one hundred students and paid the participants to complete three tasks. First, they filled out a questionnaire about their perceptions of their own reading abilities and habits in high school and college. Students provided information and opinions in response to the following questions:

- Approximately how many hours per week did you spend reading in your senior year of high school?
- Approximately what percentage of those hours were devoted to reading for your courses, in contrast to reading for your own interest or pleasure?
- Did you consider the amount of time you spent reading during your senior year in high school excessively high, moderately high, moderately how, or excessively low? Explain why.
- Did you consider yourself an excellent, above average, below average, or poor reader in high school? Explain why.
- So far this year [as of October 2], approximately how many hours per week are you spending on reading?
- Approximately what percentage of those hours are devoted to reading for your courses, in contrast to reading for your own interest or pleasure?
- Do you consider the amount of time you spend reading this year excessively high, moderately high, moderately low, or excessively low? Explain why.

- Do you now consider yourself an excellent, above average, below average, or poor reader? Explain why.

The second task required them to keep a reading journal for two consecutive weeks. We asked them to write for at least thirty minutes daily, describing in detail everything they read that day, and to produce at least ten full entries over the two weeks. For each entry, we asked the students to provide the title and author and the number of pages of each reading, indicating whether each text was read for a class, for a job, or for their interest or pleasure. Additionally, we asked students to indicate approximately how many minutes they spent reading during each day. Finally, we asked participants to focus specifically on *one* of the texts they read for each day and write about that text, responding to a series of questions. These questions were divided into five major categories: 1.) Focusing on One Specific Text, 2.) Reading Critically 3.) Drawing Relationships: Text to Self, 4.) Drawing Relationships: Text to Text, and 5.) Drawing Relationships: Text to World.[v] The following are the actual questions that we asked students to answer in response to their one "chosen" text:

Focusing on One Specific Text

1. What was the title of the text you read?
2. What was the purpose of reading this text? Why did you read it?
3. Did you choose to read this text or was it assigned? If assigned, who assigned it?
4. If assigned the text, did whoever assigned it give you instructions on how to read it? If so, what were the instructions?
5. If you chose this text for pleasure, why did you choose it?
6. How long did it take you to read the text?
7. Were you engaged in any other activity as you read the text (cooking, watching TV, etc.)?
8. Did you take a break or read straight through?

Reading Critically

1. What was the most important point the text made?
2. What were its most important secondary or supporting points?
3. Did you agree or disagree with the writer on any points?
4. Did you draw any inferences or conclusions that weren't directly stated in the text?
5. How difficult was the text to read?
6. Did you underline, highlight, or make comments in the margins? If so, describe the kinds of things you noted.
7. Did you ask questions of the text as you read? If so, describe your questions.

8. Did you look at headings and subtitles before you began to read? If so, what did they teach you?
9. What part of the reading, if any, did you skip over?
10. Why did you skip over this part, if you did?

Drawing Relationships: Text to Self

1. Did you find that what you read relates to your life in any way? If so, how?
2. Did this work inspire you in any way or stimulate your creativity? If so, how?
3. Did the text relate to your current job or a future job in any way? If so, how?
4. Did you discover anything new about your personal opinions, beliefs, or values in response to reading this text? If so, how?
5. How do you think your life experiences influence the way you read the text?

Drawing Relationships: Text to Text

1. Did you make any connections between this text and other texts you have read?
2. Does this text relate to other texts assigned in your classes? If so, how?
3. Does this text relate to other texts you have read outside of class? If so, how?
4. Did reading other texts help you understand this one? Or do you feel you needed more background information to understand the material?
5. How do you foresee this text helping you understand texts you expect to read in the future?

Drawing Relationships: Text to World

1. Did you discuss what you read with anyone? If so, with whom?
2. Who else read this text?
3. How is others' response similar to or different from your own?
4. How does this text relate to the world, to the 'bigger picture' in general?

For the third task in the study, students participated in an exit interview, in which they provided a think-aloud protocol about a self-selected 250-word portion of a textbook that they were currently reading for one of their classes. In the remainder of this article, after a brief comment on data from the intake questionnaires, we focus on what the students' reading journals taught us.

The data generated by the intake questionnaires did not suggest that the students see the reading transition from high school to college as all that dramatic. The first-year students at the University of Arkansas were reading a bit more in college than they did during their last year of high school, and they were reading a bit less for pleasure than they did during the previous year.

Students characterized the time that they spent reading during their senior year in high school as "moderately low," about 7.6 hours per week, 70 percent of which was for their classes. Nevertheless, their general perception of their reading abilities in high school was in the "above average" range.[vi] Not much seemed to change for these students when they came to college. According to the intake questionnaires, as first-year students they were still spending what they characterized as a moderately low amount of time reading, about 12.9 hours per week, 84 percent of which was for their classes, and they still perceived themselves as above-average readers.

What We Learned from the Journals, Part I: Toeing the NSSE Line

The students' two-week intensive journals in some ways fleshed out the students' self-perceptions from the intake questionnaires, but in other ways they contradicted them. Above all else, the journals offered a considerably richer picture of the students' reading lives than we had anticipated—the journals turned out to be a bountiful data source. One could certainly drop into them like an anthropologist and find several aspects of the late-adolescent reading culture that are worthy of note and, from an educationally conservative viewpoint, perplexing. For example,

- All of the students spent lots of time reading online documents.
- A substantial majority of them read their Facebook sites almost daily, sometimes for extended periods.
- Most of them read while doing something else: listening to music, checking emails and sending instant messages, watching television, and so on.

But, as fascinated as we were by the minutiae of the students' rituals, we wanted to look for bigger patterns in the journals. Initially, we simply wanted to see how our first-year students stacked up against the national numbers reported in the NSSE.

For each journal entry, we asked the participants not only to list everything they read during the course of each day but also to estimate the amount of time they had spent reading each item. All of the participants provided at least ten full entries, but only half of them were faithful recorders of texts and time. As we made a first pass through the journals of these accurate respondents, we tried to categorize the texts that they read as either "academic"—that is, texts that they read for their courses—or "nonacademic"—that is, texts that they read for pleasure, leisure, personal interest, or work. Given our interest in technologically mediated writing, moreover, we found it interesting to subdivide the "nonacademic" category into "nonacademic/technological"—reading done on a computer screen—and "nonacademic/nontechnological." The students who were faithful recorders of their texts and time spent an average of 1 hour and 24 minutes per day on academic reading, some of which—a surprisingly small proportion—was done using technology. The faithful recorders devoted an average of 54 minutes a day to nonacademic reading involving technology—Facebook profiles, emails, instant messages, Internet sites, and so on. They spent an average of 25 minutes per day on nonacademic reading that did not involve technology—magazines, books, newspapers, and so on. Thus, the faithful, categorizing respondents reported spending an average of 2 hours and 43 minutes per day on all types of reading, almost evenly divided between academic and nonacademic reading.[vii]

If we assume, however, that the faithfully categorizing respondents and the summative respondents were devoting roughly the same proportion of time to academic and nonacademic reading, their reports place these University of Arkansas first-year students right smack in the middle of that 66 percent of first-year students in the NSSE who spent fewer than 16 hours per week "preparing for class."[viii]

What We Learned from the Journals, Part II: Hints of a Reading Life

In addition to telling us how much and roughly what kinds of reading our students did, the journals also provided a fascinating window into why and how they read. Because we asked students to include in their journal entries everything that they read during the course of a day and gave them the freedom to write their "focusing on-one-specific-text" entry in response to anything they might choose, we were quite interested in the types of texts that they selected. We found an abundant and varied array.

The journals contained a grand total of 210 daily entries. Within this number, about half of the "focused" entries were about texts that students were reading for their classes, and the other half were about texts that we categorized as "nonacademic." Among the nonacademic responses, the large majority were about texts that students were reading for their personal pleasure or interest, such as employee manuals and job instructions. A smaller number were about texts they were reading either for work or for personal "business" as a student, such as documents about academic advising, academic progress, and so on. Another small percentage of nonacademic responses dealt with texts that students were reading as part of a personal program to support and, in some cases, explore their religious faith.

Considering that all of the participants in the study were full-time students, one might expect the reading that they were doing for their courses to occupy the top position in their list of intellectual priorities. Moreover, considering that the participants had reported spending 84 percent of their reading time during the first six weeks of the semester occupied with academic reading, one might expect that their nonacademic reading was done primarily for rest and relaxation.

The journal entries do not support these presumptions. Like the students in the Stanford Study of Writing, who reported having actively "performative" writing lives that transcended the writing they must do for courses (Fishman et al.), many of the students in our study described having regular, steady, full reading lives in which they engaged with a wide variety of texts for reasons both academic and nonacademic. We encountered students who, during the two-week period, were reading novels (examples: *The Fellowship of the Ring, A Handmaid's Tale,* and *Angels and Demons*), nonfiction books (*Guns, Germs, and Steel* and *Under the Banner of Heaven*), magazines (*Seventeen* and *Cosmopolitan* were favorites among the females; exercise and hunting magazines prevailed among the males), and newspapers (both the campus paper and the statewide one) for personal interest and pleasure. We found students, perhaps because of our prompting, drawing solid connections between the texts that they were reading and their emerging sense of themselves as adults in the world. One student unpacked her connection to a magazine article about the untimely death of young woman who had had an unresolved argument with her father; the journal entry described the student's own estrangement from her father following her parents' divorce. Another student noted that she connected to *The Diary of Anne Frank* because, as a Jew, she had experienced racial slurs herself. A third student described her memory of training a puppy to help her connect to part of her psychology textbook about behavioral conditioning. A fourth student explained his connection between Plato's *Republic* and Marxist governments: "Karl Marx and socialist and communist societies tried to use many of Plato's ideas in their writings and governments, but they all consistently failed, while democracy thrived and continues to spread today."

The following three brief case studies offer slightly more extended profiles of students who defy the status-quo thinking that portrays first-year college students as incapable of and uninterested in reading. Angela, Pauline, and Corey have come to college as readers of texts that speak to their own exigencies and interests.

Angela Ivy[ix] was taking four courses during the study—Italian, algebra, composition, and sociology—and she devoted some reading time to each of them. But the reading activity that occupied most of her time during the two weeks involved the Bible, plus books and articles from the popular press about contemporary issues of Christian faith. Her reports of reading experiences showed, on the one hand, a young person who was looking for confirmation of religious principles that she grew up with but, on the other hand, questioning how these principles fit into the new culture in which she was immersed at the university.

The number of minutes that Angela devoted to reading for her four courses is interesting in itself. Over the two weeks, she reported spending 325 minutes reading and studying for algebra, 215 minutes reading and studying vocabulary items for her composition class, 175 minutes reading and studying Italian, and 35 minutes reading for sociology. Compare these times with her reports for three other activities: she spent 345 minutes reading the *Bible* and books and articles dealing with Christian faith—texts that she chose to read for "interest/personal benefit." She devoted 330 minutes to reading email messages, websites (at least one of which was related to her coursework), and

Facebook entries. She spent 210 minutes reading articles in magazines and newspapers for "personal interest," but at least three of these articles were about topics that frequently emerge in contemporary discussions of religion and faith: creationism versus intelligent design, homosexuality and tolerance, and the legalization of marijuana.

Angela's journal opened with a long, questioning entry on a book called *Show Me, God* by Fred Heeren, a text that Angela says she read "by choice." The main point of the text, she wrote, "was concerning the Law of Cause and Effect—that logic demands a cause for every effect and that world/universe is an effect that demands a very great cause." She added:

> The sun, moon, and stars could not have come from nothing—that's *irrational.* Every observable fact around us can be explained in terms of something else that caused it, but when the question is about the existence of the universe itself, there is nothing in the universe to explain it—no natural explanation. I understood where the author was coming from, but just because we haven't found a natural explanation for creation doesn't mean we should just throw up our hands and say 'God did it.' (Emphasis in original)

Angela's last journal entry provided a fascinating summary of her commentary on reading texts that lead to theological questioning. She read an article entitled "The Bible Is Still Number One" in a magazine called *A Matter of Fact.* She encapsulated the main point of the article: "Prophesy and scientific foreknowledge are repeated in the Bible—giving evidence of its credibility as The Word of God." She drew a powerful connection between this text and herself: "If I could go into apologetics for a career," she wrote, "it [the article] would definitely relate to my future job." Tacitly conceding that she probably won't have this option as a career, she added, "Regardless, it's good to have a rational foundation in what you're trying to put your trust in." She saw possible connections between this text and others she might read for courses or personal interest: "The more I read about this, the more I'll have to implement into other texts I have read. It helps to have a well-rounded approach so you can look at things more objectively."

Pauline Rosario offers a powerful counterexample to those who believe that first-year students don't engage with their reading. Pauline had become fluent in English, her second language, but read regularly in her first language, Spanish, to maintain her fluency in it. She belonged to a book club, undertook a considerable amount of reading outside of class, and showed a strong ability to draw connections between her reading and her growing sense of self, the texts she has previously read, and the larger world beyond academia.

During the two-week journaling period, Pauline spent a lot of her spare time reading for pleasure. For instance, she read *One Hundred Years of Solitude* in Spanish, her native language, for the book club that she belonged to as an extracurricular activity. She commented that she read it slowly because she had difficulty with reading Spanish now that she was used to reading in English. Apparently, Pauline still valued her first language enough to put forth the effort to read the text in Spanish rather than in its translated form. She wrote, "There is one factor that is hindering my reading speed and comprehension, the book is in Spanish. Spanish was my first language but after 12 years in school, using English, it has become difficult to understand Spanish as I read it. In total I spent about an hour and a half reading the book and accomplished one and a half chapters."

Pauline even saw possibilities for drawing connections in her reading using technology. Commenting on reading emails and Web logs, she wrote, "This text obviously does not involve any academic reward, but it is very important as far as my social life goes. I did make connections with other texts (e-mails) that I've read, though, mainly because e-mails are an ongoing conversation with friends that I do not see as often. Reading this text did in fact make me understand other e-mails a little better." Pauline did not discredit the value of her personal reading or the use of electronic media because she believes that they help her explore her ideas. "As far as discovering anything about my personal opinions, this text succeeded. Because these e-mails were of a personal subject, they did relate to my life 100%. After reading these e-mails, I called a friend, so I did discuss the reading with someone else."

Finally, Pauline included this note at the end of her journal:

> I am aware that this study is to figure out the "jump" from high school to college reading; however the fact is that most of my required reading (which is not much) has nothing to do with this "jump" because what is different is not the amount of reading, but the level and wording of the text. The college text jumps to a level of reading exponentially higher than high school texts, and this is what causes the struggles for the students.

Corey Essene was enrolled in the College of Arts and Sciences Honors Program at the time of our study, and, as such, was the type of student that one might expect to take his class preparation very seriously. A superficial reading of his journal entries might lead one to question that expectation. In short, Corey seemed to blow off his required reading. On the other hand, however, his journal entries show a young man devoted to reading fantasy fiction and learning French—not so much to do well in his French class, but instead to communicate with a friend he met while traveling the previous summer and to fulfill his goal of getting a job working in the American Embassy in Paris.

Corey's first journal entry was one of only two in which he had anything substantial—or positive—to say about his assigned reading. He described his admittedly superficial reading of an essay, "The Genocidal Killer in the Mirror," simply because he and some classmates in his Honors Composition class had to meet and collectively come up with a thesis statement for an essay about it. In his next entry, however, he focused at some length on a chapter entitled "Celbedeil" in a book called *Eldest* by Christopher Paolini, which he chose to spend thirty minutes reading "to break the monotony of studying and doing homework for all of my classes." *Eldest* is clearly mainstream fantasy, the second book in a trilogy, Corey reported: "It's a story about dragons in a mythical setting. It is kind of like books I have read including Tolkien's books because it has many of the same mythical races and similar settings." Corey offered a connection-filled thought to conclude this entry: "This really relates to the real world because this symbolizes bigotry that still exists across the planet. I think that because I am aware of bigotry in society that I was able to see Paolini's throw back and symbology [sic] of these ancient grudges and beliefs. This text basically reaffirmed my passion against the ignorance of bigotry, whether it be in fiction novels, or real life and history."

In another entry, Corey turned his attention to French and made an explicit text-to-self connection, referring directly to his employment goal. He reported studying his French textbook for "about a half an hour" in his dorm room: "I read this because I am currently learning French as my second language and it is my minor. I read this also for pleasure because I enjoy learning the French language. This relates to me personally because I hope to get a job at the American embassy in Paris." Two entries later, Corey returned to the French project, describing his reading of a "long email from a friend in Paris." He added, "I read the entire text in French and it took me about ten minutes. I understood most of the letter, but I was forced to look up a few words that were not in my French vocabulary." Corey explained that he had struck a deal with Axel, a French friend whom he met traveling last summer. They agreed they would write to each other only in French: "I actually made this arrangement with Axel, most importantly, for educational purposes. Axel is fluent in English, so he is doing this as a favor to me to strengthen my French vocabulary and grammar."

In his next-to-last entry, Corey returned to some assigned reading, this time for his Fundamentals of Communication class: "The text was the basic dry, boring textbook type text, but it was highly informative. I read it in about an hour. This relates to me because I know it will help me give my assigned speech and later speeches I am to give throughout my college career and life."

We don't want to argue that Angela, Pauline, and Corey are necessarily representative of any particular population, but they do evince a strong interest in personal reading, something that status-quo thinking would assert that college students lack. Angela, Pauline, and Corey engage thoughtfully with texts; however, most of the texts that they value and connect with are not those assigned in their courses.

Rethinking Reading in College Courses

Although neither of us had Angela, Pauline, or Corey as a student in class, when we read their journals, we tended to think we might like to. Here were three students, all engaged readers, all capable to some degree of connecting their reading to their own growing sense of self and to the world around them. We venture, however, that, although Pauline might be seen as a successful college student reader, many instructors would find Angela and Corey to represent the kinds of students that they normally encounter in their courses—not very interested in the assigned course readings, not eager to "participate" in a discussion, not inclined to read any more deeply than the assignment requires.

So what did we learn about these kinds of students by reading their journals? What kinds of readers are these randomly selected University of Arkansas students? Let us unpack those questions before turning to the issue of how we urged faculty members and program administrators at our institution to think differently about reading in their courses.

First of all, our students were reading, but they were not reading studiously, either in terms of the texts they were engaging with or the manner in which they read them. Like the high school boys whose literate practices Michael Smith and Jeffrey Wilhelm describe in *Reading Don't Fix No Chevys*, the University of Arkansas students often manifested a passion for reading that was not connected to their courses. Instead, they saw the reading that they had to do for school as uninspiring, dull, and painfully required. Here was Angela's response to her sociology text: "I completely agree" with it and it "raises no questions." Corey assessed his Fundamentals of Communication reading as being self-evident, and said that he rapidly perused "The Genocidal Killer in the Mirror" just in order to generate a thesis about it. Although Angela's and Corey's responses to school-based reading, typical of those of many of the participants, were rather neutrally dismissive, other students were more adamantly critical. One student, Jennifer Respighi, described how she took only five minutes to read a sample biology lab report "because it was so boring." Another student, Katherine Quick, characterized her psychology textbook as "a brutally boring overwad" and wrote that she skipped sections "because there was no reason to read a bunch of bullshit." A third student, Walter Hope, simply opined that "my chemistry book sucks."

Many of the participants clearly rushed through their required reading simply to get it done and then move on to reading that they found more engaging. In the journals, we found daily reading schedules such as the following:

- Andrea Less, Day 5: 30 minutes reading an article for an English assignment, 20 minutes reading email and Ebay ads.
- Kathy Gravette, Day 1: 30 minutes total for reading an English assignment and the essay it required her to read, plus her art assignment, and *Cosmopolitan* magazine; Day 5: 30 minutes total for reading her English assignment ("It was difficult to read") plus *Cosmopolitan* and the newspaper.
- Fred Borg, Day 1: 45 minutes reading a selection from Descartes's *First Meditation, during* a lecture in a math class; Day 3: 20 minutes reading an essay for English.
- Tony Richardson, Day 2: 30 minutes reading an essay for English; Day 5: 96 minutes reading *The Boater's Handbook.*

In many of these reports, we would be hard pressed to find reading experiences that we would characterize as focused and contemplative.

Second, although the students generally showed some ability to draw the three types of connections that we urged them to create with our leading questions, their reported connections were not evenly distributed among the three categories. Our students seemed quite capable of making text-to-self connections—Lindsey James, for example, related her response to an article about cults to her own religious upbringing—and text-to-world connections—recall Angela's repeated connections between texts that she was reading and campus/community/world events. But it was the rare student who, like Pauline, would draw connections between and among texts that she was reading for her classes, or like William Hope, who described the connections that he drew between *Helter Skelter* and *Under the Banner of Heaven*, two books that he read for his own pleasure and interest.

Third, students are motivated by and engaged with reading, but the texts that they interact with most enthusiastically are technologically based. In addition, students have become proficient in the art of multitasking as they navigate in and out of electronic media. Virtually all of the students indicate in their journals that they spend a substantial amount of time reading online. Although some of the students' academic assignments require online research or reading on the computer, their journal entries indicate that they interact with electronic media primarily when reading for pleasure. The majority of their time reading for pleasure is spent reading and writing emails, instant messaging, or creating and perusing Facebook and MySpace profiles. In these examples, technology encourages reading for personal communication and social networking, and these purposes overlap in many ways that relate to academic study. For instance, Corey became inspired to learn French, so he emailed back and forth with a friend in France to help him acquire and enhance his reading skills. Without this incentive, Corey may not have pursued his study of French with the same enthusiasm. Pauline wrote in her journal that the significant amounts of time she spends blogging and networking with friends may have no academic reward; nevertheless, she values this kind of reading for its ability to help her network and stay connected socially. As a result of the amount of time that students spend with electronic media, their reading practices and habits have shifted with influence of these technologies. Their journal entries consistently refer to the myriad ways in which they multitask as they read. For instance, many students email and instant message their friends while surfing the Internet and reading texts on the computer. Many watch television, listen to music, or talk on their cell phones as they read their textbooks.

Given that our students seem to engage with some types of reading, what did we suggest that faculty members the University of Arkansas do to help their students engage more fully with, and read more critically, the material that they need to read for their classes? Both in campus forums sponsored by our university's Teaching and Learning Center and in internal publications, we suggested three avenues. First, we argued that faculty members need to teach students explicitly how to draw the kinds of connections that lead to engaged reading, particularly text-to-world and text-to-text connections. It's not that we think text-to-self connections are not important. We do think, however, that, as valuable as these kinds of personal connections are for initiating engaged reading, students ultimately need to be stretched beyond the boundaries of their own personal reactions. As Wayne Booth contended in *Modern Dogma and the Rhetoric of Assent,* one major function of college is to drag students "kicking and screaming, out of infantile solipsism into adult membership in an inquiring community" (13). As they read, students need to be walked through demonstrations of mature, committed, adult readers who draw connections to the world around them, both historical and current, and to other texts. One relatively easy teaching technique, the think-aloud protocol, is particularly useful. The instructor simply focuses on a passage—say, 250 words or so—from the required reading and reads it aloud to students, pausing regularly to explain to the students what connections he or she is making to his or her own life and work, to the world beyond the text, and, most important, to other texts that he or she has read. (For more on the think-aloud protocol, see Daniels and Zemelman, Chapter 5.)

Second, we suggested that faculty members and administrators need to create curriculums, co-curriculums, and extra-curriculums that invite students to engage in their reading and to connect texts that they read to their lives, their worlds, and other texts. Certainly, learning-community programs—in which students are taking two or three courses together, focusing on a common theme—foster this kind of curricular connectivity, as do service-learning and community-outreach programs, in which students accomplish necessary and useful projects that reflect principles and ideas from their reading. But even in the absence of such curricular innovations, instructors can take relatively simple steps to foster students' making connections between their courses. An instructor might ask his or her students to list and offer a one-sentence description on an index card of every other class that they are taking. Perusing the other subjects that his or her students are studying, the instructor could make an explicit effort to show how the class readings might evoke themes, issues, and motifs being raised in the other classes. In addition, the instructor might adapt and follow guidelines developed by Christopher Thaiss for first-year writing courses with a writing-across-the-curriculum orientation ("A Rubric for Understanding Writing in Different Classes and Disciplines"; see also Thaiss and Zawacki). An instructor dedicated to improving connected, engaged reading throughout the curriculum could explain explicitly to students how the documents that they must read relate directly to the aims and methods of learning that are most valued in the course environment, show clearly how the students' reading for the course should be manifest in projects and examinations, and demonstrate specifically *how* students should read the course material.

Third, we urged faculty members to look for ways to incorporate more technology into their reading assignments. It is becoming common knowledge that students engage effectively with reading done in interactive electronic contexts. For example, Gail E. Hawisher and her colleagues point out that all students have different "cultural ecologies" and therefore experience different "technological gateways" for acquiring and developing literacy, but many students have developed literacies in electronic contexts that instructors overlook or ignore. "As a result," according to Hawisher et al., "we fail to build on the literacies students already have" (676). We suggested that faculty members could enhance student learning through better engagement with reading by incorporating assignments that achieved two primary goals:

- They would provide students with opportunities to interact with electronic hyperlinked texts.
- They would engage student readers through reflection in electronic public spheres.

We urged faculty to consider incorporating such components as discussion forums through WebCT or Blackboard to help students reflect on and respond to reading assignments with their classmates, and we argued that students could also benefit from online conversations with larger discourse communities and professionals in the field of study to enhance their reading about certain topics. Setting up a Web blog or posting to an established Usenet group could help get students interested. In short, we noted that supplementing course instruction with technological materials would allow students to navigate information and to multitask in ways that would ultimately enhance their reading.

Although our study was most useful for motivating and shaping discussions at our own institution, we see merit in faculty members and administrators conducting similar studies on their own campuses; reporting the results to groups of students, instructors, and administrators; and discussing the implications of the results for teaching and learning on the campus. Indeed, we would urge any college or university serious about improving undergraduate composition and general education to examine student reading on its own campus. While the outcomes of such studies would vary according to context and region—some of our conclusions are related to the high number of fundamentalist evangelicals who attend our university—the results would generate very useful intra and inter-institutional discussions about teaching and learning.

Should the English department take the lead in conducting such studies? Not necessarily. Every English department faculty member who has been involved with writing-across-the-curriculum or writing-in-the-disciplines programs knows that they succeed best when faculty members throughout the university buy into the notion of improving learning by increasing the amount and complexity of student writing and by teaching writing consciously and explicitly in all courses. The same must be true in efforts to examine and improve student reading.

There will be resistance to such efforts. People will wonder why colleges and universities admit students who "can't read." Faculty members will opine that they lack time to teach students how to read material carefully in their courses "because there is so much I have to cover already." To anticipate and counter this resistance, any institutional effort to study whether, how, how much, and why students read must be initiated and championed by faculty members and administrators directly responsible for overseeing curriculum, instruction, and assessment of general education.

There's no need for any college or university to be apologetic about looking at students' reading habits and practices. The transition from high school to college must entail a transition to different types of reading, different amounts of reading, and different approaches to success with reading. If we intend to continue basing assignments, syllabi, and entire academic programs on student reading, then we need to know more about it.

Notes

i. See, for example, Sven Birkerts's *The Gutenberg Elegies* and Mark Edmundson's *Why Read?*

ii. The responses about the "number of assigned textbooks, books, or book-length packs of course readings" that students reported reading are also instructive: 64 percent of first-year students and 56 percent of seniors reported reading ten or fewer textbooks, books, or course packs during the academic year (38).

iii. *Reading at Risk* was not without its naysayers. In *Black Issues Book Review*, Wayne Dawkins questions the "dire picture" painted by the NEA.

iv. A 1991 study by Charlene Blackwood and her colleagues examined the pleasure reading habits of 333 college seniors in a small, public liberal arts university. Although 88 percent of the respondents reported that they read for pleasure, they did so for only about two and a half hours per week while school was in session and slightly more during vacations. In 1999, Jude Gallik surveyed the recreational reading habits of 139 first-year and upper-level students at a private, liberal arts college in Texas. Gallik found that 87 percent of the respondents devoted fewer than six hours per week to recreational reading while school was in session, a number that dropped to 75 percent during school vacations. A 1994 study by Ravi Sheorey and Kouider Mokhtari investigated the reading habits of 85 college students enrolled in an elective developmental reading course at a large public university, finding that the students read about hours per week. In a study conducted in 2000 at Texas A&M Corpus Christi, but never published, Richard Haswell and his graduate students examined practices of, and attitudes toward, "self-sponsored" and "school-sponsored" reading among 100 ninth-graders and 100 first-year college students. Haswell found that the two groups spent slightly different amounts of time each week on reading and writing: The ninth-graders reported reading 163 pages and spending 23 hours per week; the first-semester college students read 141 pages and devoted 18 hours per week. However, the ninth-graders reported reading almost twice as many pages per week of self-chosen material than did the college students, although the college students said they read one-fifth more pages of school-sponsored material per week than the ninth-graders (5). Under the auspices of the Henry J. Kaiser Family Foundation, Victoria Rideout, Donald Roberts, and Ulla Foehr studied the daily media use of more than 2,000 8- to 18-year-olds. The researchers found that subjects spent an average of 6.5 hours daily with "media": 4 hours and 16 minutes watching television and/or movies, 1 hour and 44 minutes listening to music, 1 hour and 2 minutes using the computer, and 49 minutes playing video games. Although three-quarters of the survey participants reported reading something for pleasure every day, the average time spent daily reading books, magazines, and newspapers was 43 minutes.

v. The "drawing-relationships" questions were motivated by the types of connections that Ellin Keene Oliver and Susan Zimmerman teach students to draw in *Mosaic of Thought: Teaching Comprehension in a Reader's Workshop*, a widely used resource for teacher-development programs in high schools.

vi. When examining the students' evaluations of how much time they devoted to reading in high school and college, we coded a response of "excessively high" as a 4, "moderately high" as a 3, "moderately low" as a 2, and "excessively low" as a 1. When examining the students' perceptions of their own abilities as readers, we coded a response of "excellent" as a 4, "above average" as a 3, "below average" as a 2, and "poor" as a 1.

vii. Over a seven-day week, therefore, these students devoted about 19 hours per week to reading—in other words, somewhat more than they had reported on their intake questionnaires, perhaps because the act of listing *everything* that they read during a day turned "reading" into a larger activity for these students. In contrast, the students who did not record how much time they spent reading each item, but simply provided a total number of minutes of reading per day, reported spending an average of 1 hour and 41 minutes daily on all types of reading, or about 11.8 hours per week—a bit less than they had reported on their intake questionnaires.

viii. The largest subgroup within that 66 percent is the students who reported spending 6 to 10 hours per week preparing for class—27 percent. Because the participants in our study included *everything* that they read in their daily tallies, we think it's safe to assume that the amount of time that they spent on reading *in preparation for class* probably lies within this 6to–10-hours-per-week category.

ix. By agreement with the participants, all names have been changed to pseudonyms.

Works Cited

Birkerts, Sven. *The Gutenberg Elegies: The Fate of Reading in an Electronic Age*. New York: Fawcett, 1994.

Blackwood, Charlene, et al. "Pleasure Reading by College Students: Fact or Fiction?" Paper presented at the annual meeting of the Mid-South Educational Research Association, Lexington, KY, Nov. 1991.

Booth, Wayne. *Modern Dogma and the Rhetoric of Assent*. Chicago: U of Chicago P, 1974.

Daniels, Harvey, and Steven Zemelman. *Subjects Matter: Every Teacher's Guide to Content-Area Reading*. Portsmouth, NH: Heinemann, 2004.

Dawkins, Wayne. "Is Anybody Out There? A Closer Look at the Dire Picture Unearthed in the NEA's Reading at Risk Study Turns Up Some Hopeful Signs." *Black Issues Book Review* 7.3 (May 2005): 10.

Edmundson, Mark. *Why Read?* New York: Bloomsbury, 2004.

Fishman, Jenn, Andrea Lunsford, Beth McGregor, and Mark Otuteye. "Performing Writing, Performing Literacy." *CCC* 57 (2006): 224–52.

Gallik, Jude D. "Do They Read for Pleasure: Recreational Reading Habits of College Students." *Journal of Adolescent and Adult Literacy* 42 (1999): 480–88.

Haswell, Richard. Personal correspondence. December 1, 2006.

Hawisher, Gail E., Cynthia L. Selfe, Brittney Moraski, and Melissa Pearson. "Becoming Literate in the Information Age: Cultural Ecologies and the Literacies of Technology." *CCC* 55 (2004): 642–92.

High School Survey of Student Engagement, 2005. *Getting Students Ready for College: What Student Engagement Data Can Tell Us*. 15 Dec. 2007 http://ceep.indiana.edu/hssse/pdf/college_prep_hssse05pdf.

High School Survey of Student Engagement, 2005. *What Can We Learn from High School Students*. 15 Dec. 2007 http://ceep.indiana.edu/hssse/pdf/hssse_2005_report.pdf.

National Survey of Student Engagement. *Exploring Different Dimensions of Student Engagement: 2005 Annual Survey Results*. 15 Dec. 2007 http://nsse.iub.edu/pdf/NSSE_2005_annual_report.pdf.

Oliver, Ellin Keene, and Susan Zimmerman. *Mosaic of Thought: Teaching Comprehension in a Reader's Workshop*. Portsmouth, NH: Heinemann, 1997.

Reading at Risk: A Survey of Literary Reading in America. Washington, DC: National Endowment for the Arts, 2004. 15 Dec. 2007 http://www.nea.gov/pub/ReadingAtRisk.pdf.

Rideout, Victoria, Donald F. Roberts, and Ulla G. Foehr. *Generation M: Media in the Lives of 8–18 Year Olds*. Menlo Park, CA: Kaiser Family Foundation, 2005.

Sanoff, Alvin P. "What Professors and Teachers Think: A Perception Gap over Students' Preparation." *Chronicle of Higher Education* 10 Mar. 2006. 15 Dec. 2007 http://chronicle.com/free/v52/i27/27b0091.htm.

Sheorey, Ravi, and Kouider Mokhtari. "The Reading Habits of College Students at Different Levels of Reading Proficiency." *Reading Improvement* 31 (1994): 156–66.

Smith, Michael W., and Jeffrey Wilhelm. *Reading Don't Fix No Chevys: Literacy in the Lives of Young Men*. Portsmouth, NH: Heinemann, 2002.

Thaiss, Christopher. "A Rubric for Understanding Writing in Different Classes and Disciplines." 15 Dec. 2007 http://www.mhhe.com/socscience/engligh/tc/Thaiss.

Thaiss, Christopher, and Terry Myers Zawacki. *Engaged Writers/Dynamic Disciplines*. Portsmouth, NH: Boynton/Cook, 2006.

To Read or Not to Read: A Question of National Consequence. Washington, DC: National Endowment for the Arts, 2007. 15 Dec. 2007 http://ww.nea.gov/research/ToRead.pdf.

College Composition and Communication, Volume 64, Number 3, February 2013

Motivation and Connection: Teaching Reading (and Writing) in the Composition Classroom[1]

Michael Bunn[2]

Drawing on qualitative research conducted at the University of Michigan, this article examines the extent to which composition instructors theorize and teach reading-writing connections and argues that explicitly teaching reading-writing connections may increase student motivation to complete assigned reading. The article also discusses using model texts as an effective means of teaching those connections.

Many college students see writing courses as a chore—a hurdle on the track toward graduation. At the same time, many of these students recognize the value of writing and learning to write. In extensive interviews conducted with Harvard students in the 1990s, Richard Light found that "[o]f all skills students say they want to strengthen, writing is mentioned three times more than any other. Most know they will be asked to write an enormous amount at college. Most expect this to continue after they graduate" (54). Around the same time, Thomas Hilgers and his colleagues interviewed students enrolled in upper-division writing-intensive classes in their majors at a large state university and discovered that these students valued assigned writing tasks for various reasons, most notably as an opportunity to "pursue personal goals" such as "satisfying a burning curiosity about a particular topic" or as a form of "preparation for post-college employment" (Hilgers, Hussey, and Stitt-Bergh 330–32).

In her 2009 book, *The College Fear Factor*, Rebecca D. Cox draws on five years of interviews and observations at community colleges to demonstrate that many of the students she observed value writing and writing classes even if they don't enjoy them. Cox writes that "the distinction between getting an education and enjoying it emerged as a basic theme for the vast majority of students," and among the evidence she offers is the following passage from Joy, who Cox claims "drew an explicit distinction between learning from the class and enjoying it":

> This class, I would say, is an excellent class. I think it's a necessary class that all students should have as a freshman, because it prepares you for writing papers in all different classes . . . It is a necessary evil, pretty much, because I don't know anybody who likes this class, but

1 **Citation:** Bunn, Michael. "Motivation and Connection: Teaching Reading (and Writing) in the Composition Classroom." *College Composition and Communication*, vol. 64, no. 3, Feb. 2013, pp. 496–516.

2 Michael Bunn is a full-time faculty member in the University of Southern California Writing Program and co-founder of the CCCC Special Interest Group "The Role of Reading in Composition Studies."

> it is necessary if you want to be successful in your other classes with the papers that you have to write. So I like the class on a learning standpoint. On a fun standpoint, I hate it. (53).

The students Cox followed placed a high value on writing and learning to write, even though at times they may have hated it from a "fun standpoint."

In a 2007 study of composition courses conducted at Purdue University aimed at better understanding the extent to which students transfer knowledge from one context to another, Dana Driscoll found that many students—including "students who are not in humanities-based majors but instead from majors across the curriculum"—not only value writing but also may "share some of our most basic philosophies about writing—that is, that writing is a lifelong skill and that practice with writing is the best way to improve" (89). Driscoll found that many students entered their composition courses already "positive about the value of their writing course," particularly in terms of how the work of those courses might be useful beyond college.

While many students enrolled in composition courses seem to recognize the value of learning to write, it's unclear whether students experience this same level of motivation toward assigned course reading.

Whether writing is perceived as the opportunity to investigate a topic of personal interest or viewed primarily as a "necessary evil" to help with future coursework and career aspirations, there is little doubt that many students—whether enrolled in prestigious liberal arts institutions, large state universities, or community colleges—value writing and learning to write.

But what about reading?

While many students enrolled in composition courses seem to recognize the value of learning to write, it's unclear whether students experience this same level of motivation toward assigned course reading. As Jeanne Henry notes of her own experiences of teaching reading at the collegiate level, "My freshmen were very much *able* to read; they were simply disinclined *to* read" (64, emphasis in original). David Jolliffe and Allison Harl make a similar point regarding their research on student reading at the University of Arkansas: "In short, we discovered students who were extremely engaged with their reading, but not with the reading their classes required" (600). Thus a pressing question for writing instructors is, how can we teach reading in ways that motivate students to engage with assigned course reading? Further, how can we draw upon students' own recognition of the importance of writing as a way to motivate them to read in our classes?

Over the past two decades, a handful of scholar-practitioners have explored the role that reading plays in both collegiate writing courses and composition scholarship.[i] Particularly useful are the ways that these scholars present rationales for including reading instruction in writing courses (Helmers; Horning; Salvatori), suggest reasons that reading isn't being adequately addressed within the field (Harkin; Morrow), articulate challenges that instructors—including graduate instructors—

might face when trying to teach reading in the writing classroom (Adler-Kassner and Estrem; Carillo; Ettari and Easterling; Tetreault and Center), explore approaches to reading promoted in composition textbooks (Huffman), and provide an example of how researchers might utilize qualitative methods to explore the issue of reading (Jolliffe and Harl).

What this article adds to this growing body of research is attention to some of the ways that instructors theorize and teach reading-writing connections in composition courses and how such theorization and teaching practices may affect students' motivation to complete assigned reading. As Linda Adler-Kassner and Heidi Estrem note, "Studies that focus on the contexts that *instructors* create for students' reading . . . are few and far between" (36, emphasis in original). This article is intended to help fill that gap. Examining the ways that writing instructors think about and teach reading—how they perceive connections between the processes of reading and writing and attempt to teach those connections to students—provides a more complete picture of what is happening in composition classrooms. These findings can also inform the important discussions we need to be having about which approaches to teaching reading will motivate students to engage with assigned texts and help them to read and write better.

I recently conducted qualitative research at the University of Michigan in order to examine some of the ways that instructors theorize and teach reading in composition courses and to better understand how students perceive and respond to assigned course reading. An online survey (Appendix A) was sent to instructors who were teaching, or had taught, first-year writing at the university, presenting them with a range of questions about the ways they theorize and teach reading. In total, 114 instructors were invited to complete the online survey; these instructors were all graduate students or lecturers teaching for the English Department Writing Program (EDWP) during the semester of data collection, and each of these instructors had taught at least one section of first-year writing in the past or were doing so at the time of the survey. The response rate was exactly 50 percent—57 of the 114 instructors invited to complete the online survey did so.

This article puts instructor survey and interview responses in conversation with student survey responses to shed some light on how both instructors and students think about reading as it operates in the writing classroom.

Next, interviews were conducted with 8 instructors who were teaching first-year writing at the time of our interview and who indicated on their survey that they would be willing to speak with me. Five of the interviewees were graduate student instructors (2 studying literature, 2 studying English and education, and 1 studying linguistics), and 2 were full-time faculty lecturers (who had all earned M.F.A. degrees in creative writing from the university).

After holding these interviews, I observed 4 of these interviewed instructors' classrooms during two different class sessions. In each of these four courses a four-question survey (Appendix B) was distributed to students asking for their views on the reading that they were doing for the course.

In total, I received survey responses from all 66 students present during the four class sessions—17 students each in three of the courses and 15 students in the other. Though students were given the option to decline the survey, none did so.

This article puts instructor survey and interview responses in conversation with student survey responses to shed some light on how both instructors and students think about reading as it operates in the writing classroom. Specifically, the article addresses four related questions:

1. To what extent do instructors theorize reading and writing as connected activities?
2. To what extent are instructors explicitly teaching reading-writing connections in their composition courses?
3. What effect (if any) does students' understanding of reading-writing connections have on their motivation to complete assigned reading?
4. For instructors who are explicitly teaching reading-writing connections, what are some of the specific ways they are doing it?

More fully understanding the ways that instructors theorize and teach reading writing connections is important because, as my findings suggest, explicitly teaching such connections can influence the extent to which students find course reading valuable and can affect their motivation to complete assigned reading.

In the remainder of this article I discuss a few lessons we can learn and conclusions we might draw about teaching reading based on my research findings. I begin by proposing a definition of reading that emphasizes the cooperation between readers and writers and stresses the importance of conceptualizing reading and writing as connected processes. I then examine the extent to which participating instructors at the University of Michigan theorize reading and writing as connected activities and document the ways they do (and don't) teach such connections to students. I supplement this section with responses from the student surveys to reveal whether teaching reading-writing connections explicitly seems to have any effect on student motivation to read. Next, I present and discuss the method of teaching reading-writing connections mentioned most often by instructors at Michigan: assigning model texts with the hope that students will read to identify particular techniques to try out in their own writing or read to recognize genre conventions. I conclude the article by offering a few suggestions for ways instructors might teach reading-writing connections effectively in composition courses.

Reading Defined as "Negotiation"

Readers construct meaning (at least in part) by drawing on their own personal experiences (Stein; Lindberg) and by drawing on other types of prior knowledge (Hayes; Lemke). As Deborah Brandt puts it, "readers bring to a text stores of prior knowledge about the world and about the nature of discourse that allow them to fill in the inferences and make the predictions necessary for comprehension" (119). Such interaction between reader and text suggests that the process of reading is a *negotiation* between the knowledge and purposes of the writer and the knowledge and purposes of the reader. In "A Social-Interactive Model of Writing," Martin Nystrand describes this type of negotiation: "when the respective purposes of the writer and the reader intersect as they must when the reader comprehends the writer's text, the meaning that the reader gives to the text is a unique result—a distinctive convergence or interaction—of reader and writer purpose (74).[ii] The understanding and meaning derived from texts are based not only on the characteristics of the text itself and on the reader's recognition and understanding of those characteristics, but also by a connection between writers and readers that links the knowledge and purposes of the author with the knowledge and purposes of the reader (as well as the properties of the text itself) together into a broader meaning-making activity. This negotiated meaning of texts illuminates crucial connections between the activities of reading and writing. As Nystrand puts it, "*meaning is between writer and reader*" (78, emphasis in original).

In response to this understanding of reading and writing as connected activities, a key focus of my research was to discern whether instructors conceive of reading and writing as connected activities, and the degree to which they are (or aren't) teaching reading and writing as connected processes in the classroom.

Reading-Writing Connections: Instructor Perceptions and Assumptions

Nearly 100 percent of instructors who completed the online survey (56 of 57) report that they conceptualize reading and writing as connected activities (one instructor didn't respond to the related question). Not all of those instructors explain or teach those connections to students, however. This creates a potential disconnect between instructor theorization (recognizing important connections between the processes of reading and writing) and instructor pedagogy (*not* teaching those same connections to students).

In reply to the open-ended survey question Do you believe that reading and writing are connected activities? All 56 instructors who answered the question express the belief that reading and writing are connected. Their answers distribute as follows:

Yes	25
Absolutely	15
Of course	6

Yes (or absolutely), but . . .	4
Definitely	2
Certainly	1
It is a fact, not a belief	1
They are fundamentally the same act	1
Often, but not always	1

As this distribution indicates, only 5 instructors express any form of reservation or qualify their answer in any way. For example, 2 of those instructors make a point to note that it's not *always* the case that good readers are good writers, and vice versa:

> Yes. But I have also seen struggling readers write wonderful things and struggling writers read and interpret challenging text.

> Yes. They influence each other recursively. However, in my personal life, there are people who challenge this belief for me . . . people I know who write very well, but don't read much . . . .

While all 56 of the participating instructors express the belief that reading and writing are connected activities (with 5 offering some form of qualification), this belief doesn't always translate into pedagogy.

This type of qualification doesn't really challenge the idea that reading and writing are connected, but offers a useful reminder that, in the words of 1 of these 5 instructors, it's not always an exact "one-to-one ratio."

While all 56 of the participating instructors express the belief that reading and writing are connected activities (with 5 offering some form of qualification), this belief doesn't always translate into pedagogy. In response to the question *How (if at all) do you teach a connection between reading and writing to students in first-year writing?* 10 instructors report that they *don't* explicitly teach those connections to students. This survey question elicited responses such as the following:

> Good question. I don't think I have addressed this connection explicitly.

> I don't draw connections explicitly, but I constantly tell them that the best way to improve their writing in a given genre is to read a lot in that genre.

> I'm not sure I teach that connection explicitly, though I believe the connection is made obvious by writing assignments and studies of texts.

> I'm not sure that it's something I teach directly. This may be a fault on my part. Instead of telling them the connection is important, I assume they already know or they'll see the connection as we work toward reading texts objectively.

A sentiment expressed in these responses is that instructors don't need to teach reading-writing connections explicitly or that such connections are already clear to students. As one instructor claims:

> This connection is not something necessary to parse. First of all, the students realize that by reading and questioning texts, they will better engage in analysis which will directly translate into their own writing.

This instructor's response not only assumes that students will automatically recognize how certain reading practices influence their writing, but also that such reading practices "directly translate" to student writing—both without any intervention on the part of instructors.

Another instructor discusses the assumption that students will automatically recognize connections between course reading assignments and course writing assignments. During our interview, Sally, a graduate student studying English and education, elaborated on this assumption: "I assumed today, since we're talking about narrative and they're going to be writing narratives, I assumed that [a connection between the course reading and course writing assignments] was evident. But I think we assume a lot of things, and shouldn't."[iii]

The Benefit of Explicitly Teaching Reading-Writing Connections

In our interview, Sally went on to say a bit more about why it's important for instructors to make connections between reading and writing assignments explicit to students. As she makes clear in the following excerpt, Sally believes that if instructors explicitly teach reading and writing as connected activities, students are more likely to complete assigned reading because they recognize its value in relation to the rest of the course.

> **Sally:** The reading, I believe, should always tie into what we're doing.
>
> **MB:** And when you say "what we're doing" you mean the writing assignments?
>
> **Sally:** The writing assignments. I don't think that I always make that explicit to the students? . . . I think earlier on I made it more explicit, but I think that that's something that I should continue to make explicit.
>
> **MB:** Why? Why do you think that's worth doing or important?

> **Sally:** . . . Well, one: Buy in . . . I mean student motivation, and in terms of doing the reading, they can understand why it's valuable because I've made that explicit to them. It's not valuable just because I've told them to do it. It's valuable because it's going to be applied.

In other words, students don't have to settle for the instructor's suggestion that reading is worthwhile. When reading-writing connections are made clear, students see that the reading they do will "be applied" in their writing; this helps them "buy in" to the work of the course.

Sally's view that students may be more motivated to complete assigned reading if they recognize how that reading relates to their writing is supported by the survey responses of several students. In response to the question *Are you motivated to read for this course? Why or why not?* 5 students specifically mentioned being motivated to read because the reading helped them with their writing assignments, while 9 other students mentioned that they weren't motivated to read because the texts seemed unrelated to the rest of the course. The following excerpts convey the range of those responses:

> Yes, I am motivated [to read] because all of the readings relate very directly to the essays that we are assigned.
>
> Yes, because I believe the readings really help me with writing my own paper . . . .
>
> Yes, but only to help my writing . . . .
>
> I am not motivated to read for the course because I feel the reading does not relate to what we talk about in class. It does not help me improve my writing so I am not interested in it.
>
> I sometimes know that the reading will not connect to the class, which makes it harder for me to focus and concentrate on the reading.
>
> I am not motivated to read for this course because the readings are unrelated to what we are writing about.

These responses suggest that the degree to which students are motivated to read assigned texts is influenced by whether or not they perceive connections between that reading and other aspects of the course, especially their writing assignments. Such motivation is crucial, for as Jill Fitzgerald, professor of literacy at the University of North Carolina, explains, "People must feel some urge, some motivation, some reason to read or write. If there is no urge, there is no reading and writing" (84). John Guthrie and Allan Wigfield, faculty members at the University of Maryland College of Education whose research focuses on motivation, make a similar point, that "a person reads a word or comprehends a text not only because she can do it, but because she is motivated to do it" (404).

Instructors appear to have a genuine opportunity to motivate students to complete assigned course reading. What this requires, however, is that students believe the assigned readings directly relate to, or will help them to produce, their writing assignments.[iv] If instructors *explicitly teach* reading and writing as connected activities rather than assuming that students will identify such connections on their own, students stand a far better chance of recognizing how assigned course reading relates to and can help them with their writing tasks.

> **If instructors explicitly teach reading and writing as connected activities rather than assuming that students will identify such connections on their own, students stand a far better chance of recognizing how assigned course reading relates to and can help them with their writing tasks.**

The Use of Model Texts

An important strategy for teaching reading-writing connections surfaced again and again as instructors answered a range of survey questions, and most notably in responses to the question *How (if at all) do you teach a connection between reading and writing to students in first-year writing?* Assigning model texts is discussed by 17 different instructors and referred to a total of 27 times throughout the surveys.[4] These model texts—mostly published pieces, though sample student papers are occasionally mentioned as well—are primarily discussed in two different ways: as displays of writing techniques and strategies that students can identify and then try in their own writing, or as examples of the specific genre that students will eventually be assigned to write.[v] What distinguishes these two types of reading—which both utilize model texts selected and assigned by the instructor—from many other approaches is that they emphasize reading as a means to learn *about writing*, not as a means to better understand a topic, issue, or worldview. These two uses of model texts call on students to study the text with an eye toward their own eventual writing, to read in a way that greatly resembles what I have described elsewhere as *reading like a writer* ("How").

Several survey respondents mention the first of these two purposes for assigning model texts: wanting students to identify specific writerly techniques or writing strategies that they can try out in their own writing. Here is a sampling of those responses:

> I ask students to pay attention to various techniques utilized by the authors and "steal" the ones they find helpful for their own writing.

> I ask them to engage with the texts they read by responding to them in writing (challenging them, asking questions, etc.) and then to pull out strategies to use in their own writing.

> We ask a lot of questions of texts that are relevant to the essay they are in the process of

> writing to help them ask questions from which they can write. I also focus heavily on the structure and rhetorical approaches used in the published essays we read, pointing out that these are models for them to use in their own essays.
>
> We'll examine the strategies used in introductions and conclusions in the published texts to get students thinking about what strategies they may want to use in their essay. Students should use the published readings as models, essentially looking for things they appreciate and want to use in their own work.

In each of these responses the instructor describes using model texts to demonstrate strategies and structural techniques that students can adopt in their own writing. The idea is that students will recognize elements to which they responded as a reader and use these elements in their own assigned writings.

> Sally presents a specific classroom activity intended to encourage students to read for what they can use in their own writing:
>
> [W]e've been sort of informally keeping a personal style journal where after we read a text and we've examined it for structure and we've looked at the argument, we also talk about the aesthetic piece. What did they notice that they like, and what can they take from that text to try out in their own writing?
>
> So, if we found a really good example of a parallel sentence, if they have never tried that before, then they make a note of it and they've got it in the text so that they can refer back to it.

This exercise prompts students to read with an eye toward their own writing by locating specific strategies and techniques that they intend to use and reinforces the idea that both texts and reading serve purposes beyond the transmission of content.

Another instructor describes in a survey response how he or she encourages students to reflect upon the specific ways that they imitate assigned texts:

> I have students analyze claims, evidence, organization, metaphors, and language in articles we read. I encourage them to adopt one or two strategies in their papers using imitation in their writing. I ask them to try to make it seamless (to not let me see it). However, I ask them to write a submission note about their writing process, and in this, they are invited to explain how they mimicked a writer we have read and what the experience felt like as well as if they believe the result is rhetorically effective.

By requiring students to reflect on their adoption of techniques and strategies they locate in the model text and compose a submission note in which they assess the effectiveness of this borrowing, this instructor prompts students to identify and consider direct connections between their course reading and writing.[vi] The submission note and student paper serve as tangible proof that the reading done for the course has influenced the student's writing.

The other primary reason that instructors offer for assigning model texts is that they want to provide students with an example of a *genre* in which the students will eventually be asked to write.[vii] This use of model texts asks students to look at the overall structure of the text or the conventions associated with a particular genre, rather than focus on individual writerly techniques and strategies that they can adopt, as we see in the following two examples from the instructors' surveys:

> We read examples of the kinds of essays they would be writing—descriptive narratives, researched arguments, etc. I subscribe to the theory that students should read models of the genre in which they will be writing.
>
> If I'm teaching prosody, it makes sense to use metered poetry. If I'm teaching the personal essay, it makes sense to use other personal essays as models. The same can be said for the teaching of other genres.

Instructors assign these texts intending for students to read them as models of genre, but it remains unclear whether instructors are actually teaching students *how* to do this. While the majority of instructors who report assigning model texts so that students can adopt techniques and strategies mention taking time in class to show students how to read for them, this is not the case for most of the instructors who reported assigning model texts as examples of genre. This is a potential disconnect in the course: instructors want students to read for genre conventions but fail to explain this to students or teach them how to do it.

During our interview, Don, a full-time lecturer, noted that this is a potential problem because students don't necessarily know how to read for genre conventions or how to use the texts to improve their own writing:

> It can't be like whoa, look at these four models. Let's just do what they're doing. They can't really—can't really see what's happening in those pieces. I think they see an analytical essay and like—I use the word analytical essay because you know it is a kind of genre. You know but to them it's totally *not* a genre, and I think they're kind of blind to most of what is happening.

Don suggests that students are ill-equipped to use model texts effectively on their own. This view is confirmed by at least one student who explained in a survey response, "I am not very motivated to read for this course because I never really know what to look for in the reading." If instructors can teach students how to read and use model texts, they may be able to combat this sort of lack of motivation on the part of students. It's not enough to merely assign certain kinds of texts. After conducting his own study of student writers using model texts, Peter Smagorinsky reached a similar conclusion, warning, "Simply reading a model piece of writing . . . is insufficient to teach young writers how to produce compositions . . . most novices need more direct instruction" (174).

Teaching Model Texts Effectively: An Example

One of the instructors I interviewed and observed, Tawnya, a graduate student studying literature, attempts to provide the kind of "direct instruction" that Smagorinsky recommends by being very explicit with students about potential connections between their assigned reading and their writing assignments:

> **Tawnya:** For both of the papers they've done so far, I've given them readings that do what I'm asking them to do, with the hopes that when they sit down . . . they can re-read it and say "Okay, how can I use this as a template for my writing?"
>
> **MB:** And when you say "ask them to do," you mean readings that are demonstrating a genre or something?
>
> **Tawnya:** Right, so the first one was a descriptive analysis, and the second one was the review, due tomorrow. And then for the third one as well, which is more of a standard argumentative paper, I will do the same, so that they can use it as a template . . . .

By encouraging students to use these texts as models and read with an eye toward their own eventual writing—to read them as examples of the specific genre in which they will be writing—Tawnya helps students to connect the assigned reading to their writing tasks.

Her belief that reading in this way helps students improve their writing is a belief shared by many of her students. In response to the question *Do you find the reading that you do for this course helpful in improving your writing?* Tawnya had the highest total number (14) and percentage (82 percent) of students who said *yes*. The following three responses represent how nearly every student in her class mentioned the benefit of reading texts that serve as models for their writing assignments:

By encouraging students to use these texts as models and read with an eye toward their own eventual writing—to read them as examples of the specific genre in which they will be writing—Tawnya helps students to connect the assigned reading to their writing tasks.

> The readings are useful because they typically display the style of writing that needs to be utilized in the upcoming paper. For example: in preparation for writing a critique of a live performance, we will read different styles of critiques from various periodicals.

> The reading done for this class is helpful because it usually relates to a paper we are going to write. This makes the process of writing papers easier by giving students a reference.
>
> Yes, I do because the readings we do are often the same as the paper we are writing. When we discuss the readings we look at things they have done well and we might want to do in our papers.

This third comment suggests that at least some of the students in Tawnya's course are developing their understanding of specific writerly strategies and techniques in addition to understanding genre conventions: they are locating things in the assigned texts that the author has "done well" and that they "might want to do" in their papers.

A key to Tawnya's success is that beyond simply assigning models of specific genres, she talks with students about how they should be reading the model texts. Tawnya's students get direct instruction in how to read model texts for *both* writerly strategies they can adopt and for genre conventions.[viii] While observing Tawnya's course, I witnessed this kind of explicit instruction firsthand. Tawnya initiated discussion of the assigned essay by telling students, "I thought maybe we could go through this part-by-part and talk about . . . [how] he is doing an analysis and his use of detail, his ability to state his thesis and what he's thinking. It should hopefully help you." She then directed the students to reread the first paragraph. When they were finished, she asked the class, "What did you think of this introduction? Why was it either effective or ineffective at pulling you in as a reader?"

Throughout the discussion that ensued, Tawnya pushed the students to explain in specific detail why they did or didn't find the introduction effective. She also led students to examine some of the specific choices the author had made. For example, she asked the class to consider the pros and cons of only discussing two areas of the country in an essay dealing with the polarization of America. Two students offered responses to her question:

> I thought the pros were because he only focused on two places he could go into more in-depth analysis of the places, but because he only focused on two places, while maybe fundamentally red and blue states are still there, there are still differences everywhere. So if he wanted to make a more specific essay he should focus on those two, but if he wanted to get a really good grasp of the difference between red and blue he should have covered more ground.
>
> I think it works for his purposes because these places are so polar opposite.

Both of these students responded insightfully to the author's strategy of only covering two locations in the essay, particularly the first student who offered an alternative strategy that the author *might* have used (as well as a rationale for that alternative). In proposing an alternative strategy for composing the essay, this student displays the kind of understanding about writing strategy that can develop when instructors take the time to teach students to read in this way. A bit later in the same discussion, Tawnya asked the students to look at a specific metaphor operating in the text and told them that they too could use a metaphor to help structure their next paper: "This is another kind of strategy you can use in papers is coming up with a metaphor that describes what you're trying to say. So you analyze your performance, and then you come up with a clever way of expressing it to your audience." With this move, Tawnya directs students' attention to a specific technique operating in the model text and tells them explicitly that they can make a similar move in their own writing. It's difficult to imagine a more straightforward way of connecting the reading and writing that students do.

I present Tawnya's approach as a successful example of teaching reading through the use of model texts for a couple of important reasons. First, she assigns students to read model texts with the *dual* purpose of reading for individual writing techniques and strategies that they can try out, and of reading the text as an example of the genre that they will be working in themselves. She prompts students to use the model texts in both ways simultaneously; this means that students get direct instruction in how to use the model texts for both purposes, each of which can be helpful as they think about their own writing. Second, she demonstrates for her students *how* she would like them to read, and while doing so she emphasizes connections between the reading they are doing and their writing assignments. She has carefully considered how her reading and writing assignments connect and makes an effort to help students recognize those connections.

"Let's say we were going to bring you to campus and arrange for you to speak with all of our writing instructors. What would you tell them? What would you say that could help us improve the ways we teach reading?"

Conclusion

A few weeks after I finished analyzing my data, I had the opportunity talk about my research with the director of writing from another Midwestern university and one of his faculty colleagues. As I told them about my findings and about the apparent need for instructors to teach reading-writing connections explicitly, his colleague looked over at me and asked, "Let's say we were going to bring you to campus and arrange for you to speak with all of our writing instructors. What would you tell them? What would you say that could help us improve the ways we teach reading?"

There are several suggestions I would like to make to a room full of writing instructors about how to teach reading. Here is where I might start:

- I'd think about the extent to which and the ways in which I perceive reading and writing to be connected activities. This pedagogical awareness can help me to design a course in which the reading and writing assignments build upon and reinforce each other. It's clear from the interviews with instructors at Michigan and from several years of working with new writing instructors at three different institutions that many instructors begin designing their course by *first* selecting the texts to be read, often with little consideration for how those texts connect to course writing assignments.

- Selecting the readings first—independent of the course writing tasks—makes it far harder for us to conceive of how the reading and writing tasks connect and increases the likelihood that they won't connect. If instead we select readings and design writing prompts simultaneously, there is a far greater chance that we will be aware of connections between the two and be able to articulate those connections to students.
- I'd talk with students during class about the connections between assignments. Students indicated in their survey responses that they were more or less motivated to read assigned texts depending upon whether they viewed that reading as relevant to their writing assignments. This simple step to explain the scaffolding we've done can help generate motivation on the part of students to complete assigned reading and can help them to understand that reading and writing are connected activities.
- Assigning students to read model texts isn't enough; students usually don't know how to read for writerly techniques or for genre conventions on their own. We must teach students *how* to read model texts in ways that will inform the eventual writing that they will do and teach them to read in ways that help them to develop their understanding of writerly strategies and techniques *and* that help them to identify genre conventions so that they are better prepared to write in those genres.

Teaching reading in terms of its connections to writing can motivate students to read and increase the likelihood that they find success in both activities. It can lead students to value reading as an integral aspect of learning to write. It can help students develop their understanding of writerly strategies and techniques. Most of us firmly believe that reading improves writing. Let's make sure that we are teaching reading in ways that make this happen for students.

Appendix A: Instructor Survey

1. How many semesters of first-year writing have you taught, including this one?
2. How many total writing courses have you taught, including this one?
3. Do students arrive (at the university) prepared to read at the college level?
4. What kinds of reading do students do for your first-year writing course?

5. Do you teach students to read visual images or nonwritten texts? If so, what do you do?
6. What is the reading skill, or particular reading approach, that is most important or beneficial for students to learn in first-year writing?
7. Do you teach students to do a particular kind of reading or adopt a particular reading approach?
8. Do you believe that reading and writing are connected activities?
9. How (if at all) do you teach a connection between reading and writing to students in first-year writing?
10. Are there any differences between the ways that you ask students to read the writing produced by their classmates and the ways you ask them to read published texts? If so, what are the differences?
11. Are there any classroom activities or assignments that are better suited to use one type of text as opposed to the other—either published writing or student-produced writing? Please explain your answer.
12. Please discuss a few of the factors that have most influenced your ideas about how to teach, or not to teach, reading in first-year writing.

Appendix B: Student Survey

1. Do you find the reading that you do for this course helpful in improving your writing? Why or why not?
2. Do you have a preference between reading published writing or the writing produced by your classmates? Please explain your answer.
3. Are you motivated to read for this course? Why or why not?
4. Have you learned about possible connection(s) between reading and writing in this course? If yes, what have you learned?

Notes

i. The topic of reading has received increased attention in the past few years. In 2009, the journal *Open Words: Access and English Studies* devoted its entire spring issue to articles exploring college-level reading—including some discussion of reading's place within collegiate writing courses. In 2010, the journal *Reader: Essays in Reader-Oriented Theory, Criticism, and Pedagogy* devoted its fall issue to exploring disciplinary ways of teaching reading, including attention to some of the ways that reading is taught in composition. Most recently, at the 2012 Conference on College Composition and Communication in St. Louis, a new annual Special Interest Group dedicated to exploring "The Role of Reading in Composition Studies" met for the first time.

ii. Kathleen McCormick prefers an "interactive" model of reading that she believes stresses that "first, both readers and texts contribute to the reading process and second, that both texts and readers are themselves ideologically situated" (69). However, I prefer Nystrand's description of reading as a "negotiation" over other conceptions of reading, including Louise Rosenblatt's notion of "transaction," because negotiation—more than any other term—implies the degree of cooperation and even compromise needed for writers and readers to make meaning effectively from a text. Negotiation implies that two parties—in this case the writer and reader—are approaching the enterprise with the *mutual* goal of creating meaning.

iii. All instructor and student names are pseudonyms.

iv. This emphasis on model texts may be common at other institutions as well. While conducting a comprehensive study of writing in the undergraduate curriculum at the University of Pittsburgh, David Bartholomae and Beth Matway found a similar use of model texts among faculty from a variety of disciplines: "Many of those interviewed use models in their teaching—either examples of student papers or examples of professional writing—in order to give students a point of reference for genre, format, and style."

v. Although they don't specifically mention the use of model texts, Linda Adler-Kassner and Heidi Estrem found that writing instructors at Eastern Michigan University had "three relatively clear purposes for reading within the program. *Content-based* reading . . . asks students to summarize and interpret, to consider connections between ideas, and to use reading to develop ideas. *Process-based* reading focuses on the work of the writer/researcher, scrutinizing the text to look at the decisions made by the writer in the process of textual production as a possible model for students' own writing/research work. *Structure-based* reading asks students to focus on the conventions reflected in and used to shape content; the emphasis is on developing genre awareness so that student writers can make conscious decisions about how to use different genres and conventions, and can make conscious choices about how, when, or whether to use them" (40–41). The second two of these purposes—*process-based* and *structure-based* reading—seem nearly identical to the two primary ways that instructors participating in my research describe wanting students to read in conjunction with model texts.

vi. These submission notes are similar to Jeffrey Sommers's "student-teacher memos' in that they are each "intended to take both student and teacher behind the paper, into the composing process which produced the draft" (77). Sommers asks students to submit a memo with each writing assignment aimed at helping students to "describe and comment on their composing processes" (78). This surveyed instructor's "submission note" may actually do more, however, to help students connect the process of reading with the process of writing, since Sommers's questions focus almost exclusively on writing and the student's written text.

vii. Throughout this article I use the term *genre* to indicate a category or type of text (e.g., a review, an opinion column, an argumentative essay) in the traditional literary sense. While I'm aware that other conceptions of genre transcend this limited conception and construct genre as a way to define various situations and social actions, it's clear that instructor participants (such as Don) were using the term exclusively to indicate forms and types of writing.

viii. Although Tawnya shows that these two uses of model texts—as providing techniques to adopt and as examples of genre—aren't mutually exclusive, nearly every instructor who mentions using model texts refers to either one use or the other, but not both.

Works Cited

Adler-Kassner, Linda, and Heidi Estrem. "Reading Practices in the Writing Classroom." *WPA* 31.1/2 (2007): 35–47. Print.

Bartholomae, David, and Beth Matway. "The Pittsburgh Study of Writing." *Across the Disciplines* 7 (Oct. 2010). Web.

Brandt, Deborah. "Social Foundations of Reading and Writing." *Convergences: Transactions in Reading and Writing.* Ed. Bruce Petersen. Urbana: NCTE, 1986. 115–26. Print.

Bunn, Michael. "How to Read like a Writer." *Writing Spaces: Readings on Writing.* Vol. 2. Ed. Charles Lowe and Pavel Zemliansky. Anderson: Parlor P, 2011. 71–86. Web.

Carillo, Ellen C. "Making Reading Visible in the Classroom." *Currents in Teaching and Learning* 1.2 (2009). 37–41. Web.

Cox, Rebecca D. *The College Fear Factor*. Cambridge: Harvard UP, 2009. Print.

Driscoll, Dana. "Pedagogy of Transfer: Impacts of Student and Instructor Attitudes." Diss. Purdue U, 2009. Web.

Ettari, Gary, and Heather C. Easterling. "Reading (and) the Profession." *Reader* 47 (Fall 2002): 9–37. Print.

Fitzgerald, Jill. "Reading and Writing as 'Mind Meeting.'" *Reading and Writing Together: New Perspectives for the Classroom.* Ed. Timothy Shanahan. Norwood: Christopher-Gordon, 1990. 81–97. Print.

Guthrie, John, and Allan Wigfield. "Engagement and Motivation in Reading." *Handbook of Reading Research.* Vol. 3. Ed.

Michael L. Kamil, Peter B. Mosenthal, P. David Pearson, and Rebecca Barr. Mahwah: Lawrence Erlbaum, 2000. Print.

Harkin, Patricia. "The Reception of ReaderResponse Theory." *College Composition and Communication* 56.3 (2005): 410–25. Print.

Hayes, John. "A New Framework for Understanding Cognition and Affect in Writing." Ruddell and Unrau 1399–430.

Helmers, Marguerite, ed. *Intertexts: Reading Pedagogy in College Writing Classrooms*. Mahwah: Lawrence Erlbaum, 2003. Print.

Henry, Jeanne. "Cultivating Reading Workshop: New Theory into New Practice." *Open Words* 3.1 (2009): 1–4. Print.

Hilgers, Thomas, Edna Lardizaball Hussey, and Monica Stitt-Bergh. "'As You're Writing, You Have These Epiphanies': What College Students Say about Writing and Learning in Their Majors." *Written Communication* 16.3 (1999): 317–53. Print.

Horning, Alice. "Reading Across the Curriculum as the Key to Student Success." *Across the Disciplines* 4 (May 2007). Web.

Huffman, Debrah. "Toward Modes of Reading in Composition." *Reader* 60 (Fall 2010): 204–30. Print.

Jolliffe, David, and Allison Harl. "Studying the 'Reading Transition' from High School to College: What Are Our Students Reading and Why?" *College English* 70.6 (2008): 599–617. Print.

Lemke, Jay. "Social Semiotics: A New Model for Literacy Education." *Classrooms and Literacy*. Ed. David Bloome. Norwood: Ablex, 1989. 289–309. Print.

Light, Richard. *Making the Most of College: Students Speak their Minds*. Cambridge: Harvard UP, 2001. Print.

Lindberg, Gary. "Coming to Words: Writing as Process and the Reading of Literature." *Only Connect*. Ed. Thomas Newkirk. Upper Montclair: Boynton/ Cook, 1986. 143–57. Print.

McCormick, Kathleen. *The Culture of Reading / The Teaching of English*. Manchester: U. of Manchester P, 1994. Print.

Morrow, Nancy. "The Role of Reading in the Composition Classroom." *JAC* 17:3 (1997): 453–72. Print.

Nystrand, Martin. "A Social-Interactive Model of Writing." *Written Communication* 6.1 (1989): 66–85. Print.

Rosenblatt, Louise. "The Transactional Theory of Reading and Writing." Ruddell and Unrau 1363–98.

Ruddell, Robert, and Norman Unrau, eds. *Theoretical Models and Processes of Reading.* 5th ed. Newark: International Reading Association, 2004. Print.

Salvatori, Mariolina. "Conversations with Texts: Reading in the Teaching of Composition." *College English* 58.4 (1996): 440–54. Print.

Smagorinsky, Peter. "How Reading Model Essays Affects Writers." In *Reading/Writing Connections: Learning from Research.* Ed. Judith W. Irwin and Mary Anne Doyle. Newark: International Reading Association, 1992. 160–76. Print.

Sommers, Jeffrey. "Behind the Paper: Using the Student-Teacher Memo." *College Composition and Communication* 39.1 (1988): 77–80. Print.

Stein, Victoria. "Elaboration: Using What You Know." *Reading-to-Write: Exploring Cognitive and Social Process.* Ed. Linda Flower et al. Oxford: Oxford UP, 1990. 144–155. Print.

Tetreault, Diane DeVido, and Carole Center. "But I'm Not a Reading Teacher!" *Open Words* 3.1 (2009): 45–61. Print.

College Composition and Communication, Volume 33, Number 1, 1982

From Story to Essay: Reading and Writing[1]

Anthony R. Petrosky[2]

Most of the work in reading, response to literature, and composition has gone on independently. Few people have crossed the boundaries of their disciplines to examine the relationships between these aspects of human understanding. Consequently, both research and pedagogy are hard pressed to describe and apply integrated notions of these three aspects of language.

As a result of separate instruction and assessment of progress in reading, literature, and composition, curricula in language are fragmented to the point where literature is often kept out of reading, and composition instruction seldom includes reading or study of literary works, except as models of writing. We even train teachers to be one kind of teacher, say a reading specialist, and not the other. Our obsessions with specialization pose unnecessary and artificial problems that have serious consequences for students. How can they learn to play the spectrum of discourse, as James Moffett says, when the spectrum is broken into wholly independent components, and otherwise intelligent people go around claiming that we can not ask students to write about their reading because the writing confounds reading, especially the assessment of reading ability.[i]

Although I do not intend to discuss assessment, the implications will, I hope, be clear. I do intend to focus on the relationships between reading, response to literature, and composition from theoretical and pedagogical perspectives. In order to do this, I need to first draw attention to research and theory in reading, and then show how recent reading research is telling us the same things about understanding that we know from literary and composition research. Essentially, my argument is that our comprehension of texts, whether they are literary or not, is more an act of composition—for understanding is composing—than of information retrieval, and that the best possible representation of our understandings of texts begins with certain kinds of compositions, not multiple-choice tests or written free responses.

I also want to claim that this process of writing in response to reading is heavily subjective, and, as such, depends on the reader's models of reality; the text, and the context in which it occurs. We

1 **Citation:** Petrosky, Anthony. "From Story to Essay: From Reading to Writing." *College Composition and Communication*, vol. 33, no. 1, 1982, pp. 19–37.

2 Anthony Petrosky is Associate Professor of English Education at the University of Pittsburgh. A poet and researcher as well as a teacher, he has published essays in *Research in the Teaching of English*, *English Journal*, *The Journal of Basic Writing*, *The Mathematics Teacher*, and *The Science Journal*, among other professional periodicals, and he has published three chapbooks of poetry. With his wife, he edits and publishes fiction and poetry under his own imprint, The Slow Loris Press.

set our expectations and goals for understanding, in other words, according to our personal frames of reference, according to the particular kind of text we face, and according to the group of people we are interacting with. We need, therefore, to share, read, and comment on each other's written responses if we are to understand ourselves as readers and writers and, equally important, if we are to understand the myriad aspects of texts.

Along the way to making these claims, I first review the radical change in thinking about reading that has come about over the past decade—change that goes from seeing reading as straight information retrieval to seeing it as a process dependent on and subject to readers' models of reality (in the technical jargon of reading, "schema"), which are mental configurations or maps built from prior knowledge, feelings, personality, and culture which readers then apply to, or impose on, new experiences. I then tie these notions of reading into the work of Louise Rosenblatt, Norman Holland, and David Bleich in literary study to demonstrate that these three theorists are, basically, making the same claims about reading as the reading people. After making these connections, my attention turns to demonstrating how comprehension of texts—the putting together of understanding—is the same kind of putting together, or composing, that David Bartholomae discusses when he talks about writers, especially basic writers, as people caught within their own worlds to the point where it is difficult for them to see how they must change their private discourse to meet the demands of public discourse. I will argue, like Bartholomae, that there is a way out of these worlds and that comprehension, like composition, means making public what is private—a process dependent on explication, illustration, and critical examination of perceptions and ideas.

Finally, I come full circle and make a very simple claim that in order to help students understand the texts they read and their response, we need to ask them to write about the texts they read. I demonstrate the differences between written free response to texts and a response heuristic taken from the work of David Bleich; and, consequently, I argue that Bleich's response heuristic is a good beginning point for teaching students how to represent their comprehension in writing.

We must begin, I think, by reseeing our language use as a whole, not as discrete pieces. Reading, responding, and composing are aspects of understanding, and theories that attempt to account for them outside of their interactions with each other run the serious risk of building reductive models of human understanding. Yet we continually focus our attention on them as if they exist in isolation from one another. Consequently, we end up with theories of comprehension, for example, that discount any reliance on composition or extended response. In the same vein, reading researchers are careful not to contaminate assessments of comprehension by asking readers for extended written or oral response to texts. Generally, this kind of research looks to memory as if it were an exact and orderly storehouse, identical for everyone, that can account for comprehension. But by eliminating extended written or oral discourse as a representation of comprehension, we box ourselves into the position of equating comprehension with definitions of recall that ignore the constructive roles of affect and interpretation in remembering. Comprehension can not be simple literal recall for recall is, as F. Bartlett pointed out in 1932,[ii] never simple and hardly literal. Readers recall, either accurately or inaccurately, for reasons, and those reasons are driven by affect, cognitive frameworks (or, in Bartlett's language, "schemata"), and the context in which the reading and recalling are taking place. To put it another way, the process of recollecting usurps the reality that is recollected.

Putting these arguments aside for a moment, there is another problem with representing comprehension through recall rather than through some kind of structured response that leads to a dialectic which represents the interaction of readers with a text. When we tell students that their job is to remember information or details from texts they read, we limit their senses of reading to one narrow slice of the whole domain of reading and, in effect, we tell them that reading is the kind of activity we do when we have to pass tests based on information in textbooks. And whereas this certainly goes on in schools, it is not the kind of reading that teaches how to think—it teaches, instead, how to memorize and regurgitate. The reading that teaches us how to think lets us read without the pressures of recall and then, when we are finished, it begs us to speak our minds about what we have read and, in the process, it asks us to substantiate our interpretations and opinions—our readings—with evidence from our lives and the texts. When we only ask students to recall or engage in quick, easy-answer type discussions about their reading, we do not give them a chance to form interpretations and opinions with documentation from themselves and texts. One of the best ways to begin giving them this chance is, I will argue, to ask them to write about readings, using Bleich's response heuristic.

To pick up the main threads of my argument, let me say that I think there is compelling evidence to support the claim that comprehension is heavily subjective and is a function of the reader's prior knowledge, the text, and the context. I also think we can argue that we compose as we comprehend, and that our composition arises from these same factors: the text, our affective and cognitive frameworks (or prior knowledge), and the context for reading. When we put together our comprehension—however consciously or unconsciously—the "putting together" is more an act of composition than of information retrieval. And if, as I argue, comprehension is heavily dependent on these three factors, then a convincing representation of it must focus on how they enter into our responses as public statements derived from private experience. To see how we do this, we can and should turn to extended written response to texts. If we take this stance toward comprehension, then it is not enough for readers to demonstrate their comprehension by saying what they perceive in texts (as multiple-choice tests and quick, easy-answer type discussions lead them to do);[iii] they have to explain why they see what they do by explicating the forces that drive their discussions, because they often see things differently for legitimate reasons. The authority for their explanations comes, then, from the personal associations (that is, from their prior knowledge)—the thoughts and feelings they generate in response to what they read—that flesh out their connections to the texts and from textual evidence. And just as the believability or credibility of a text comes from these associations, comprehension arises from an immersion in the particulars of texts, readers' knowledge, and contexts.

These response compositions are best judged, I want to argue, by the standards usually applied to academic essays: adequacy of elaboration, coherence, clarity, and aptness of illustration. This kind of academic discourse derives its validity from examples and illustrations that anchor the explanations and generalizations in readers' knowledge. The knowledge bases, in the case of reading, are readers' prior experiences, the texts, and the contexts for reading. The personal narratives—which are, in fact, illustrations and examples of personal knowledge—that reveal readers' approaches to comprehending link readers to texts in the same way that examples and illustrations link writers to essays by connecting statements, generalizations, explanations, and conclusions to the knowledge or evidence that informs them.

When we see reading, then, as composing, we see also the need for readers to have ways to express and explain the connections between their prior knowledge and the texts they read. Clearly, this kind of meaning-making requires something more than multiple-choice questions or quick, easy-answer type discussions. If we are looking for compositions that begin to represent comprehension, then there are two elements, I would argue, that must be present in the composition. There must be, of course, reference to and reconstruction of the text to some degree; but there must be, also, reference to and reconstruction of the reader's associations—the reader's schema—so we, the reader's public, can see how he or she is putting it all together.

Recent research in reading by people like Robert Anderson,[iv] David Rumelhart,[v] and Robert Schank and Robert Abelson[vi] focuses on readers as meaning-makers in reading and gives us a theoretical base for making connections between reading, response to literature, and composing as similar processes sharing both the dependence on peoples' models of reality (or, schemata) and the essential "putting together" as the act of constructing meaning from words, text, prior knowledge, and feelings. Basically, and although their research differs in large and small ways, they represent reading as a process arising from the interactions of texts, readers, and contexts. As Marilyn Jager Adams and Allan Collins put it, "A fundamental assumption of schema-theoretic approaches to language comprehension is that spoken or written text does not in itself carry meaning. Rather, a text only provides direction for the listener or reader as to how he should retrieve or construct the intended meaning from his own, previously acquired knowledge."[vii] Schemata—frequently referred to as "plans" (Schank and Abelson), "frames" (Minsky), and "scripts" (Schank and Abelson)—are knowledge structures that provide a framework from which we view the world, including texts. What we know and can know, then, is dependent on what we already know and believe. Current thinking along these lines[viii] suggests that schemata consist of categories that control our perceptions of both format and content in our reading. In other words, as our models of reality develop in breadth and depth through our experience, we develop categories for our knowledge that help us organize what we know, believe, and feel. This organized knowledge, then, influences both the shape and content of our comprehension, and by extension, of our response and writing.

Prior to this work in schema-theoretic approaches to comprehension, researchers tended to see reading as the act of retrieving information from a text with little or no consideration for the reader as a meaning-maker in a relative and interpretive process. In contrast, the schema-theoretic approach says, simply, that readers put together their comprehension from not just the text, but from the interactions of their personal knowledge, feelings, and experiences with the text under the constraints of the context for reading. This is quite a radical change from seeing reading as the straightforward retrieval of information.

Somewhat the same kind of turnabout in our understanding of reading has taken place in literature. When scholars like I. A. Richards[ix] first started to wonder publicly why their students made so many unique interpretations of works of literature, they set in motion the thinking that eventually yielded the notion that readers transact with texts using their personal models of reality to construct meaning and interpretations. Currently, variations on this position are championed by Louise Rosenblatt,[x] who maintains that reading is a transaction between readers and texts; Norman Holland,[xi] who asserts that this transaction is dependent on the reader's personality; and David Bleich,[xii] who contends that reading is essentially and necessarily subjective.

Rosenblatt, unlike Holland or Bleich, makes an important distinction between readers' purposes for reading. She argues for two basic stances towards texts, efferent and aesthetic (actually she sees them as ends of a continuum). When readers approach a text efferently, they look only for information, not an aesthetic experience. When they approach a text aesthetically, their primary concern "is with what happens *during* the actual reading event. . . . In aesthetic reading, the reader's attention is centered directly on what he is living through during this relationship with a particular text."[xiii] And while she argues for close attention to texts by readers as the way of letting them confirm the accuracy of their comprehension, she also argues for equally close attention to "what that particular juxtaposition of words stirs up within each reader."[xiv] Like schema-theoretic approaches to comprehension, Rosenblatt's transactive model—built on the work of John Dewey and Arthur F. Bentley[xv]—emphasizes the role of the knower's prior knowledge in knowing. Her distinction between efferent and aesthetic stances, like the current emphasis on context for reading, gives us a way of discussing the problems of students who read everything like textbooks. And while it is certainly true that readers can take these stances towards anything they read, the process of reading is in all cases transactive. Although Rosenblatt does not herself assert the point, writing about reading is one of the best ways to get students to unravel their transactions so that we can see how they understand and, in the process, help them learn to elaborate, clarify, and illustrate their responses by reference to the associations and prior knowledge that inform them.

Norman Holland also views reading as a transaction. Although he does not discuss efferent and aesthetic reading, nor the contexts for reading, he sees the process as a transaction where comprehension is completely dependent on the reader's fixed, invariant identity—the unchanging core of personality formed, according to Holland, in the early months of life. David Bleich, on the other hand, working from a subjective paradigm of knowledge, a paradigm that assumes knowledge is always relative and unique to the knower, argues that the constraints of the text are trivial because they can be changed by individual, idiosyncratic action. Unlike Rosenblatt and Holland, he is unwilling to admit the constraints of the texts because, as he claims, "they function as any real object functions, since they can be changed by subjective action."[xvi] Bleich's views are radical, and he is, I think, too easily seduced by what he refers to as "subjective action"—the possibilities of people seeing things differently because of their unique models of reality. Even though we can, as he says, change things, including texts, by subjective action, we in fact do not always do this. And, furthermore, we share an enormous set of beliefs and expectations that make it possible for us to understand each other. Bleich argues persuasively, though, for the power of the individual's unique experience to control interpretation and for the power of the community that must then evolve when readers come together to determine reality. He takes the position that texts are symbolizations resymbolized, understood, and interpreted within the context of a community. The community channels and defines reality through the dialectic that ensues when readers get together in various contexts to understand texts and each other. For Bleich, the only way to demonstrate comprehension is through extended discourse where readers become writers who articulate their understandings of and connections to the text in their responses. Response is, then, an expression and explanation of comprehension; and comprehension means using writing to explicate the connections between our models of reality—our prior knowledge—and the texts we recreate in light of them.

Unlike retrieval models of reading, this approach gives readers a way to discuss their thoughts, feelings, and references while making meaning for themselves by writing expressive and explanatory prose in response to their readings. Essentially, *they are asked to write, first, what they perceive in the text, and then how they feel about what they see, and finally what associations—thoughts and feelings—inform and follow from their perceptions.* This "response" heuristic yields an essay that represents comprehension much more accurately than multiple-choice questions, quick-and-easy-answer type discussions, or free responses. This approach to writing about reading is derived from a powerful heuristic—explanation conducted by description and association—that is used widely in philosophical, psychoanalytic, and psychological inquiry. It can tease out structured response and, therefore, encourage respondents to discover their orientations to just about anything. Like all frequently repeated experiences, its effect is paradigmatic, altering the way we "see" and respond, "affecting by analogy much beyond the immediately seen . . ."[xvii] When used as a writing prompt, it yields a first draft of what can, with revision based on comments from a teacher or a group of students, become a sophisticated essay. Within the past ten years, the field of composition has begun to concern itself with the same heuristic. David Bartholomae, working towards a pedagogy for basic writers,[xviii] has found that writing produced by basic writers relies heavily on the writers' unarticulated knowledge, with little or no exposition of that knowledge through examples, illustrations, and details. He maintains that a characteristic of a sophisticated essay, on the other hand, is the writer's critical examination, through examples and illustrations, of the assumptions, beliefs, and knowledge that inform the writing. In other words, Bartholomae contends that the roots of public academic discourse rest in the writer's subjectivity—that is, in the power of the writer's unique experience and prior knowledge, which control perceptions and interpretations. One of the important distinctions between good and bad public academic discourse is, then, that good public discourse articulates this prior knowledge or individual point of view so that it is accessible to others who need the information in order to understand the writer and his or her contexts. Once a student writer has made this information accessible, he or she can then, with help from the teacher and other students, go back to his or her other essay and begin a critical examination of both the essay and the assumptions underlying it.

Bartholomae's approach to composition asks writers to do what Bleich's heuristic for writing responses asks readers to do: use examples and illustrations as the basis for explanations, generalizations, and critical examinations. The examples and illustrations in a response come from the reader's associations, beliefs, assumptions, knowledge, and perceptions of the text. Writing about reading in this way gives readers a way to make meaning for themselves through a process of discovery rooted in inferential thinking.

Roland Barthes,[xix] discussing writing in a more global sense, extends the metaphor of a writer's "schemata" to help us see the role of personal background and cultural conventions in writing. He expands the notion of personal influences on writing to include not only the "familiar personal past" of the writer but also influences beyond the immediate control of the writer, such as the pressures of history and tradition that limit and define writing and its conventions. So in a narrow sense writers, like readers, are influenced in responding by the exigencies of their familiar personal past, but they are also influenced in responding and writing by pressures beyond their immediate awareness, such as the broad cultural expectations and influences of history and tradition—frames and schemata of much more inclusive proportions.

In summary, one of the most interesting results of connecting reading, literary, and composition theory and pedagogy is that they yield similar explanations of human understanding as a process rooted in the individual's knowledge and feelings and characterized by the fundamental act of making meaning, whether it be through reading, responding, or writing. When we read, we comprehend by putting together impressions of the text with our personal, cultural, and contextual models of reality. When we write, we compose by making meaning from available information, our personal knowledge, and the cultural and contextual frames we happen to find ourselves in. Our theoretical understandings of these processes are converging, as I pointed out, around the central role of human understanding—be it of texts or the world—as a process of composing.

The pedagogical implications of making these theoretical connections are actually quite simple: readers and writers need help in the form of heuristics and dialogue to articulate their understandings of texts, themselves, and the world. Bleich's response heuristic works to this end by giving students a way to flesh out the models of reality that inform their understandings of texts. Once this happens and students have explained their readings, they can enter into critical discussions with teachers and other students that lead them to examine their readings *and* the assumptions that inform them.[xx]

Let me now turn to an example. Here is a response that a student, Dan, wrote in a free response style with no direction except to write a statement that would represent his understanding of William Faulkner's "A Rose For Emily." Prior to this response, he had written in a free response style after reading Donald Barthelme's "The Balloon," and Shakespeare's sonnet 138. It is characteristic of the eight free responses he wrote in a graduate seminar on reading and psychology that I taught at the University of Pittsburgh in 1981. His free responses, like almost everyone else's in the seminar, tended to be sketchy and unfocused.

Upon Reading "A Rose for Emily"

How beautiful:

How otherwise?

The thing's as we expect and Wouldn't, couldn't change.

No blemish Emily But hybrid

Of the stubborn rose

That yields diverse perversity.

That yields perverse integrity And loyalty and spoils

All notion garden walks

Are through once briar and thicket catch to tear.

Maybe that would be enough if I had any confidence in my poetry. The temptation is to say it again, now in prose, but the thing is so fleeting . . . I guess that's why poetry seemed like the right way to express it. I wonder if I can capture how "A Rose for Emily" affects me in any other way? It's almost a violation of something strong and basic in me

> to pull this wonderful mess of emotion out, so fishnet tangled up, and give it a shape it shouldn't have.
>
> I love William Faulkner for doing this to me. And he took me so by surprise. I rushed to get the story in the first few pages and suffered reader's doldrums in the next few and was cynical when toward the end I wondered if Estella might appear chasing after a story to hide in. And then, the man himself lay in the bed, and sweetly, no, I can't understand it either, I don't know why it's with such a rush of pleasure that I see it, Emily had joined him there. I thought so many things that were the same thing when Faulkner finished writing. I thought, Yes, that's right, of course she'd done this thing. It's not so hard to understand or even wish it as a romantic and symbolic act. It's those crazy people who are always giving us the symbols. They must be the only ones with any vision.

Links with the text are missing from this response, and it is difficult to see why Dan says the things he does. It is particularly difficult to see why this story moves him as much as he claims it does. And even though I like the poetic sense of his response, I have to admit, finally, that I need more from Dan if I am to understand his understanding of the story.

Before going on to look at Dan's use of the heuristic in his response to *The Great Gatsby,* I think another glimpse at one of his free responses will help me complete the picture of free response that I am trying to paint. For this example, I turn to Dan's response to Robert Frost's poem, "Once By The Pacific." The poem begins with someone looking out at the ocean and seeing waves shatter on the rocks, "forming a misty din." It builds to an awesome foreboding of the sea's destructive power and, finally, in the last stanza God enters to put out the light.

Although Dan wrote this as a free response, it is one of the last such responses and came at a time in the semester when he was growing frustrated with the sketchy, unfocused nature of the free responses. Here he deliberately moves his attention to a central idea and tries to focus his response on the poem—more so than he did on the story in his response to "A Rose For Emily." But, again, it does not work; he begins well enough with a statement defining his attempt to find a central idea, but he finally ends up digressing into what he claims Frost makes him see and, finally, a private association he has with Niagara Falls.

> **Response To "Once By The Pacific"'**
>
> What to say. How to begin. What central idea to express and tie in with "Once By The Pacific." I don"t know. I see dusk at all the ocean spots I've stood in—as a boy with jellyfish in the Atlantic, as an adolescent with the black sand and the hucksters in the Mediterranean, as a young man with my insecurities in an inlet, on a peninsula, on the edge of a continent in any water anywhere stretching my imagination out and out.

> Great water, I conclude, had life. Frost hasn't surprised that reaction in me. So what has he done? He has made me answer, Yes, that's right—if tales come carried from the tale giver they will reach shore on wing if they are good and on wave if they are ominous and bad. He has made me answer, Yes, the word will be too loud to hear, too spendrift to be held for long before, once shattered into bits of night, new words, greater than before, succeed those old. And he has made me answer, Yes, the earth absorbs initial shocks to fall back upon upright earth, but it is *someone* who had best put affairs in order, for what continent will make a man secure?
>
> He makes me see a privileged man alone, exposed, host-like by the door he is standing, privy to a drama played out. And he is not surprised and he does not seem to be afraid. Another, look, another hurries on below, over washing slabs of stone, wraps up his eyes under his coat, about his business, off to supper, and privy to nothing. No eyes, no ears for hearing any noise save the muttering he gives way to—the gust that swallows it.
>
> The caves of Niagara. Creep along the narrow caves, edge along the walls of the caves of Niagara and hear what you can see at the mouths of the caves. Hear the thunder unabated as the water walls explode forever hour upon hour. Come closer to the cruelty, let it last at you. See death in the mouths of the caves of Niagara and ask what sort of man can be here and think his own thoughts, not hear the roar and change.
>
> He makes me remember. He makes me know what I know.

While the first two paragraphs seem, to me, to be the barest beginnings of a response that other readers can understand, he never quite puts the response together with his private associations that drive it so we could see the links he might be making in his mind. We end up with the barest structure of a response that lacks support in the form of explicit connections between what Dan sees in the poem and why he sees what he does. As a reader, my reaction is puzzlement. I am left with a handful of important unanswered questions. Why, for instance, is he so heavy-handed in the second paragraph? Why is there a second man in the third stanza? What does this person represent? And, finally, how is this association to Niagara Falls connected to his reading of the poem? What is it that Dan knows from Niagara that this poem makes him remember?

All in all, Dan's attempt at a more focused response with the free response format is only a little better, a little clearer than his response to "A Rose For Emily," and, as we will see, is nowhere near as clear and explicit as his response to *The Great Gatsby,* where he uses the response heuristic. There is, though, an aspect of Dan's response to the Frost poem that deserves some attention because it highlights the relative uselessness of personal associations in a response unless they are connected in some explicit way to the reader's impressions or interpretations of the text. Dan's first and last paragraphs of this response are free associations very much in the manner of what the response heuristic is meant to produce; but unlike the associations encouraged by the response heuristic they are not connected to statements of perception or interpretation, so they appear to come from and go nowhere.

When Dan began to use Bleich's response heuristic—writing first what he perceived in the text, then how he felt about what he saw, and finally what associations followed from his perceptions—his responses blossomed into three and four-page single-spaced essays that flip back and forth between sections of the texts and specific personal references. The following selection from his response to *The Great Gatsby* is typical of the way he interrelates the text with his memories and associations. He tells us, in short, how he relates to the text he writes about. This is part of his first response from the heuristic.

> Nick's house. The first thing I remember, having just finished Gatsby, is Nick's house. It sits hidden (mostly by grass) and because it is hidden, it provides Nick with a good private spot for making observations and for making judgements. I like the house. I think its walls are probably white and rough and the rooms crowded with furniture. It is always warm, and it is always a smarter place to be than is Gatsby's. Houses are important to me. I always think of my childhood *in* some house. My favorite house was in Butler, Pa. I spent a romantic adolescence there, writing awful short stories on Sunday mornings while my parents were in church, smoking my father's Camel cigarettes on the sly, feeling very grown up and melancholy. It was in this house that I spent a year convalescing after an operation that straightened my spine from a radical curve into a soft curve. I was encased in plaster from my head to my knees—helpless. Every Sunday morning, after he came back from church, my father, a practical, even rough business man, ministered to my needs. And though my mother spent her time during the week doing the same things and doing them with more finesse and doing them gently, it is with greater fondness that I remember the way my father roughed me up with rowels and brushes and soapy water. My room was on the second floor and looked out over a small reservoir completely surrounded by old trees. I watched the seasons change and start to change again before I was on my feet again. And if it hadn't happened, I wouldn't know the depth of my father's love for me.

Nick's house reminds him of his favorite childhood house where he grew close to his father. Clearly, he has strong feelings about the whole scene that the house brings to mind and, in a direct way, these feelings shape his stance towards the text. Dan's use of his family as a sounding board for characters and events in the text is one of the recurring characteristics of his affective and cognitive framework. In his response to *Gatsby,* he develops every textual reference into a statement about some member of his family. He discusses Fitzgerald's humor, and then begins discussing his father by beginning with his sense of humor. Later on in the same response, he discusses the scene in the hotel room where Tom Buchanan confronts Gatsby with his fabricated story of his life, and then he slips into a monologue on his relationship with his brother by referring to Gatsby's relationship with Tom. The response heuristic teases out these kinds of references and Dan was one of the two people in the seminar who continually returned to their families in their responses.

When Dan wrote using Bleich's response heuristic in response to *Gatsby,* he developed his statements around characters and events that related to recollections of his family, but he also wrote, for the first time during the semester, statements that began with specific retellings of the text, then moved to explanations of his connections to the text *vis a vis* his feelings and associations; finally, he concluded by generalizing from his discussion.

Not everyone in the seminar wrote from family recollections, and not everyone had Dan's initial success with the response heuristic. One student, Bob—a clinical psychologist—managed to double the length of his responses using Bleich's heuristic, but still his responses were not explicit enough to be accessible to others in the class. He relentlessly saw everything in the stories and poems from a clinical perspective. He would not discuss a character or event unless he could frame the discussion as an illustration of a clinical phenomenon. He saw Faulkner's Emily, for instance, as a person who never understood her options in life; and, therefore, she needed therapy to help her see these options. He saw *Gatsby* as a book that "carried some good descriptions of character behavior disorders." He continually placed himself in the role of a therapist and he took great pleasure from treating characters as patients. His responses prompted lengthy seminar discussions—most of which were devoted to fleshing out what he was saying—and he literally recreated every story and poem in light of his clinical experiences.

Millie, another student in the seminar, had a difficult time writing responses that articulated the prior experiences underlying her perceptions and judgments. Here are the first two paragraphs of her response to *Gatsby.* They are typical of her two-page response to this book. Notice how they never quite get off the ground, although the barest bones of the heuristic are evident—perceptions of the text, feelings, and spare associations. She stops short of the depth of explanation that Dan achieves in his response to *Gatsby,* and she did not at all try to interpret texts as we will see Dan doing later in his response to Penelope Mortimer's *The Pumpkin Eater.* Notice, too, how Millie introduces pertinent information about her associations with Nick's sense of powerlessness when Tom and Gatsby begin to fight, but she does not develop that discussion into any kind of elaborated description or explanation that might allow us to get a concrete sense of her perception of the powerlessness that she attributes to Nick.

> Whenever I think over what I remember from the novel, sensory impressions come to mind first. One of the most vivid impressions is dust. The grayness in the valley of ashes between the City and the Eggs depresses me. I can see the bareness and sterility of the

> landscape and Myrtle's body lying in the dusty road. I can also visualize the grayness of Wilson's face. The valley of ashes reminds me of a depressing strip of highway leading into New Kensington which is littered with shacks, coal tipples, junked cars, and greasy diners. This strip puts the rider in the right frame of mind for entering New Kensington, "a good place to work, trade, and live."
>
> Another memorable sensory impression is the heat. I can feel the enervating heat the afternoon Nick first visits Daisy and Tom. I am oppressed by the boiling tense environment the afternoon the couples go to the city. It's no surprise to me that violent activity explodes because the oppressive air keeps swelling along with the palpable tension between Tom and Gatsby. I know how the heat enervates me and makes me short tempered. I love summer storms that finally give some relief from oppressive heat. I know how Nick must have felt as the tension built between Gatsby and Tom. I've been in unpleasant situations like the one that afternoon and I was powerless to stop the inevitable progression that led to a violent outburst.

While Millie does *tell* us that she understands the tension and powerlessness that Nick must have felt, she does not give us the description and explanation that would allow us to see or understand her experience with powerlessness so we might know what it means to her. Her narrative is thin compared to Dan's, and as such it is less compelling than Dan's. In short, Millie begins to use the heuristic, but unlike Dan, she stops short and does not make the commitment to description and explanation through association with prior personal knowledge that Dan does. Consequently, I have only a vague sense of the prior knowledge driving her response; in order to have a more concrete sense of her associations with the text, I need more explanation. My response was to ask her to say more—to specifically tell the story of that afternoon she felt powerless and then to tell how her sense of powerlessness is related to Nick's. And although I kept asking her for more explanation and critical examination, she never did write anything nearly as sophisticated as Dan.

Dan's response to Penelope Mortimer's *The Pumpkin Eater* is another good example of how the response heuristic helps him discuss his associations with the story, so that unlike Millie's response to *Gatsby,* his response gives us a good sense of the mental map that is guiding his reactions. But this response also differs in an important way from his earlier *Gatsby* response in that it takes a more critical, speculative stance towards the text. The second paragraph—presented below—goes beyond the description of houses in his *Gatsby* response by exploring "desperation" and commenting on what Mrs. Armitage might have felt in her desperate state. Notice, too, how this paragraph follows a pattern. First, he describes Mrs. Armitage, confused and desperate, awaking in Giles' bedroom (a perception of the text); then Dan recalls the desperation of his brother and he explains that experience as a comment on desperation (a statement of his feelings couched in the associations); finally, he concludes by generalizing from his discussion. Dan cues to this scene because he has strong associations with desperation. He tells us what those associations are so that we can see why this scene is important enough for him to want to discuss it, and then he takes his experience with desperation and turns it into critical speculation on desperation and Mrs. Armitage's situation.

> A awakes. Eleven hours unconscious in Giles' bedroom. Night? Lace day? I can't say, but were I to film the scene the lights would burn without shades from the sockets and the room would be sick with their paleness. Giles tells A the truth about Jake's calls and she is desperate to go. She is confused with so much sleep, disoriented and not certain about time. She goes, and what is left behind is the room—rumpled, stale, yellow with some bright spots chat turn out to be bare lights. And I am reminded chat what surrounds me when I awake and just before I sleep and as I work has a profound effect upon whether I stay all sane. And I remember how one evening my brother David and I sat arguing in our room, our parents insulated downstairs with their papers from our racket and thumping around. I held my head in my hands and wailed chat he had to clean up the room, for he'd made a mess. He became frightened and set to work without delay. I was calm again before long. But I also had a new kind of memory and one chat had come too early in the life of a boy—I had done something and felt some way without reason and without control and had scared myself and David. Face to face with an altered consciousness chat would test me again in dreams and in wakefulness whenever it was time to be a little crazy. Desperate. David slipped over the edge before any of the rest of us, though, and did it without witness. I could have helped had I known he was nuts because I had seen the ocher side though I hadn't embraced it. I could have helped, and I remember how it isn't good to be desperate all alone.

Dan's last paragraph in the same response is another good example of the same pattern. First, he describes Jake's father in the context of a haunting statement he left behind when he died; then he recalls a boy from his youth and relates a moving story about his death; and, finally, he concludes the response by generalizing about death and memory. Notice, too, how explicit his links are to the text in this response compared with those in his responses to "A Rose For Emily" and "Once by the Pacific." His connections are much more visible and concrete in his responses, like this one, that follow from the heuristic than they are in his responses, like the one to "A Rose For Emily," that are essentially free response. Here too, he goes beyond his earlier *Gatsby* response by making a critical judgment in guessing "that Mortimer is claiming Jake's father purposely held back important things for the reasons A suspects." Once Dan makes the interpretive judgment, he goes on to explore it and its implications by commenting on private and public feelings. We get a good sense of the mental map that directs his explorations because he re creates the experience that bears directly—or, at lcast, associativcly—on his scnsc of public and privatc fcelings.

> I felt close to the strange character of Jake's father. We don't know a lot about him, but he left behind a haunting statement in which the nature of God is examined. A calls it his only great statement and accuses him of leaving his life still uninvolved because the statement came after his death. I guess that Mortimer is claiming Jake's father purposely held back important things for the reasons A suspects. Good. We peer into people's lives and make them ordinary by it. Holding portions away from public view seems a small, dignified price to pay, whatever the results. One's children don't know the depths of your feelings toward God. Small price for owning something private, that. I can feel a reaction against the process that we are all currently undergoing rising up in me. We are peering into one another's lives, and worse, we assist one another. Billy Fennick. A boy from my youth named Billy taught me how to set trees on fire and to smoke. He was bad for me. He went to the Navy and never came home because he drowned. His submarine went under and didn't come up. He was as close to me, to my hands, as this typewriter once and then he was under the sea drowning. My friend Billy. And do you know what I wondered when I heard? I wondered if he saw my face and heard me laugh when he talked dirty. Because Billy left nothing. The submarine was lost. Billy never came home, even dead. But, in my little age, I was convinced if he had thought of me, he left me behind. I was his statement and the sign of his involvement with the world. That sort of mystic link with the dead is important to me. It is not ordinary, first of all, and I think the dead deserve being remembered unusually. And second of all, those kinds of memories give the living a chance to make amends for the shortcomings of living so close beside the people we love that the only thing that makes them important to us is their death.

Dan's responses are particularly moving, but then so were almost everyone's in the seminar once we began using Bleich's response format. But the responses were not only moving, they had explanatory power because they used examples and illustrations derived from associations as a way of revealing the readers' mental maps that were guiding their responses. There was very little explaining or illustrating in the free responses and in the responses, like Millie's, that only flirted with the heuristic. Generally, readers free responded in terms of what they liked, and then they drew conclusions or generalizations about the work, about some aspect of it, or about reality. And while it was interesting to see these varied and individual perceptions, they were not compelling as acts of comprehension in the ways essays are compelling when they illustrate with examples to flesh out the knowledge—personal, factual, or textual—that shapes one's comprehension.

Throughout the seminar we duplicated and shared our responses so that at the end of the semester we had complete sets of responses from everyone in the group. We used these as the basis for our theoretical and literary discussions. The final project for the seminar was a self-study paper.

The group members were asked to write case studies on their reading. They examined all of their responses in light of the readings and discussions. From this, they wrote case reports of themselves as readers. The papers were interesting for a number of reasons. First, everyone looked for and found consistent patterns in their readings that indicated how they were using their personal knowledge to create both the format and content of their responses. Second, the readers took varied theoretical stances to explain their readings, but regardless of their bent, they were able to explain them. And third, they recognized that they wrote considerably more sophisticated papers when they used the response heuristic. By having a way to flesh out the personal knowledge that informed their comprehension, they were better able to explain themselves to each other. And while I would be hard pressed to argue that elaboration like this will always lead to more sophisticated response—for I can certainly imagine elaborated but empty responses—I do think that this kind of elaboration and explanation is a necessary beginning to more critical examinations of texts and the assumptions underlying readers' readings of them.

Teaching reading this way means teaching composition as the most compelling and persuasive representation of comprehension. If we are willing to consider that comprehension is more than limited recall and retelling (although it certainly contains these), and if we are willing to see reading as a kind of transaction between readers and texts in specific contexts, then we need to ask readers to represent their comprehension through composition by asking them to follow a sequence of assignments that begins with Bleich's response heuristic and then moves to more critical examination of responses and the assumptions underlying them.

When readers in my seminar used Bleich's response heuristic, their responses began with references to the text and then moved into personal narratives that told the story of their associations with the text. The personal narratives served a function similar to that served by examples and illustrations in essays—they fleshed out assumptions, feelings, and prior knowledge to give authority to what the author had to say. When these examples and illustrations are missing from essays, the writing becomes a set of empty assertions with little or no evidence to give them authority. And like essays that follow conventions but say nothing, they turn into a kind of "themewriting."[xxi] The same is true of the responses the readers in my seminar wrote when they followed the free response format. Like Dan in his response to "A Rose for Emily," they wrote vague statements that were difficult to understand and were like essays without compelling examples and illustrations—responses that lacked evidence and failed to show the essential connections of knower to known.

Statements of comprehension are most compelling, on the other hand, when they make connections between knower and known, text and reader, reading and context. And, equally important, when we ask readers to write about their readings using Bleich's response heuristic, we are asking them to engage in one of the most fundamental intellectual processes. We ask them to use a basic heuristic of inquiry. The process is similar to making interpretations and documenting them; as such, it is fundamental to the beginnings of any dialogue or dialectic that must ensue when people come together to understand reality. Writing plays a crucial role in this heuristic because it can commit and compel the reader to discover meaning by articulating one's responses in extended discourse that is meant to be public within the community of the classroom.

Once readers have used Bleich's heuristic to generate a response, the class can move to a discussion of everyone's responses, and then, using comments from the group and from the teacher, the readers can begin treating their responses as both critical statements whose assumptions and stances need to be examined, questioned, and discussed, and as pieces of writing that can be revised and edited. By following a procedure like this, students can accumulate experience in reading, writing about their reading, discussing each other's reading, commenting on responses as pieces of writing, and revising and editing. Teachers, on the other hand, need to learn how to read responses with an eye to helping students flesh out the personal knowledge and critical judgments that inform them. In order to do this, I read and wrote along with my students. I am convinced that doing this is necessary if the teacher is to become a member in the community of readers; but, perhaps more importantly, I am convinced that doing it is necessary because it teaches me how to talk about responses in the context of trying to help students do what I am trying to do for myself. The entire process is, I think, one of the most meaningful ways to integrate reading and writing in composition, reading, and literature classes.[xxii]

Notes

i. This argument that we should not ask students to write about their reading because the writing confounds our assessment of their reading is a familiar one in assessment circles. I first encountered it in its most entrenched form when I held a contract to develop test specifications and items for the third national assessment of reading and literature. It resides, I believe, in the notion that reading and writing are discrete mental processes—a notion that I hope this paper begins to dispel.

ii. F. C. Bartlett, *Remembering* (Cambridge: Cambridge University Press, 1932). The term "schemata" is used by Bartlett to include both affective and cognitive frameworks, but it is often the case that people quoting him use it only to mean cognitive frameworks. The varied use of the term has lead me to prefer "models of reality'" or "frames" in lieu of "schemata."

iii. For decades multiple-choice tests have dominated reading comprehension assessment and instruction. College skills programs have students read short paragraphs and answer multiplechoice questions as comprehension instruction, and classrooms at all levels of education are dominated by quick, easy-answer type discussions of texts. Finally, from the third national assessment of reading and literature, we have empirical evidence indicating that students at ages 9, 13, and 17 do much better on multiple-choice questions than on essays that require them to explain answers to multiple-choice questions. About 70%

of all 17-year-olds can do the multiple-choice questions while only 20 to 30% can adequately explain and substantiate their answers. To me, this is a clear indication of the kinds of instruction students are getting in reading and literature classes—a situation that must change if we are going to move beyond superficial reading and literature instruction.

iv. Robert Anderson, "The Notion of Schemata and the Educational Enterprise," in R. Anderson, R. Spiro, and W. Montague, eds., *Schooling and the Acquisition of Knowledge* (Hillsdale, New Jersey: Erlbaum, 1977).

v. David Rumelhart, "Schemata: The Building Blocks of Cognition," in R. Spiro, B. Bruce, and W. Brewer, eds., *Theoretical Issues in Reading and Comprehension* (Hillsdale, New Jersey: Erlbaum, 1980).

vi. Robert Schank and Robert Abelson, *Scripts, Plans, Goals, and Understanding* (Hillsdale, New Jersey: Erlbaum, 1977).

vii. Marylin Jager Adams and Allan Collins, *A Schema-Theoretic View of Reading* (Urbana, IL: Center for the Study of Reading, 1977). It is interesting, I think, to see both the idea of retrieval and construction applied to reading in this quotation. Although the gist of the statement is clearly along the lines of readers constructing meaning, there is still a tension in the author's reluctance to completely give up the retrieval notion of reading. This is, I think, typical of the tensions in the field of reading.

viii. Robert De Beaugrande, "Design Criteria for Process Models of Reading," *Reading Research Quarterly,* 16 (February, 1981), 261–315.

ix. I. A. Richards, *Practical Criticism: A Study of Literary judgment* (New York: Harcourt Brace, 1929).

x. Louise Rosenblatt, *The Reader, The Text, The Poem: The Transactional Theory of the Literary Work* (Carbondale, Ill.: Southern Illinois University Press, 1978).

xi. Norman N. Holland, *5 Readers Reading* (New Haven: Yale University Press, 1975).

xii. David Bleich, *Subjective Criticism* (Baltimore: John Hopkins University Press, 1978). Although I have taken the response heuristic from this book, there is much more here for the reader who wants to go beyond the heuristic to critical examinations of responses and texts.

xiii. Rosenblatt, pp. 24–25.

xiv. Rosenblatt, p. 137.

xv. John Dewey and Arthur F. Bentley, *Knowing and the Known* (Boston: Beacon Press, 1949).

xvi. Bleich, p. 112.

xvii. John Fowles, *Daniel Martin* (Boston: Little, Brown and Company, 1977). Fowles talks about reading and writing throughout this marvelous book. His comments are as insightful as the best reading and writing research.

xviii. David Bartholomae, "Teaching Basic Writing: An Alternative to Basic *Skills," Journal of Basic Writing* (Spring/Summer, 1979), 85–109.

xix. Roland Barthes, *Writing Degree Zero and Elements of Semiology* (Boston: Beacon Press, 1970). This is one of the most helpful books for understanding writing in the contexts of history and tradition, governed by cultural codes and conventions. Even though Barthes changed his position on writing well before his death, his work here seems relevant to reading and writing.

xx. See David Bartholomae and Anthony Petrosky, "Facts, Artifacts, and Counterfacts: A Basic Reading and Writing Course for the College Curriculum," in Marilyn Sternglass and Douglas Butturff, eds., *Building the Bridges Between Reading and Writing* (Akron, Ohio: L&S Books, 1981) for a more detailed discussion of a basic reading and writing pedagogy emanating from these notions of comprehension as composition.

xxi. William E. Coles, Jr., *The Plural I: The Teaching of Writing* (New York: Holt, Rinehart, and Winston, 1978). Coles characterizes writing that says nothing but says it well as "themewriting." He claims, and my experience supports his claim, that students learn how to do this kind of writing in schools where teachers spend little or no time commenting on the meaning and content of papers, but, rather, spend time teaching composition forms and formats.

xxii. A version of this paper was originally presented at the New York University Language and Reading Conference, New York City, May, 1981. I am grateful to my friends and colleagues Arthur Applebee, David Bartholomae, Charles Cooper, and Susan Wall for their careful readings of earlier drafts.

College English, Volume 45, Number 7, November 1983

Reading and Writing a Text: Correlations between Reading and Writing Patterns[1]

Mariolina Salvatori[2]

> The capacity to participate in verbally complex texts is not widely fostered in our educational system, and desirable habits of reflection, interpretation, and evaluation are not widespread. These are goals that should engender powerful reforms in language training and literary education. But none of these are attainable if good literary works of art are envisioned as the province of only a small, highly trained elite. Once the literary work is seen as part of the fabric of individual lives, the gap may be at least narrowed, without relinquishing recognition of standards of excellence.
>
> —Louise M. Rosenblatt, *The Reader, the Text, the Poem* (Carbondale, Ill.: Southern Illinois University Press, 1978), p. 143

At present the teaching of literature and composition are characterized by an artificial separation between the activities of reading and those of writing.[3] Although there is no question that a number

1 **Citation:** Salvatori, Mariolina "Reading and Writing a Text: Correlations between Reading and Writing Patterns." *College English*, vol. 45, no. 7, 1983, pp. 656–666.

2 Mariolina Salvatori teaches English and comparative literature and composition at the University of Pittsburgh. She has previously published articles on ltalo Svevo, Cesare Pavese, and the immigrant novel. Her research interests include the modern Italian novel, the literature of aging, and reader response theory, especially its applications to composition.

3 There are some who advocate such a " separatist" view. For example, E. D. Hirsch's argument is based on problematic assumptions about both the teaching of composition (i.e., for Hirsch, "the teaching of writing skills") and the teaching of literature (i.e., knowledge *about* rather than *through* literature): "Everyone accepts literacy as a goal of schooling, but the planners of school curricula are not always sure just where the *skills of writing* should be taught. *Should it be connected with* literary instruction in classes on poetry and fiction? Or should it be kept with the *humbler language arts* of spelling and punctuation? . . . Everything I have learned from my researches points toward the correctness of the second point of view—that composition is a *craft* which cannot properly be subsumed under any conventional subject matter. . . . In talking with many university teachers of composition, I have become convinced that one reason for the desire to mix composition with other instructional goals is the ignorance that besets us all about effective ways to teach composition. We know a lot more about literature than we know about teaching the craft of prose. In our anxious ignorance on that subject, we commit ourselves to goals that are more 'humanistic' than mere composition." *The Philosophy of Composition* (Chicago: University of Chicago Press, 1977), p. 140 italics mine.

of conveniences attend this separation, the division can be dangerous if it seems to suggest that the processes of the one activity, in theory and in practice, are antithetical to the teaching of the other, and if it implicitly sets up a qualitative and value-laden distinction between the reading of inexperienced and experienced readers.

The exclusion of literary texts from most composition curricula may be seen as the indirect, though not accidental, result of the influence of some literary theories that place their main emphasis on the elaborate analysis of the structures and the meanings of a literary text.[4] While these theories presuppose a highly trained reader—which the beginning writing student is not—they usually neglect to account for, and to explain, the complex activities of that reader's mind as she or he receives, responds to, and generates those meanings.

Paradigmatic of this approach to the reading (and the teaching) of a literary text is Tzvetan Todorov's assertion that "since reading is so hard to observe," and "introspection is uncertain, psycho-sociological investigation is tedious . . . it is . . . with a kind of relief that we find the work of construction represented in fiction itself, a much more convenient place for study [since] a text always contains within itself directions for its own consumption."[5] But to know that a text contains within itself "directions for its own consumption" is already to know how to read and respond to those directions. The reader, in other words, is not only aware of the great variety of activities entailed in the reading of a fictional text, but because of this awareness, has also developed the appropriate skills to perform such reading. How he or she has managed to develop those skills remains, to a large extent, a mystery. The reading of elaborate texts remains the province of knowledgeable critics whose expertise inexperienced students can only vaguely imitate through the memorization of an empty literary nomenclature, achieving at best knowledge *about* rather than *through* literature.

When the reading of literary texts is envisioned in these terms, then there is, and there should be, no use for them in composition classes. But the loss can be considerable because, as Louise M. Rosenblatt points out:

---

4 See Hirsch's specious argument for the separation of literature and composition: "For it can be shown that knowing how to write is different from knowing about literature. The proof is simple. Numbers of graduate students in literature are unable to write well, yet they do demonstrably know a great deal about literature, much more than a freshman could possibly learn in a composition course. Whatever the theory may have been under which the teaching of literature was thought to be closely connected with writing skills, that theory has been shown to be incorrect by this simply empirical test" (p. 141). But it may be argued that the "empirical test" shows something else, i.e., that the teaching of literature as *information* about genres, poetic forms, images and metaphors, etc., rather than *exploration* of how a reader's mind interacts with a text to compose meanings, might be responsible for this arbitrary distinction between the activities of writing and reading.

5 "Reading as Construction," in *The Reader in the Text,* eds. Susan R. Suleiman and Inge Crosman (Princeton. N.J.: Princeton University Press, 1980), pp. 67, 77.

> Literary texts provide us with a widely broadened "other" through which to define ourselves and our world. Reflection on our meshing with the text can foster the process of self-definition in a variety of ways. . . . The reader, reflecting on the world of the poem or play or novel as he conceived it and on his responses to that world, can achieve a certain self-awareness, a certain perspective on his own preoccupations, his own system of values. (pp. 145, 146)[6]

For this "self-awareness" to be brought about, literature ought to be taught as a way of exploring, understanding, and reflecting on the strategies by which readers—all readers—generate meanings in the act of reading; only through this approach can the teaching of literature become a useful means for composition teachers to foster in their students those reflective habits of mind that can, and will, contribute to the students becoming better writers.

The advantage of seeing the activities of reading and writing as inseparable was suggested by Andrea A. Lunsford, who came to the conclusion that "the teacher of writing must automatically and always be a teacher of reading as well." The implications of her observations on remedial writers were that

> all language skills are related—[the] level of reading comprehension is related to complexity of sentence formation (or syntactic maturity) and . . . both are related to mature, synthetic thought-processes. Our students were all both poor readers and poor writers, and their gains in these two areas clearly paralleled each other. Furthermore, as our students' ability to manipulate syntactic structures improved so did their ability to draw inferences and make logical connections.[7]

My experience with basic reading and writing students, as well as with more advanced ones, confirms Lunsford's conclusions about students' parallel development in the two activities. But my research suggests that the improvement in writers' ability to manipulate syntactic structures—their

6 See also George Dillon's refutation of Hirsch's views in *Constructing Texts: Elements of a Theory of Composition and Style* (Bloomington: Indiana University Press, 1981). Dillon's premise is that constructing texts embraces the activities of reader and writer, comprehension and composition. Similar arguments are made by David Bartholomae, "Integrating Reading and Writing: A Research Report," paper read at the Conference on College Composition and Communication, March 1978: and Ann E. Berthoff: "We need research projects in teaching reading and writing together. Because literature tends to crowd our writing, some have exiled it from the composition classroom. This is a solution that creates further problems. We need teachers who know how to relate critical reading to composing—not by finding topics to write about in the assigned reading but by identifying how forming is central to both reading and writing" (*The Making of Meaning: Metaphors, Models and Maxims for Writing Teachers* [Upper Montclair, N.J.: Boynton Cook, 1981], p. 10). Finally, see Bruce T. Petersen, "Writing about Responses: A Unified Model of Reading, Interpretation, and Composition," *College English,* 44 (1982), 459–468.

7 "What We Know—and Don't Know—About Remedial Writing," *College Composition and Communication,* 29 (1978), 49, 51.

maturity as writers—is the result, rather than the cause, of their increased ability to engage in, and to be reflexive about, the reading of highly complex texts. However, if the two language activities are indeed related, the important question need not be "what causes what," but rather how to teach composition so as to benefit from the interrelationship of the two activities.[8]

I want to suggest an answer to this latter question by describing the writing of one of my students. Mary was a student in the fall of 1981 in the Basic Reading and Writing Seminar, a course at the University of Pittsburgh that serves students whose test scores place them at the lowest 10% of the freshman class. The course, which is team taught, was designed by David Bartholomae and Anthony Petrosky.

In response to an early assignment which asks the student to write about a significant event in her life and to explain why she sees it as significant, Mary wrote about the time she, as a lifeguard, saved the life of a child.

> I was watching the kids in my area and there was two kids, around eight or nine, playing around by dunking each other. All of a sudden the one boy started bobbin for air. So I blew a long blast from my whistle, that was a signal that a guard was leaving their chair and going in for a save. I then dove into the water and start swimming over toward the kid. Once I got there, I got him out of the water with some assistance from the other guards. We then took him into the first aid room and he was okay but he was just shook up. . . .
>
> This experience is very significant because, I was able to help someone who needed it. It made me feel good because I carried out my job and responsibilities the way I should have . . . since that was my first save I will never forget it. . . . I will always remember that incident, that I could help someone when they needed me.

Although the teaching of composition is perhaps the least of Wolfgang Iser's concerns, some of his ideas about reading will help us understand what is happening in Mary's writing and what we can do about it. His description of the processes by which readers produce meanings as they interact with a text sheds considerable light on the reasons why students adopt ineffective reading strategies and helps us to discover important correlations between their reading patterns and the writing patterns they use to compose their responses to a text.[9]

In *The Act of Reading* (Baltimore, Md.: Johns Hopkins University Press, 1978) Iser claims that

8 See Marilyn Sternglass, "Sentence-Combining and the Reading of Sentences," *CCC*, 31 (1980), 325–328; and "Assessing Reading, Writing, and Reasoning," *CE*, 43 (1981), 269–275.

9 The "interactional" or "transactional" view of reading, vigorously and convincingly advocated by reader response theorists and psycholinguists in the 1970s, was formulated by Louise Rosenblatt in 1938 in *Literature as Exploration* at a time when practitioners and interpreters of the tenets of New Criticism placed absolute emphasis on the technique of literary texts.

> central to the reading of every literary work is the *interaction* between its structure and its recipient. . . . The literary work has two poles . . . the author's text . . . and the realization of it accomplished by the reader. (p. 106, my italics)

The work itself, then, is neither identical with the text nor with its realization, "but must be situated somewhere between the two." In other words, the work is "indeterminate" and "dynamic," or better, indeterminate because continuously dynamic. In the act of its reading the work cannot, nor should, be reduced to one meaning, to one perspective; the reader should not deny the possibility of subsequent revisions of meanings, subsequent modifications of perspectives. Unfortunately it is mostly against the indeterminacy and the dynamism of a literary work that our students defend themselves by reducing it either to the assumed reality of the text (i.e., the message, the information, the main idea, all conceived as stable, finite units), or to their own subjectivity (i.e., "I can relate to this," "I cannot relate to this," which are often spurious judgments based on ephemeral associations or pre-established perspectives). In either case reading becomes a one-way activity rather than a process by which, as Iser suggests, a reader passes through the various perspectives offered by the text, relates the different patterns and views to one another, and in so doing "sets the work in motion and himself in motion, too." Iser's language suggests throughout the kinetic, transactional, and participatory nature of the reading process which an excessive emphasis on either pole would annul.

According to Iser the transaction between text and reader is an event brought about and regulated by the reader's simultaneous engagement in the two contrasting and mutually monitoring activities of "consistency building" and the "wandering viewpoint." The activity of the wandering viewpoint tends to flesh out, to reorganize, and to proliferate the meanings a text proposes, and thus it generates a reader's revision of previous perspectives. The activity of consistency building, on the other hand, tends to stabilize ambiguities and to select segments from a text that confirm "familiar" meanings, and thus it generally prevents a reader's revision of perspectives.[10] Apparently, of the two activities, consistency building is the one that readers most instinctively tend to engage in, particularly when the texts they read are characterized by "blanks" or "gaps" of indeterminacy (i.e., when things are implied rather than said) which need to be "filled" with "projections," hypotheses—themselves always subject to revision—about how to "supply what is meant from what is not said" (p. 111). The more a text contains such "gaps," the more a reader may need to engage in the activity of the wandering viewpoint in order to check the stabilizing, and potentially reductive, tendency of consistency building. At the same time he or she must monitor, through consistency building, the potentially

10 This is how Iser explains the reason for the tendency to confirm familiar meanings: "One of the factors conditioning this selection is that in reading we think the thoughts of another person. Whatever these thoughts may be, they must to a greater or lesser degree represent an unfamiliar experience, containing elements which at any one moment must be partially inaccessible to us. For this reason, our selections tend first to be guided by those parts of our experience that still seem to be familiar" (*The Act of Reading,* p. 126).

excessive "wandering" of the wandering viewpoint. By providing us with a metaphorical language for identifying these otherwise imperceptible activities, Iser helps us to seek ways of modifying them and of thus enabling our students to become reflexive about and to improve their reading patterns.

The reading process, then, is an extremely complicated activity in which the mind is at one and the same time relaxed and alert, expanding meanings as it selects and modifies them, confronting the blanks and filling them with constantly modifiable projections produced by inter-textual and intra-textual connections. Because of the nature of the reading process, each reading remains as "indeterminate" as the text that it is a response to. But this is precisely the kind of activity—demanding, challenging, constantly structuring them as they structure it—that our students are either reluctant or have not been trained to see as reading. Specifically, it is with the indeterminacy of the text that they have their major difficulties. In their responses to a literary text most students do perform that one action, consistency building, that is central to the reading activity, and they identify what they consider the main idea. They fail, however, to realize that the identification of one idea among many others is only one step toward a more complete and dynamic reading. They perform one synthesis rather than various syntheses and tend to settle too soon, too quickly, for a kind of incomplete, "blocked" reading. Interestingly, the same "blocked" pattern has a tendency to characterize their writing as well; they lift various segments out of the text and then combine them through arbitrary sequential connections (usually coordinate conjunctions)—a composing mode that is marked by a consistent restriction of options to explore and develop ideas. The most telling signal is perhaps the absence of complex sentences and subordinations. As Ann E. Berthoff says in *The Making of Meaning,*

> the most difficult aspect of teaching writing as process and of considering it the result of something that is nurtured and brought along, not mechanically produced, is that our students do not like uncertainty (who does?); they find it hard to tolerate ambiguity and are tempted to what psychologists call "premature closure." They want the writing to be over and done with. (p. 22)

Berthoff's observation stresses the similarity between the essentially dynamic nature of the reading and writing activities. It is then plausible to suggest that by enabling students to tolerate and confront ambiguities and uncertainties in the reading process, we can help them eventually to learn to deal with the uncertainties and ambiguities that they themselves generate in the process of writing their own texts.

For example, in Mary's account of her saving a child, her past is like a "text" she is skimming through but not interacting with. (I am obviously suggesting here that in constructing a response, be it to a text or to a personal experience, we employ similar organizational strategies.) By structuring her narrative through an action-reaction, cause-effect pattern she prevents herself from pausing and examining the enormous implications of what she has accomplished. Furthermore in the conclusion Mary does not engage with her text by filling the blanks between " all of a sudden" and a flurry of phrases describing action ("so I blew the whistle," "I then dove," "once I got there"). She glosses over these gaps, and thereby reduces the significance of her experience to the blandness of "helping someone who needed it," the satisfaction of a "job well done." The synthesizing activity through which she should have grouped and modified the phases[11] of the text she has written—thereby enlarging, enriching, and modifying her viewpoint on the save from a "job well done" to a perspective that can include and acknowledge the enormous significance of her action—has been halted by an excess of consistency building. The text merely reproduces a sequence of actions; it does not compose those actions into a pattern that reveals their significance. The wandering viewpoint has not established the interaction between text and reader, because although she is writing about that experience from the perspective of the present, her viewpoint is fixed in the past at the moment when she had to act quickly, without time to think about what she was doing, why, and what it all meant.

The same kind of lack of interaction with the text, the same excess of consistency building, is evident in Mary's response to a later assignment. The students had read and discussed Maya Angelou's *I Know Why the Caged Bird Sings.* During class discussion, however, Mary was silent and content to account for her silence by saying: "I cannot relate to the story." She was right, of course, although not the way she meant it. In her written response to the in-class assignment that asked her to read a particular chapter of the book and write about what she thought was significant about the narrative, she could not effectively "relate," that is, "synthesize" the various segments of the text. She could not, in Iser's words, set the work in motion, and herself in motion too.

> One of the important points Maya made was even though the workers didn't receive very much for there work they kept on trying. *They would come in dragging* and tried and Maya *said* it *was painful to watch.* Even though they are so exhausted they all said that they was going to the service that was going to be held . . . *This seems important because they didn't have very much* and they ·was all look upon by the white people yet they kept trying. Then they mention about charity which I thought was important because none of them had ever been exposed to it, except within their own town maybe. What I saying is when they would go into town like when Maya and Momma went to the dentist they was look down upon. . . .
>
> Another point *I thought was* important was after service when they was going home and it was mention about the white folks having everything and they said it was better to suffer for a while. than spend eternity in hell. This was important because they felt that

---

11 "Phase" is an Iserian term. I prefer it to the psycholinguistic term "chunk" which suggests too finite a unit and which would contradict the concept of "indeterminacy" and of blending perspectives.

> after all this was over there would be a better life for them. Which points out the that the white folks would be looking up to them because of how ignorant they was to them.
>
> At the end of the chapter when it was said that reality began its tedious crawl back into their reasoning. After all, they were needy and hungry. . . . *I guess Maya was saying* that we have to go back to this type of living but hoping it would soon change and change for the better. (My emphasis)

In this reading Mary extracts various segments of the text which she then simply reproduces in the order of their appearance (One of the important points . . . Then they mention . . . Another point . . . At the end of the chapter). Her response is "blocked" in the same way at the consistency building step. The various blocks are connected primarily by means of sentences that restate "what Maya said," or that comment, and only tentatively, on the importance of what Maya said. "I think it is important," "Maya said," "this seems important," and "I guess Maya was saying." The tentativeness is guesswork, not qualification. What Mary is showing is that she doesn't know why anything is said or in what senses it might be important.

Further, in her reading of Angelou's text, confronted with the "unfamiliar" experience of the blacks, Mary has been guided in her selection by those elements in the text that seem "familiar." While she selects the blacks' docility and faithfulness as important points, she fails, for example, to acknowledge Maya's critical view of their passivity. Within the text there are considerable differences—gaps—between Maya's and the other blacks' viewpoint. By not relating these different perspectives to one another, Mary structures herself as a reader and writer who reacts to only one phase of the text (the blacks' positive view of their own docility) rather than interacts with the whole (the blacks' positive view of their own docility and Maya's negative view of it). She thus domesticates the virtuality of the text in terms of what she seems to recognize as a "familiar" notion.

Mary kept writing about herself and the texts she read and we kept responding to the texts she composed, explaining to her the effect of her use of language. Our strategy was to move her from the assumption that reading is the extraction of segments from a text and sequential rearrangement of them, to an awareness that reading is construction, the composing of oneself and the text through interaction with it.

At about mid-term, like the other students, she was required to construct her theory of adolescence through critical "reading" of three significant events in her life. Her text in this case was a composite one, a text made up of what she herself had already written in response to three previous assignments. The exercise took many weeks, many rewritings, and plenty of editing. As she continued to read the three phases of her life, Mary started to see and make connections between them to synthesize segments that earlier had had no relationship for her. No longer was she positioning herself outside the text. She was in the text, moving back and forth, her wandering viewpoint grouping and regrouping the three phases in such a way as to suggest, at least at moments, her involvement in an active process of meaning-making. She was in the process of composing herself as a composer of her own reality. In one sense, the moments are small, but they are vital.

"The day had finally come," says the writer, when "my only sister was getting married." Mary goes on to explain how close she was to her sister who had always taken care of her. Then she goes on to say:

> I was really happy for her that she was getting married, *but* I was also sad because she would be moving away from Pgh . . . two special people were going to be moving away. I felt like they were trying to hurt me by moving, *but* I knew that they had not planned it that way . . . I felt like they didn't want me around; I felt unwanted by them. They said I could go visit them, but I really didn't think they wanted that because I was still thinking that they didn't want anything to do with me. . . . I was used to having them around and now they were gone. I felt like someone had taken a part of me away. (My emphasis)

What is remarkable in Mary's account of her confusion at being left behind is this basic writer's movement, back and forth between her perspective and their perspective on "leaving." As she composes her text Mary passes through the various perspectives and relates them to one another. Her interpretation and their interpretation coexist; the opposing views are acknowledged as such, and structured, through language, as such. It is the *but,* the conjunction of disjunction, that signals this moment of awareness, the writer's acknowledgment of a blank of indeterminacy she refuses to reduce to either one interpretation or another. Although the grammatical present is not in the text, it is now, at the moment of composing, that Mary enacts the beginning of her understanding of the complexity of human relationships, and the complexity of herself as one who is able to embody such complexity. Important also is the way in which, as Mary composes her response to the reading of her own personal text, she branches out to include a segment from a text she had previously read but had not, as she put it, "related to." She is now making not only inter but intra-textual relations.

> For example, in the book, *I Know Why the Caged Bird Sings,* when Baily said he was going to sea, Maya was *hurt* because she never knew life without him around. This was the same situation. I was close to Lianne as Maya and Baily were. . . . Now it hurts that they are away, because I would like to share with them the *excitement* I felt when I had to save *this little boy* at work. . . . (My emphasis)

From "Maya was hurt," to "now it hurts"; the first hurt, the pain of being left behind, is moved to the second, the regret of not being able to share with them, to give them, part of the "excitement" she felt saving "this little boy." In her previous text Mary simply "felt good"; the boy she saved was just "this one boy." The give-and-take that at this moment marks her relationship to others, the transaction ("Now it hurts that they are away . . . I would like to share with them the excitement . . ."), becomes a correlative of the type of relationship she establishes with the texts she reads and writes (she now is enriched by and enriches Maya's perspective). Mary is decidedly not yet a fluent writer, but she has begun to learn that she produces meaning.

In one of her last in-class assignments Mary had to read a chapter from Margaret Mead's *Coming of Age in Samoa* and write about what she thought was important in the chapter and why. Here are two of the key moments in her essay:

> Margaret Mead's main point *is* that "adolescence is not necessarily a time of stress and strain, but that cultural conditions make it so." Margaret Mead *is saying* that . . . For instance . . .
>
> Margaret Mead *breaks down* her main point in this chapter and *tells* us. . . . (My emphasis)

The tentativeness that had characterized her earlier responses to *I Know Why* has disappeared. For all its clumsiness Mary's writing here conveys the impression that she knows what Margaret Mead is saying, and that she knows, too, that her own view of adolescence can accommodate both agreement and disagreement with Mead's view. She is enacting her realization that reading is construction, a matter of composing oneself and the text through interaction with it. Her reading experience with this text is located in her present moment of consciousness. And once more, Mary's use of *but* marks the gap of indeterminacy that puts into motion text and reader in the meaning-making activity:

> I *agree* with what Margaret Mead is saying about . . . *but I* feel that this could be hard because the American girl is faced with a decision and then from that she is faced with more. *It is like a tree,* the first decision is the trunk and then there are so many branches of decision to make. (My emphasis)

For Mary reading is no longer "distance" from the text, nor reduction of it through a sequential reproduction that fixes its "virtuality." She replaces the former "blocks" in her response with a certain type of confusion, but her confusion is both necessary and meaningful. The tree metaphor, for instance, "inscribes" Mary's presence in her text, as she generates a "reading," the first so far, that is not determined by a specific text. So though the thoughts have not been clearly sifted out, Mary seems to be experiencing a sense of urgency that suggests the need to articulate something discovered at the moment of its discovery. "The most important point to me in this chapter," she writes at the end of her essay,

> is that *if you are able to survive* the choices and decisions that society places on you during adolescence, *society will accept you as a young adult.* For the Samoan adolescents the

> choices are minimal. . . . But for me, I feel I am accustomed to these decisions in life and I accept them as my way of living. (My emphasis)

There is no such "point" in Margaret Mead's chapter. The point is Mary's, a point she has generated in her reading of the chapter, a meaning she has constructed by enlarging the horizon of Mead's text to include the text she wrote about her life.

Mary may not yet be a fluent writer. Mary may never come to be the kind of fluent writer who consistently "draws the reader into her text." But as we read the whole text she has composed during the fourteen weeks of the term, we can map the specific moments of a development. Having learned to be the kind of reader who, through the activity of a more dynamic "wandering viewpoint," reorganizes and modifies minimal acts of comprehension ("consistency building") into larger patterns; having learnt to participate in "verbally complex texts" by engaging with the experiences and the views of others, and by applying "desirable habits of reflection, interpretation, and evaluation," Mary has had the experience that moves her from a writer who merely reproduces the texts she reads and writes about, to a writer who more actively interacts with the text she composes as that text composes her.

If Mary had been placed in a composition class in which the only or main focus had been on writing, it is possible that she would have achieved the same kind of proficiency she now shows as a writer. Having improved as a writer, however, would not necessarily mean that she would have improved as a reader. Although it is an open question still how much more one learns about composing one's own texts when reading the texts of others, my current research suggests that although the two activities are interconnected, the activity of reading seems to subsume the activity of writing to a greater extent than most composition pedagogy presumes.

QUESTIONS ON CHAPTER 6: READINGS ON READING

READING AND WRITING TO COMPREHEND

1. **Choose a reading strategy** from Chapter 2 that will help you determine how the essays you read in this chapter define reading. What is reading's relationship to writing?
2. **Rhetorically read and annotate** the essays in this chapter with a particular focus on the purpose of each.
3. **Rhetorically read and annotate** the essays in this chapter with a particular focus on the argument of each, as well as the evidence that each author uses to support this argument.

READING AND WRITING TO RESPOND

4. **Develop a synthesis** in which you put at least 3 of the selections from this chapter into conversation with each other. Be sure to find a place for your own intellectual response in the conversation (see Chapter 3 for help with syntheses).

READING AND WRITING TO APPLY AND REFLECT

5. **Apply and Reflect.** As noted in the introduction to this chapter, many of this chapter's selections focus on students. Choose one of the essays from this chapter and test out its argument about students. Reflecting on your own experience as a student, how accurate is the author's argument about students? In what ways does the argument reflect your own experiences? In what ways do your experiences challenge the argument?

REFLECTING ON YOUR READING STRATEGIES AND ANNOTATIONS

Consider the different reading strategies you applied while reading the selections in this chapter. Which were most useful for understanding each text? For determining each text's purpose? For writing a synthesis? For reflecting on your experiences as a student? Anticipate future uses of these reading strategies in this class, in other classes, and in other contexts. Consider previous courses and contexts in which these strategies would have been helpful.

Chapter 7. Reading, Writing, and Technology

Communication technologies have been moving at an incredibly fast pace for decades now and show no signs of slowing down. For years, email has been seen as passé in the face of newer technologies such as Twitter, Instagram, and Snapchat, which undoubtedly will be quickly replaced by other technologies—maybe even by the time you are reading this! Although you have likely heard people blame technology for decreasing literacy abilities, research shows that people are reading and writing more than ever before. A great deal of that writing may be happening online and, perhaps, in the form of text-messages. The reading may occur on Instagram or in eBooks rather than in hard-covered books. But, does that matter? Does that not "count?" Certainly what we read and write, as well as how we read and write, are affected by the technologies we use to do so. The selections in this chapter explore those relationships.

As you read the essays in this chapter, avoid the temptation to see the authors of these pieces *as either for or against* technology (see Chapter 4 for more on the problems with binary thinking). Instead, think about these authors as inquiring into technology. More often than not, to locate these authors as staunchly opposed to or in support of technology is to oversimplify their positions and the point of their pieces.

PRIOR TO READING EACH SELECTION IN THIS CHAPTER

Look at the questions after each reading. What are you expected to do after reading this selection? In other words, what are your purposes for reading? Although you will be asked to apply particular reading strategies in order to complete some of the tasks, others will leave the choice of strategy up to you. Refer to the descriptions of the reading strategies in Chapter 2 and decide which will be most useful in helping you accomplish those tasks. Remember that you will be reading each selection multiple times and, therefore, will have additional opportunities to apply different reading strategies.

READINGS

The Book Stops Here

By Daniel H. Pink

This essay explores the origins of Wikipedia, as well as early critiques of the enormous online encyclopedia. Pink addresses how Wikipedia grew so quickly and how, in the process, it redefined what encyclopedias are and how they function.

You will be required to purchase a subscription after you visit *Wired* a certain number of times. Keep this in mind as you are working with this reading.

Visit https://www.wired.com/2005/03/wiki/

Questions about "The Book Stops Here"

READING AND WRITING TO COMPREHEND

1. **Rhetorically read and annotate**. In "The Book Stops Here," Pink writes, "Wikipedia represents a belief in the supremacy of reason and the goodness of others." What does he mean? Read and annotate Pink's piece with specific attention to his argument and the types of evidence he uses to make his argument (see Chapter 2 for help with rhetorical reading).
2. **Summarize.** Looking back at your annotations, complete a paragraph-long summary of Pink's argument and the evidence he uses to make it.

READING AND WRITING TO RESPOND

3. **Compose.** Using your summary and annotations (see questions 1 and 2), write an intellectual response to Pink. Where do you stand on these issues? (See Chapter 3 for help with writing intellectual responses.)

READING AND WRITING TO APPLY AND REFLECT

4. **Apply and Reflect.** Pink's article was written more than ten years ago, which raises questions about its relevance today. Spend time browsing Wikipedia with Pink's

argument or one of his claims in mind. To what extent does what you find on Wikipedia support what Pink has to say? To what extent does today's Wikipedia challenge Pink's argument and claims?

5. **Multimodal Option.** Pink's article was written more than ten years ago, which raises questions about its relevance today. Spend time browsing Wikipedia with Pink's argument or one of his claims in mind. To what extent does what you find on Wikipedia support what Pink has to say? To what extent does today's Wikipedia challenge Pink's argument and claims? Develop a multimodal project that indicates your answers to these questions.

Scan this Book

By Kevin Kelly

The New York Times Magazine

Scan This Book!

This essay explores the digitization of books. Kelly describes how libraries and corporations around the world are digitizing printed books thereby allowing readers to read books online and to move seamlessly from one online book to another through links and tags. Kelly considers what this technology means for readers, reading, copyright law, and libraries.

You will be required to purchase a subscription after you visit *The New York Times Magazine* a certain number of times. Keep this in mind as you are working with this reading.

Visit https://www.nytimes.com/2006/05/14/magazine/14publishing.html

Questions about "Scan this Book"

READING AND WRITING TO COMPREHEND

1. **Rhetorically read and annotate.** In "Scan This Book!," Kelly writes, "Indeed, the only way for books to retain their waning authority in our culture is to wire their texts into the universal library." What does Kelly mean? Why does he use the term "waning?" Read and annotate his piece using one of the reading strategies that you believe will help you understand this quote and its importance to his argument.

2. **Summarize.** Using your annotations in response to question 1, summarize Kelly's argument.

3. **Consider.** Kelly spends a lot of time talking about copyright in this piece. How and why does this matter to his argument?

READING AND WRITING TO RESPOND

4. **Compose.** Using your annotations and your answers to questions 1 through 3, write an intellectual response to address Kelly's argument (see Chapter 3 for help with intellectual responses).

READING AND WRITING TO APPLY AND REFLECT

5. **Reread and compose.** Reread Kelly's text twice in order to apply the Believing/Doubting Game reading strategy. Referring to your annotations from these readings, write a letter to a specific audience of your choice that supports (i.e. "believes") Kelly's argument. You may choose to write to a friend, a parent, or a professor, for example (see Chapter 2 for help with the Believing/Doubting Game strategy).

6. **Compose.** Referring to your annotations indicating your "doubts," write a letter to the author, Kelly, explaining these doubts. Now, look back at your two letters, as well as your intellectual response if you completed one. How do they compare? *So what?*

A Head for Detail

By Clive Thompson

FAST COMPANY

This essay tells the story of seventy-two-year-old computer scientist Gordon Bell whose goal is to never forget anything. With the help of technology, including tiny cameras and audio recorders, Bell is conducting an experiment in "lifelogging" by capturing every aspect of his day-to-day existence. Bell's lifelogging experiment allows Thompson to raise questions about the role of human memory in a world where technology can remember for you.

Visit https://www.fastcompany.com/58044/head-detail

Questions about "A Head for Detail"

READING AND WRITING TO COMPREHEND

1. **Choose.** In this piece, Thompson describes Gordon Bell's experiment in lifelogging. Choose a reading strategy that you believe will help you understand what is involved in lifelogging.

2. **Consider.** As Thompson describes Bell's experiment, there are moments where Thompson's feelings about and attitude toward the experiment emerge, feelings and attitudes that likely affect the reader. Rhetorically read Thompson's piece with an eye toward the kinds of appeals he makes to readers (see Chapter 2 for help with rhetorical reading). What does Thompson want readers to think? How do you know?

3. **Read and reannotate.** Thompson not only develops his position on lifelogging, but he includes what memory experts and others in related fields have to say about similar experiments. Reread and re-annotate Thompson's piece applying a reading strategy that allows you to write a brief summary of the positions he describes.

READING AND WRITING TO RESPOND

4. **Consider.** Using the summary you developed for question 3, write an intellectual response to Thompson's and the others' positions. Where do you stand on these issues? (see Chapter 3 for help with writing intellectual responses)

READING AND WRITING TO APPLY AND REFLECT

5. **Reflect** on Thompson's statement toward the end of his piece: "Whatever it all means, Bell will likely be the first person on the planet to find out." What do you think the implications of "it all" is? Why do you think Thompson doesn't define or more precisely explain what he means by "it all?"

Escape the Echo Chamber

By C. Thi Nguyen

Focusing on echo chambers and epistemic bubbles, this essay explores how the Internet has made it especially easy for like-minded people to engage only with each other and circulate ideas and perspectives among themselves with which they all already agree. The essay also address why it is so hard to escape this phenomenon.

Visit https://aeon.co/essays/why-its-as-hard-to-escape-an-echo-chamber-as-it-is-to-flee-a-cult.

Questions about "Escape the Echo Chamber"

READING AND WRITING TO COMPREHEND

1. **Consider.** In "Escape the Echo Chamber," Nguyen writes, "All it takes to enter an echo chamber is a momentary lapse of intellectual vigilance." What does he mean?
2. **Rhetorically read and annotate** Nguyen's piece with specific attention to his argument and the types of evidence he uses to make his argument (see Chapter 2 for help with rhetorical reading).
3. **Summarize.** Looking back at your annotations, complete a paragraph-long summary of Nguyen's argument and the evidence he uses to make it.

READING AND WRITING TO RESPOND

4. **Consider.** Using your annotations and summary, write from a position you occupy—whether that of a student, a parent, an American, an activist—and explore the implications of Nguyen's argument for you and others that occupy that position (see Chapter 3 for help with intellectual responses).
5. **Multimodal Option.** Using your annotations and summary, and responding from a position you occupy—whether that of a student, a parent, an American, an activ-

ist—develop a response to Nguyen that brings in more than one mode to explore the implications of his argument for you and others that occupy that position.

READING AND WRITING TO APPLY AND REFLECT

6. **Reread and apply.** Reread Nguyen's piece using a reading strategy that helps you understand the distinction and importance of the distinction between epistemic bubbles and echo chambers. Apply these terms to an event (political or otherwise), phenomenon, or a trend. How helpful are these terms in thinking about your subject? To what extent does the distinction between echo chambers and epistemic bubbles (as Nguyen describes it) matter.

The Pace of Modern Life

Anonymous

This comic is comprised of a series of quotations dating back to the 1800s on the subject of modern life. Since the term "modern" itself is relative, this comic allows readers to imagine connections among different periods in history.

Published by xkcd.com.
Visit https://xkcd.com/1227/

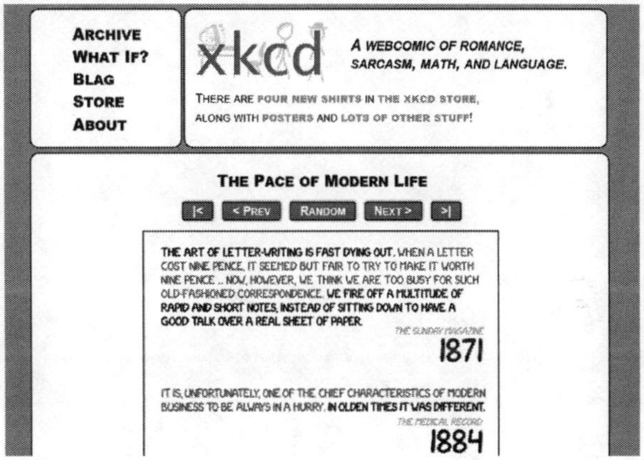

THE ART OF LETTER-WRITING IS FAST DYING OUT. WHEN A LETTER COST NINE PENCE, IT SEEMED BUT FAIR TO TRY TO MAKE IT WORTH NINE PENCE ... NOW, HOWEVER, WE THINK WE ARE TOO BUSY FOR SUCH OLD-FASHIONED CORRESPONDENCE. **WE FIRE OFF A MULTITUDE OF RAPID AND SHORT NOTES, INSTEAD OF SITTING DOWN TO HAVE A GOOD TALK OVER A REAL SHEET OF PAPER.**

THE SUNDAY MAGAZINE

1871

IT IS, UNFORTUNATELY, ONE OF THE CHIEF CHARACTERISTICS OF MODERN BUSINESS TO BE ALWAYS IN A HURRY. **IN OLDEN TIMES IT WAS DIFFERENT.**

THE MEDICAL RECORD

1884

WITH THE ADVENT OF CHEAP NEWSPAPERS AND SUPERIOR MEANS OF LOCOMOTION ... THE DREAMY QUIET OLD DAYS ARE OVER ... FOR **MEN NOW LIVE THINK AND WORK AT EXPRESS SPEED**. THEY HAVE THEIR *MERCURY* OR *POST* LAID ON THEIR BREAKFAST TABLE IN THE EARLY MORNING, AND IF THEY ARE TOO HURRIED TO SNATCH FROM IT THE NEWS DURING THAT MEAL, THEY CARRY IT OFF, TO BE **SULKILY READ AS THEY TRAVEL ... LEAVING THEM NO TIME TO TALK WITH THE FRIEND WHO MAY SHARE THE COMPARTMENT WITH THEM** ... THE HURRY AND BUSTLE OF MODERN LIFE ... LACKS THE QUIET AND REPOSE OF THE PERIOD WHEN OUR FOREFATHERS, THE DAY'S WORK DONE, TOOK THEIR EASE ...

WILLIAM SMITH, *MORLEY: ANCIENT AND MODERN*

1886

CONVERSATION IS SAID TO BE A LOST ART ... GOOD TALK PRESUPPOSES LEISURE, BOTH FOR PREPARATION AND ENJOYMENT. **THE AGE OF LEISURE IS DEAD, AND THE ART OF CONVERSATION IS DYING.**

FRANK LESLIE'S POPULAR MONTHLY, VOLUME 29

1890

INTELLECTUAL LAZINESS AND THE HURRY OF THE AGE HAVE PRODUCED **A CRAVING FOR LITERARY NIPS.** THE TORPID BRAIN ... HAS GROWN TOO WEAK FOR SUSTAINED THOUGHT.

THERE NEVER WAS AN AGE IN WHICH SO MANY PEOPLE WERE ABLE TO WRITE BADLY.

ISRAEL ZANGWILL, *THE BACHELORS' CLUB*

1891

THE ART OF PURE LINE ENGRAVING IS DYING OUT. WE LIVE AT TOO FAST A RATE TO ALLOW FOR THE PREPARATION OF SUCH PLATES AS OUR FATHERS APPRECIATED. IF A PICTURE CATCHES THE PUBLIC FANCY, THE PUBLIC MUST HAVE AN ETCHED OR A PHOTOGRAVURED COPY OF IT WITHIN A MONTH OR TWO OF ITS APPEARANCE, THE DAYS WHEN ENGRAVERS WERE WONT TO SPEND TWO OR THREE YEARS OVER A SINGLE PLATE ARE FOR EVER GONE.

JOURNAL OF THE INSTITUTE OF JAMAICA, VOLUME I

1892

SO MUCH IS EXHIBITED TO THE EYE THAT **NOTHING IS LEFT TO THE IMAGINATION.** IT SOMETIMES SEEMS ALMOST POSSIBLE THAT THE MODERN WORLD MIGHT BE CHOKED BY ITS OWN RICHES, **AND HUMAN FACULTY DWINDLE AWAY AMID THE MILLION INVENTIONS THAT HAVE BEEN INTRODUCED TO RENDER ITS EXERCISE UNNECESSARY.**

THE ARTICLES IN THE *QUARTERLIES* EXTEND TO THIRTY OR MORE PAGES, BUT **THIRTY PAGES IS NOW TOO MUCH**. SO WE WITNESS A FURTHER CONDENSING PROCESS AND, WE HAVE THE *FORTNIGHTLY* AND THE *CONTEMPORARY* WHICH REDUCE THIRTY PAGES TO **FIFTEEN PAGES** SO THAT YOU MAY READ A LARGER NUMBER OF ARTICLES IN A SHORTER TIME AND IN A SHORTER FORM. AS IF THIS LAST CONDENSING PROCESS WERE NOT ENOUGH THE CONDENSED ARTICLES OF THESE PERIODICALS ARE **FURTHER CONDENSED** BY THE DAILY PAPERS, WHICH WILL GIVE YOU **A SUMMARY OF THE SUMMARY** OF ALL THAT HAS BEEN WRITTEN ABOUT EVERYTHING.

THOSE WHO ARE DIPPING INTO SO MANY SUBJECTS AND GATHERING INFORMATION IN A SUMMARY AND SUPERFICIAL FORM LOSE THE HABIT OF SETTLING DOWN TO GREAT WORKS.

EPHEMERAL LITERATURE IS DRIVING OUT THE GREAT CLASSICS OF THE PRESENT AND THE PAST ... **HURRIED READING CAN NEVER BE GOOD READING.**

G. J. GOSCHEN, *FIRST ANNUAL ADDRESS TO THE STUDENTS*, TOYNBEE HALL, LONDON

1894

THE EXISTENCE OF **MENTAL AND NERVOUS DEGENERATION AMONG A GROWING CLASS OF PEOPLE**, ESPECIALLY IN LARGE CITIES, IS AN OBVIOUS PHENOMENON ... THE MANIA FOR STIMULANTS ... DISEASES OF THE MIND ARE ALMOST AS NUMEROUS AS THE DISEASES OF THE BODY ... THIS INTELLECTUAL CONDITION IS CHARACTERIZED BY **A BRAIN INCAPABLE OF NORMAL WORKING ... IN A LARGE MEASURE DUE TO THE HURRY AND EXCITEMENT OF MODERN LIFE**, WITH ITS FACILITIES FOR RAPID LOCOMOTION AND **ALMOST INSTANTANEOUS COMMUNICATION BETWEEN REMOTE POINTS OF THE GLOBE** ...

THE CHURCHMAN, VOLUME 71

1895

IF WE **TEACH THE CHILDREN HOW TO PLAY** AND ENCOURAGE THEM IN THEIR SPORTS ... **INSTEAD OF SHUTTING THEM IN BADLY VENTILATED SCHOOLROOMS**, THE NEXT GENERATION WILL BE MORE JOYOUS AND WILL BE HEALTHIER THAN THE PRESENT ONE.

PUBLIC OPINION: A COMPREHENSIVE SUMMARY OF THE PRESS THROUGHOUT THE WORLD, VOLUME 18

1895

THE CAUSE OF THE ... INCREASE IN NERVOUS DISEASE IS **INCREASED DEMAND MADE BY THE CONDITIONS OF MODERN LIFE UPON THE BRAIN**. EVERYTHING IS DONE IN A HURRY. **WE TALK ACROSS A CONTINENT, TELEGRAPH ACROSS AN OCEAN**, TAKE A TRIP TO CHICAGO FOR AN HOUR'S TALK ... **WE TAKE EVEN OUR PLEASURES SADLY AND MAKE A TASK OF OUR PLAY** ... WHAT WONDER IF THE PRESSURE IS ALMOST MORE THAN OUR NERVES CAN BEAR.

G. SHRADY (FROM P. C. KNAPP)
"ARE NERVOUS DISEASES INCREASING?" *MEDICAL RECORD*

1896

THE MANAGERS OF SENSATIONAL NEWSPAPERS ... DO NOT TRY TO EDUCATE THEIR READERS AND MAKE THEM BETTER, BUT TEND TO **CREATE PERVERTED TASTES AND DEVELOP VICIOUS TENDENCIES**. THE OWNERS OF THESE PAPERS SEEM TO HAVE BUT ONE PURPOSE, AND THAT IS TO INCREASE THEIR CIRCULATION.

MEDICAL BRIEF, VOLUME 26

1898

TO TAKE SUFFICIENT TIME FOR OUR MEALS SEEMS FREQUENTLY IMPOSSIBLE ON ACCOUNT OF THE DEMANDS ON OUR TIME MADE BY OUR BUSINESS ... WE ACT ON THE APPARENT BELIEF THAT ALL OF OUR BUSINESS IS SO PRESSING THAT WE MUST JUMP ON THE QUICKEST CAR HOME, EAT OUR DINNER IN THE MOST HURRIED WAY, MAKE THE CLOSEST CONNECTION FOR A CAR RETURNING ...

LOUIS JOHN RETTGER,
STUDIES IN ADVANCED PHYSIOLOGY

1898

IN THESE DAYS OF INCREASING RAPID ARTIFICIAL LOCOMOTION, **MAY I BE PERMITTED TO SAY A WORD IN FAVOUR OF A VERY WORTHY AND VALUABLE OLD FRIEND OF MINE, MR. LONG WALK?**

I AM AFRAID THAT THIS GOOD GENTLEMAN IS IN DANGER OF GETTING NEGLECTED, IF NOT FORGOTTEN. WE LIVE IN DAYS OF WATER TRIPS AND LAND TRIPS, EXCURSIONS BY SEA, ROAD AND RAIL–BICYCLES AND TRICYCLES, TRAM CARS AND MOTOR CARS ... BUT IN MY HUMBLE OPINION, GOOD HONEST WALKING EXERCISE FOR HEALTH BEATS ALL OTHER KINDS OF LOCOMOTION INTO A COCKED HAT.

T. THATCHER, "A PLEA FOR A LONG WALK",
THE PUBLISHERS' CIRCULAR

1902

THE ART OF CONVERSATION IS ALMOST A LOST ONE. **PEOPLE TALK AS THEY RIDE BICYCLES–AT A RUSH–WITHOUT PAUSING TO CONSIDER THEIR SURROUNDINGS** ... WHAT HAS BEEN GENERALLY UNDERSTOOD AS CULTURED SOCIETY IS RAPIDLY DETERIORATING INTO BASENESS AND VOLUNTARY IGNORANCE. **THE PROFESSION OF LETTERS IS SO LITTLE UNDERSTOOD**, AND SO FAR FROM BEING SERIOUSLY APPRECIATED, THAT ... NEWSPAPERS ARE FULL, NOT OF THOUGHTFUL HONESTLY EXPRESSED PUBLIC OPINION ON THE AFFAIRS OF THE

NATION, BUT OF VAPID PERSONALITIES INTERESTING TO NONE SAVE GOSSIPS AND BUSY BODIES.

MARIE CORELLI,
FREE OPINIONS, FREELY EXPRESSED

1905

THERE IS A GREAT **TENDENCY AMONG THE CHILDREN OF TODAY TO REBEL AGAINST RESTRAINT**, NOT ONLY THAT PLACED UPON THEM BY THE WILL OF THE PARENT, BUT AGAINST ANY RESTRAINT OR LIMITATION OF WHAT THEY CONSIDER THEIR RIGHTS ... THIS FACT HAS FILLED WELL MINDED PEOPLE WITH GREAT APPREHENSIONS FOR THE FUTURE.

REV. HENRY HUSSMANN,
THE AUTHORITY OF PARENTS

1906

OUR MODERN FAMILY GATHERING, SILENT AROUND THE FIRE, **EACH INDIVIDUAL WITH HIS HEAD BURIED IN HIS FAVOURITE MAGAZINE**, IS THE SOMEWHAT NATURAL OUTCOME OF THE BANISHMENT OF COLLOQUY FROM THE SCHOOL ...

THE JOURNAL OF EDUCATION, VOLUME 29

1907

PLAYS IN THEATRES AT THE PRESENT TIME PRESENT SPECTACLES AND **DEAL OPENLY WITH SITUATIONS WHICH NO PERSON WOULD HAVE DARED TO MENTION IN GENERAL SOCIETY FORTY YEARS AGO** ... THE CURRENT REPRESENTATIONS OF **NUDE MEN AND WOMEN IN THE DAILY JOURNALS** AND THE ILLUSTRATED MAGAZINES WOULD HAVE EXCLUDED SUCH PERIODICALS FROM ALL RESPECTABLE FAMILIES TWO DECADES AGO ... THOSE WHO HAVE BEEN DIVORCED ... FORTY AND FIFTY YEARS AGO LOST AT ONCE AND IRREVOCABLY THEIR

Questions about "The Pace of Modern Life"

READING AND WRITING TO COMPREHEND

1. **Choose.** Although not as clearly as the more traditional reading selections in this chapter, "The Pace of Modern Life" makes an argument. Choose a reading strategy that will allow you to summarize this argument and complete a brief summary.

2. **Apply** the mapping strategy to this reading to help you understand how the different quotations work together (see Chapter 2 for help with mapping).

READING AND WRITING TO RESPOND

3. **Reread and Synthesize.** Re-read "The Pace of Modern Life" using a reading strategy of your choice in order to consider how you could connect this text to the others in this chapter. Write a synthesis of at least 3 selections in the chapter, including "The Pace of Modern Life" (see Chapter 3 for help with syntheses). Be sure to include your intellectual response (see Chapter 3 for help with intellectual responses) in the synthesis.

READING AND WRITING TO APPLY AND REFLECT

4. **Reread and Compile.** Re-read "The Pace of Modern Life" using the RLW strategy in order to develop your own text using the same techniques. Compile a series of quotations that allow you to make an argument on a subject of your choice.

5. **Reflect.** How does the form of the text, which is comprised of unattributed quotations, affect how you read the text? Did you approach this text differently from other texts? Explain your answer.

6. **Multimodal Option.** Develop a multimodal project that compiles a series of quotations allowing you to make an argument on a subject of your choice.

LONG WRITING ASSIGNMENTS BASED ON READINGS IN CHAPTER 7: READING, WRITING, AND TECHNOLOGY

1. The authors of the selections in this chapter are concerned with the contemporary place of technology, as well as the future role of technology. Yet, many authors consistently look to the past, to history, as well. In order to inquire into the role that history plays in this larger discussion about technology, **write** an essay that explores how at least two of the authors address history. **Develop** an academic argument that addresses why history is so important to the discussion about current and future technologies (see Chapter 4 for help with developing an academic argument). **Revisit** the annotations you already have on the texts to determine how

helpful those are. It is likely that you will need to **reread** the selections by applying a reading strategy that you think will be most effective for completing this particular assignment.

2. **Multimodal Option.** Develop a multimodal project that allows you to make an argument about the importance of history to these more contemporary discussions of technology.

3. Whether exploring Wikipedia or digital libraries, several of the selections in this chapter describe how technology breathes life into otherwise static objects. Reread the selections in this chapter in order to see how authors describe the difference between the static object and the more dynamic product. Choose a technological advance that you believe has created a more dynamic version of something. Make sure your object is not addressed in this chapter of readings. View this advance through the lens of the authors' arguments from this chapter. To what extent does the object support what the authors have to say? To what extent does it challenge the authors' argument? **Revisit** the annotations you already have on the texts to determine how helpful those are. It is likely that you will need to **reread** the selections by applying a reading strategy that you think will be most effective for completing this particular assignment.

4. The authors of the selections in this chapter rely on the three rhetorical appeals (ethos, pathos, and logos) to differing degrees. **Write** an essay in which you explore which method of persuasion seems most common, and develop an argument as to why that type of appeal is the preferred one when it comes to this subject (see Chapter 2 for help with rhetorical appeals). **Revisit** the annotations you already have on the texts to determine how helpful those are. You will likely need to **reread** the selections by applying a reading strategy that you think will be most effective for completing this particular assignment.

5. Many of the selections in this chapter were written about a decade ago. **Develop** an essay—using one of the author's arguments as a lens—in which you explore a current technology or a handful of related, current technologies in order to discover what the author might say about these. In other words, extend the author's argument so that it addresses a current technology. What would the author notice about your chosen technology? What observations might the author make? What

position might the author take in relation to its use(s)? Ground your answers to these questions in evidence from the text. **Revisit** the annotations you already have on the texts to determine how helpful those are. You will likely need to **reread** the selections by applying a reading strategy that you think will be most effective for completing this particular assignment.

6. **Multimodal Option.** Explore a current technology or a handful of related, current technologies in order to discover what an author of one of the texts in this chapter might say about these. In other words, extend the author's argument so that it addresses a current technology. What would the author notice about your chosen technology? What observations might the author make? What position might the author take in relation to its use(s)? Use the very form of technology that you have chosen in order to extend the author's argument so that it addresses this technology.

REFLECTING ON YOUR READING STRATEGIES AND ANNOTATIONS

Consider the different reading strategies you applied while reading the selections in this chapter. Which were most useful for understanding the text? For writing a summary? For figuring out what you think? For responding to the text? For imitating an author's style? Anticipate future uses of these reading strategies in this class, in other classes, and in other contexts. Consider previous courses and contexts in which these strategies would have been helpful.

Chapter 8. Expertise and Technology

This chapter includes selections that address the relationship between expertise and technology. Opening with Plato's "Allegory of the Cave," this chapter relies on a broad definition of technology in which technology is defined as a tool or instrument. In "Allegory of the Cave," a dialogue between Socrates and his student Glaucon, Socrates reflects on—among other things—the relationship between teacher and student or expert and novice, and he considers the best way for teachers to share their expertise. The technology piece comes in the form of the tool that Socrates uses to make his points, namely the technology of puppets, which play an important role in this allegory. While readers may not readily recognize a puppet—a child's toy—as a form of technology—when technology is defined as a tool or an instrument, then the puppets used in the allegory can be understood as technologies and, more specifically, communication technologies that allow Socrates to argue his points. Moreover, the puppets also become virtual reality technologies in that they are used to explore reality. In fact, drawing on the work of Grau and Dibbell, cyberlaw scholar Greg Lastowka argues that virtual reality technologies of today do not differ all that much from prior technologies. Lastowka notes that "puppetry, costumes, painting, photography, film and robotics provide essentially the same sorts of pleasures and anxieties we derive from more recent virtual technologies" (482). He continues, "The shock and thrill we experience by watching a three-dimensional film like *Avatar* is just the latest way in which we find pleasure in the confusion between reality and artifice" (482).

The three other selections in this chapter traffic in more common definitions of technology as Lanier's "Digital Maoism," Howe's "The Rise of Crowdsourcing," and McGrath's "It Should Happen to You" explore Wikipedia, the open source software movement, and YouTube, respectively. Because these pieces were written several years ago, readers are given a glimpse into these worlds as they were still coalescing and their products were nowhere near as mainstream or as popular as they are today. These early perspectives on brand new technologies (YouTube was less than a year old when McGrath wrote his piece!) give readers rare access to the early responses to them, as well as the opportunity to reflect on how they have changed since their inception.

For Further Reading

Lastowka, Greg. "Defining the Virtual." *The Oxford Handbook of Virtuality*, edited by Mark Grimshaw, Oxford UP, pp. 481–495.

Mark Grimshaw, editor. *The Oxford Handbook of Virtuality.* Oxford UP, 2014.

PRIOR TO READING EACH SELECTION IN THIS CHAPTER

Look at the questions after each reading. What are you expected to do after reading this selection? In other words, what are your purposes for reading? Although you will be asked to apply particular reading strategies in order to complete some of the tasks, others will leave the choice of strategy up to you. Refer to the descriptions of the reading strategies in Chapter 2 and decide which will be most useful in helping you accomplish those tasks. Remember that you will be reading each selection multiple times and, therefore, will have additional opportunities to apply different reading strategies.

READINGS

The Allegory of the Cave

By Plato

The "Allegory of the Cave" is a philosophical theory that Plato puts forth in *The Republic*. Plato presents his theory as a dialogue between Glaucon, a student, and Socrates, his mentor or teacher. The piece raises questions about knowledge and how we come to know and understand the world around us.

Plato. "The Allegory of the Cave." *The Republic*, Book VII. Available through Project Gutenberg at http://www.gutenberg.org/files/1497/1497-h/1497-h.htm#link2H_4_0010. (Follow the "Read this Book Online" link and scroll down to Book VII.)

BOOK VII

And now, I said, let me show in a figure how far our nature is enlightened or unenlightened:—Behold! human beings living in a underground den, which has a mouth open towards the light and reaching all along the den; here they have been from their childhood, and have their legs and necks chained so that they cannot move, and can only see before them, being prevented by the chains from turning round their heads. Above and behind them a fire is blazing at a distance, and between the fire and the prisoners there is a raised way; and you will see, if you look, a low wall built along the way, like the screen which marionette players have in front of them, over which they show the puppets.

I see.

And do you see, I said, men passing along the wall carrying all sorts of vessels, and statues and figures of animals made of wood and stone and various materials, which appear over the wall? Some of them are talking, others silent.

You have shown me a strange image, and they are strange prisoners.

Like ourselves, I replied; and they see only their own shadows, or the shadows of one another, which the fire throws on the opposite wall of the cave?

True, he said; how could they see anything but the shadows if they were never allowed to move their heads?

And of the objects which are being carried in like manner they would only see the shadows?

Yes, he said.

And if they were able to converse with one another, would they not suppose that they were naming what was actually before them?

Very true.

And suppose further that the prison had an echo which came from the other side, would they not be sure to fancy when one of the passers-by spoke that the voice which they heard came from the passing shadow?

No question, he replied.

To them, I said, the truth would be literally nothing but the shadows of the images.

That is certain.

And now look again, and see what will naturally follow if the prisoners are released and disabused of their error. At first, when any of them is liberated and compelled suddenly to stand up and turn his neck round and walk and look towards the light, he will suffer sharp pains; the glare will distress him, and he will be unable to see the realities of which in his former state he had seen the shadows; and then conceive some one saying to him, that what he saw before was an illusion, but that now, when he is approaching nearer to being and his eye is turned towards more real existence, he has a clearer vision,—what will be his reply? And you may further imagine that his instructor is pointing to the objects as they pass and requiring him to name them,—will he not be perplexed? Will he not fancy that the shadows which he formerly saw are truer than the objects which are now shown to him?

Far truer.

And if he is compelled to look straight at the light, will he not have a pain in his eyes which will make him turn away to take refuge in the objects of vision which he can see, and which he will conceive to be in reality clearer than the things which are now being shown to him?

True, he said.

And suppose once more, that he is reluctantly dragged up a steep and rugged ascent, and held fast until he is forced into the presence of the sun himself, is he not likely to be pained and irritated? When he approaches the light his eyes will be dazzled, and he will not be able to see anything at all of what are now called realities.

Not all in a moment, he said.

He will require to grow accustomed to the sight of the upper world. And first he will see the shadows best, next the reflections of men and other objects in the water, and then the objects themselves; then he will gaze upon the light of the moon and the stars and the spangled heaven; and he will see the sky and the stars by night better than the sun or the light of the sun by day?

Certainly.

Last of all he will be able to see the sun, and not mere reflections of him in the water, but he will see him in his own proper place, and not in another; and he will contemplate him as he is.

Certainly.

He will then proceed to argue that this is he who gives the season and the years, and is the guardian of all that is in the visible world, and in a certain way the cause of all things which he and his fellows have been accustomed to behold?

Clearly, he said, he would first see the sun and then reason about him.

And when he remembered his old habitation, and the wisdom of the den and his fellow-prisoners, do you not suppose that he would felicitate himself on the change, and pity them?

Certainly, he would.

And if they were in the habit of conferring honours among themselves on those who were quickest to observe the passing shadows and to remark which of them went before, and which followed after, and which were together; and who were therefore best able to draw conclusions as to the future, do you think that he would care for such honours and glories, or envy the possessors of them? Would he not say with Homer,

'Better to be the poor servant of a poor master,'

and to endure anything, rather than think as they do and live after their manner?

Yes, he said, I think that he would rather suffer anything than entertain these false notions and live in this miserable manner.

Imagine once more, I said, such an one coming suddenly out of the sun to be replaced in his old situation; would he not be certain to have his eyes full of darkness?

To be sure, he said.

And if there were a contest, and he had to compete in measuring the shadows with the prisoners who had never moved out of the den, while his sight was still weak, and before his eyes had become steady (and the time which would be needed to acquire this new habit of sight might be very considerable), would he not be ridiculous? Men would say of him that up he went and down he came without his eyes; and that it was better not even to think of ascending; and if any one tried to loose another and lead him up to the light, let them only catch the offender, and they would put him to death.

No question, he said.

This entire allegory, I said, you may now append, dear Glaucon, to the previous argument; the prison-house is the world of sight, the light of the fire is the sun, and you will not misapprehend me if you interpret the journey upwards to be the ascent of the soul into the intellectual world according to my poor belief, which, at your desire, I have expressed—whether rightly or wrongly God knows. But, whether true or false, my opinion is that in the world of knowledge the idea of good appears last of all, and is seen only with an effort; and, when seen, is also inferred to be the universal author of all things beautiful and right, parent of light and of the lord of light in this visible world, and the immediate source of reason and truth in the intellectual; and that this is the power upon which he who would act rationally either in public or private life must have his eye fixed.

I agree, he said, as far as I am able to understand you.

Moreover, I said, you must not wonder that those who attain to this beatific vision are unwilling to descend to human affairs; for their souls are ever hastening into the upper world where they desire to dwell; which desire of theirs is very natural, if our allegory may be trusted.

Yes, very natural.

And is there anything surprising in one who passes from divine contemplations to the evil state of man, misbehaving himself in a ridiculous manner; if, while his eyes are blinking and before he has become accustomed to the surrounding darkness, he is compelled to fight in courts of law, or in other places, about the images or the shadows of images of justice, and is endeavouring to meet the conceptions of those who have never yet seen absolute justice?

Anything but surprising, he replied.

Any one who has common sense will remember that the bewilderments of the eyes are of two kinds, and arise from two causes, either from coming out of the light or from going into the light, which is true of the mind's eye, quite as much as of the bodily eye; and he who remembers this when he sees any one whose vision is perplexed and weak, will not be too ready to laugh; he will first ask whether that soul of man has come out of the brighter life, and is unable to see because unaccustomed to the dark, or having turned from darkness to the day is dazzled by excess of light. And he will count the one happy in his condition and state of being, and he will pity the other; or, if he have a mind to laugh at the soul which comes from below into the light, there will be more reason in this than in the laugh which greets him who returns from above out of the light into the den.

That, he said, is a very just distinction.

But then, if I am right, certain professors of education must be wrong when they say that they can put a knowledge into the soul which was not there before, like sight into blind eyes.

They undoubtedly say this, he replied.

Whereas, our argument shows that the power and capacity of learning exists in the soul already; and that just as the eye was unable to turn from darkness to light without the whole body, so too the instrument of knowledge can only by the movement of the whole soul be turned from the world of becoming into that of being, and learn by degrees to endure the sight of being, and of the brightest and best of being, or in other words, of the good.

Very true.

And must there not be some art which will effect conversion in the easiest and quickest manner; not implanting the faculty of sight, for that exists already, but has been turned in the wrong direction, and is looking away from the truth?

Yes, he said, such an art may be presumed.

And whereas the other so-called virtues of the soul seem to be akin to bodily qualities, for even when they are not originally innate they can be implanted later by habit and exercise, the virtue of wisdom more than anything else contains a divine element which always remains, and by this conversion is rendered useful and profitable; or, on the other hand, hurtful and useless. Did you never observe the narrow intelligence flashing from the keen eye of a clever rogue—how eager he is, how clearly his paltry soul sees the way to his end; he is the reverse of blind, but his keen eye-sight is forced into the service of evil, and he is mischievous in proportion to his cleverness?

Very true, he said.

But what if there had been a circumcision of such natures in the days of their youth; and they had been severed from those sensual pleasures, such as eating and drinking, which, like leaden weights, were attached to them at their birth, and which drag them down and turn the vision of their souls upon the things that are below—if, I say, they had been released from these impediments and turned in the opposite direction, the very same faculty in them would have seen the truth as keenly as they see what their eyes are turned to now.

Very likely.

Yes, I said; and there is another thing which is likely, or rather a necessary inference from what has preceded, that neither the uneducated and uninformed of the truth, nor yet those who never make an end of their education, will be able ministers of State; not the former, because they have no single aim of duty which is the rule of all their actions, private as well as public; nor the latter, because they will not act at all except upon compulsion, fancying that they are already dwelling apart in the islands of the blest.

Very true, he replied.

Then, I said, the business of us who are the founders of the State will be to compel the best minds to attain that knowledge which we have already shown to be the greatest of all—they must continue to ascend until they arrive at the good; but when they have ascended and seen enough we must not allow them to do as they do now.

What do you mean?

I mean that they remain in the upper world: but this must not be allowed; they must be made to descend again among the prisoners in the den, and partake of their labours and honours, whether they are worth having or not.

But is not this unjust? he said; ought we to give them a worse life, when they might have a better?

You have again forgotten, my friend, I said, the intention of the legislator, who did not aim at making any one class in the State happy above the rest; the happiness was to be in the whole State, and he held the citizens together by persuasion and necessity, making them benefactors of the State, and therefore benefactors of one another; to this end he created them, not to please themselves, but to be his instruments in binding up the State.

True, he said, I had forgotten.

Observe, Glaucon, that there will be no injustice in compelling our philosophers to have a care and providence of others; we shall explain to them that in other States, men of their class are not obliged to share in the toils of politics: and this is reasonable, for they grow up at their own sweet will, and the government would rather not have them. Being self-taught, they cannot be expected to show any gratitude for a culture which they have never received. But we have brought you into the world to be rulers of the hive, kings of yourselves and of the other citizens, and have educated you far better and more perfectly than they have been educated, and you are better able to share in the double duty. Wherefore each of you, when his turn comes, must go down to the general underground abode, and get the habit of seeing in the dark. When you have acquired the habit, you will see ten thousand times better than the inhabitants of the den, and you will know what the several images are, and what they represent, because you have seen the beautiful and just and good in their truth. And thus our State, which is also yours, will be a reality, and not a dream only, and will be administered in a spirit unlike that of other States, in which men fight with one another about shadows only and are distracted in the struggle for power, which in their eyes is a great good. Whereas the truth is that the State in which the rulers are most reluctant to govern is always the best and most quietly governed, and the State in which they are most eager, the worst.

Quite true, he replied.

And will our pupils, when they hear this, refuse to take their turn at the toils of State, when they are allowed to spend the greater part of their time with one another in the heavenly light?

Impossible, he answered; for they are just men, and the commands which we impose upon them are just; there can be no doubt that every one of them will take office as a stern necessity, and not after the fashion of our present rulers of State.

Yes, my friend, I said; and there lies the point. You must contrive for your future rulers another and a better life than that of a ruler, and then you may have a well-ordered State; for only in the State which offers this, will they rule who are truly rich, not in silver and gold, but in virtue and wisdom, which are the true blessings of life. Whereas if they go to the administration of public affairs, poor and hungering after their own private advantage, thinking that hence they are to snatch the chief good, order there can never be; for they will be fighting about office, and the civil and domestic broils which thus arise will be the ruin of the rulers themselves and of the whole State.

Most true, he replied.

And the only life which looks down upon the life of political ambition is that of true philosophy. Do you know of any other?

Indeed, I do not, he said.

And those who govern ought not to be lovers of the task? For, if they are, there will be rival lovers, and they will fight.

No question.

Who then are those whom we shall compel to be guardians? Surely they will be the men who are wisest about affairs of State, and by whom the State is best administered, and who at the same time have other honours and another and a better life than that of politics?

They are the men, and I will choose them, he replied.

And now shall we consider in what way such guardians will be produced, and how they are to be brought from darkness to light,—as some are said to have ascended from the world below to the gods?

By all means, he replied.

The process, I said, is not the turning over of an oyster-shell (In allusion to a game in which two parties fled or pursued according as an oyster-shell which was thrown into the air fell with the dark or light side uppermost.), but the turning round of a soul passing from a day which is little better than night to the true day of being, that is, the ascent from below, which we affirm to be true philosophy?

Quite so.

And should we not enquire what sort of knowledge has the power of effecting such a change?

Certainly.

What sort of knowledge is there which would draw the soul from becoming to being? And another consideration has just occurred to me: You will remember that our young men are to be warrior athletes?

Yes, that was said.

Then this new kind of knowledge must have an additional quality?

What quality?

Usefulness in war.

Yes, if possible.

There were two parts in our former scheme of education, were there not?

Just so.

There was gymnastic which presided over the growth and decay of the body, and may therefore be regarded as having to do with generation and corruption?

True.

Then that is not the knowledge which we are seeking to discover?

No.

But what do you say of music, which also entered to a certain extent into our former scheme?

Music, he said, as you will remember, was the counterpart of gymnastic, and trained the guardians by the influences of habit, by harmony making them harmonious, by rhythm rhythmical, but not giving them science; and the words, whether fabulous or possibly true, had kindred elements of rhythm and harmony in them. But in music there was nothing which tended to that good which you are now seeking.

You are most accurate, I said, in your recollection; in music there certainly was nothing of the kind. But what branch of knowledge is there, my dear Glaucon, which is of the desired nature; since all the useful arts were reckoned mean by us?

Undoubtedly; and yet if music and gymnastic are excluded, and the arts are also excluded, what remains?

Well, I said, there may be nothing left of our special subjects; and then we shall have to take something which is not special, but of universal application.

What may that be?

A something which all arts and sciences and intelligences use in common, and which every one first has to learn among the elements of education.

What is that?

The little matter of distinguishing one, two, and three—in a word, number and calculation:—do not all arts and sciences necessarily partake of them?

Yes.

Then the art of war partakes of them?

To be sure.

Then Palamedes, whenever he appears in tragedy, proves Agamemnon ridiculously unfit to be a general. Did you never remark how he declares that he had invented number, and had numbered the ships and set in array the ranks of the army at Troy; which implies that they had never been numbered before, and Agamemnon must be supposed literally to have been incapable of counting his own feet—how could he if he was ignorant of number? And if that is true, what sort of general must he have been?

I should say a very strange one, if this was as you say.

Can we deny that a warrior should have a knowledge of arithmetic?

Certainly he should, if he is to have the smallest understanding of military tactics, or indeed, I should rather say, if he is to be a man at all.

I should like to know whether you have the same notion which I have of this study?

What is your notion?

It appears to me to be a study of the kind which we are seeking, and which leads naturally to reflection, but never to have been rightly used; for the true use of it is simply to draw the soul towards being.

Will you explain your meaning? he said.

I will try, I said; and I wish you would share the enquiry with me, and say 'yes' or 'no' when I attempt to distinguish in my own mind what branches of knowledge have this attracting power, in order that we may have clearer proof that arithmetic is, as I suspect, one of them.

Explain, he said.

I mean to say that objects of sense are of two kinds; some of them do not invite thought because the sense is an adequate judge of them; while in the case of other objects sense is so untrustworthy that further enquiry is imperatively demanded.

You are clearly referring, he said, to the manner in which the senses are imposed upon by distance, and by painting in light and shade.

No, I said, that is not at all my meaning.

Then what is your meaning?

When speaking of uninviting objects, I mean those which do not pass from one sensation to the opposite; inviting objects are those which do; in this latter case the sense coming upon the object, whether at a distance or near, gives no more vivid idea of anything in particular than of its opposite. An illustration will make my meaning clearer:—here are three fingers—a little finger, a second finger, and a middle finger.

Very good.

You may suppose that they are seen quite close: And here comes the point.

What is it?

Each of them equally appears a finger, whether seen in the middle or at the extremity, whether white or black, or thick or thin—it makes no difference; a finger is a finger all the same. In these cases a man is not compelled to ask of thought the question what is a finger? for the sight never intimates to the mind that a finger is other than a finger.

True.

And therefore, I said, as we might expect, there is nothing here which invites or excites intelligence.

There is not, he said.

But is this equally true of the greatness and smallness of the fingers? Can sight adequately perceive them? and is no difference made by the circumstance that one of the fingers is in the middle and another at the extremity? And in like manner does the touch adequately perceive the qualities of thickness or thinness, of softness or hardness? And so of the other senses; do they give perfect intimations of such matters? Is not their mode of operation on this wise—the sense which is concerned with the quality of hardness is necessarily concerned also with the quality of softness, and only intimates to the soul that the same thing is felt to be both hard and soft?

You are quite right, he said.

And must not the soul be perplexed at this intimation which the sense gives of a hard which is also soft? What, again, is the meaning of light and heavy, if that which is light is also heavy, and that which is heavy, light?

Yes, he said, these intimations which the soul receives are very curious and require to be explained.

Yes, I said, and in these perplexities the soul naturally summons to her aid calculation and intelligence, that she may see whether the several objects announced to her are one or two.

True.

And if they turn out to be two, is not each of them one and different?

Certainly.

And if each is one, and both are two, she will conceive the two as in a state of division, for if there were undivided they could only be conceived of as one?

True.

The eye certainly did see both small and great, but only in a confused manner; they were not distinguished.

Yes.

Whereas the thinking mind, intending to light up the chaos, was compelled to reverse the process, and look at small and great as separate and not confused.

Very true.

Was not this the beginning of the enquiry 'What is great?' and 'What is small?'

Exactly so.

And thus arose the distinction of the visible and the intelligible.

Most true.

This was what I meant when I spoke of impressions which invited the intellect, or the reverse—those which are simultaneous with opposite impressions, invite thought; those which are not simultaneous do not.

I understand, he said, and agree with you.

And to which class do unity and number belong?

I do not know, he replied.

Think a little and you will see that what has preceded will supply the answer; for if simple unity could be adequately perceived by the sight or by any other sense, then, as we were saying in the case of the finger, there would be nothing to attract towards being; but when there is some contradiction always present, and one is the reverse of one and involves the conception of plurality, then thought begins to be aroused within us, and the soul perplexed and wanting to arrive at a decision asks 'What is absolute unity?' This is the way in which the study of the one has a power of drawing and converting the mind to the contemplation of true being.

And surely, he said, this occurs notably in the case of one; for we see the same thing to be both one and infinite in multitude?

Yes, I said; and this being true of one must be equally true of all number?

Certainly.

And all arithmetic and calculation have to do with number?

Yes.

And they appear to lead the mind towards truth?

Yes, in a very remarkable manner.

Then this is knowledge of the kind for which we are seeking, having a double use, military and philosophical; for the man of war must learn the art of number or he will not know how to array his troops, and the philosopher also, because he has to rise out of the sea of change and lay hold of true being, and therefore he must be an arithmetician.

That is true.

And our guardian is both warrior and philosopher?

Certainly.

Then this is a kind of knowledge which legislation may fitly prescribe; and we must endeavour to persuade those who are to be the principal men of our State to go and learn arithmetic, not as amateurs, but they must carry on the study until they see the nature of numbers with the mind only; nor again, like merchants or retail-traders, with a view to buying or selling, but for the sake of their military use, and of the soul herself; and because this will be the easiest way for her to pass from becoming to truth and being.

That is excellent, he said.

Yes, I said, and now having spoken of it, I must add how charming the science is! and in how many ways it conduces to our desired end, if pursued in the spirit of a philosopher, and not of a shopkeeper!

How do you mean?

I mean, as I was saying, that arithmetic has a very great and elevating effect, compelling the soul to reason about abstract number, and rebelling against the introduction of visible or tangible objects into the argument. You know how steadily the masters of the art repel and ridicule any one who attempts to divide absolute unity when he is calculating, and if you divide, they multiply (Meaning either (1) that they integrate the number because they deny the possibility of fractions; or (2) that division is regarded by them as a process of multiplication, for the fractions of one continue to be units.), taking care that one shall continue one and not become lost in fractions.

That is very true.

Now, suppose a person were to say to them: O my friends, what are these wonderful numbers about which you are reasoning, in which, as you say, there is a unity such as you demand, and each unit is equal, invariable, indivisible,—what would they answer?

They would answer, as I should conceive, that they were speaking of those numbers which can only be realized in thought.

Then you see that this knowledge may be truly called necessary, necessitating as it clearly does the use of the pure intelligence in the attainment of pure truth?

Yes; that is a marked characteristic of it.

And have you further observed, that those who have a natural talent for calculation are generally quick at every other kind of knowledge; and even the dull, if they have had an arithmetical training, although they may derive no other advantage from it, always become much quicker than they would otherwise have been.

Very true, he said.

And indeed, you will not easily find a more difficult study, and not many as difficult.

You will not.

And, for all these reasons, arithmetic is a kind of knowledge in which the best natures should be trained, and which must not be given up.

I agree.

Let this then be made one of our subjects of education. And next, shall we enquire whether the kindred science also concerns us?

You mean geometry?

Exactly so.

Clearly, he said, we are concerned with that part of geometry which relates to war; for in pitching a camp, or taking up a position, or closing or extending the lines of an army, or any other military manoeuvre, whether in actual battle or on a march, it will make all the difference whether a general is or is not a geometrician.

Yes, I said, but for that purpose a very little of either geometry or calculation will be enough; the question relates rather to the greater and more advanced part of geometry—whether that tends in any degree to make more easy the vision of the idea of good; and thither, as I was saying, all things tend which compel the soul to turn her gaze towards that place, where is the full perfection of being, which she ought, by all means, to behold.

True, he said.

Then if geometry compels us to view being, it concerns us; if becoming only, it does not concern us?

Yes, that is what we assert.

Yet anybody who has the least acquaintance with geometry will not deny that such a conception of the science is in flat contradiction to the ordinary language of geometricians.

How so?

They have in view practice only, and are always speaking, in a narrow and ridiculous manner, of squaring and extending and applying and the like—they confuse the necessities of geometry with those of daily life; whereas knowledge is the real object of the whole science.

Certainly, he said.

Then must not a further admission be made?

What admission?

That the knowledge at which geometry aims is knowledge of the eternal, and not of aught perishing and transient.

That, he replied, may be readily allowed, and is true.

Then, my noble friend, geometry will draw the soul towards truth, and create the spirit of philosophy, and raise up that which is now unhappily allowed to fall down.

Nothing will be more likely to have such an effect.

Then nothing should be more sternly laid down than that the inhabitants of your fair city should by all means learn geometry. Moreover the science has indirect effects, which are not small.

Of what kind? he said.

There are the military advantages of which you spoke, I said; and in all departments of knowledge, as experience proves, any one who has studied geometry is infinitely quicker of apprehension than one who has not.

Yes indeed, he said, there is an infinite difference between them.

Then shall we propose this as a second branch of knowledge which our youth will study?

Let us do so, he replied.

And suppose we make astronomy the third—what do you say?

I am strongly inclined to it, he said; the observation of the seasons and of months and years is as essential to the general as it is to the farmer or sailor.

I am amused, I said, at your fear of the world, which makes you guard against the appearance of insisting upon useless studies; and I quite admit the difficulty of believing that in every man there is an eye of the soul which, when by other pursuits lost and dimmed, is by these purified and re-illumined; and is more precious far than ten thousand bodily eyes, for by it alone is truth seen. Now there are two classes of persons: one class of those who will agree with you and will take your words as a revelation; another class to whom they will be utterly unmeaning, and who will naturally deem them to be idle tales, for they see no sort of profit which is to be obtained from them. And therefore you had better decide at once with which of the two you are proposing to argue. You will very likely say with neither, and that your chief aim in carrying on the argument is your own improvement; at the same time you do not grudge to others any benefit which they may receive.

I think that I should prefer to carry on the argument mainly on my own behalf.

Then take a step backward, for we have gone wrong in the order of the sciences.

What was the mistake? he said.

After plane geometry, I said, we proceeded at once to solids in revolution, instead of taking solids in themselves; whereas after the second dimension the third, which is concerned with cubes and dimensions of depth, ought to have followed.

That is true, Socrates; but so little seems to be known as yet about these subjects.

Why, yes, I said, and for two reasons:—in the first place, no government patronises them; this leads to a want of energy in the pursuit of them, and they are difficult; in the second place, students cannot learn them unless they have a director. But then a director can hardly be found, and even if he could, as matters now stand, the students, who are very conceited, would not attend to him. That, however, would be otherwise if the whole State became the director of these studies and gave honour to them; then disciples would want to come, and there would be continuous and earnest search, and discoveries would be made; since even now, disregarded as they are by the world, and maimed of their fair proportions, and although none of their votaries can tell the use of them, still these studies force their way by their natural charm, and very likely, if they had the help of the State, they would some day emerge into light.

Yes, he said, there is a remarkable charm in them. But I do not clearly understand the change in the order. First you began with a geometry of plane surfaces?

Yes, I said.

And you placed astronomy next, and then you made a step backward?

Yes, and I have delayed you by my hurry; the ludicrous state of solid geometry, which, in natural order, should have followed, made me pass over this branch and go on to astronomy, or motion of solids.

True, he said.

Then assuming that the science now omitted would come into existence if encouraged by the State, let us go on to astronomy, which will be fourth.

The right order, he replied. And now, Socrates, as you rebuked the vulgar manner in which I praised astronomy before, my praise shall be given in your own spirit. For every one, as I think, must see that astronomy compels the soul to look upwards and leads us from this world to another.

Every one but myself, I said; to every one else this may be clear, but not to me.

And what then would you say?

I should rather say that those who elevate astronomy into philosophy appear to me to make us look downwards and not upwards.

What do you mean? he asked.

You, I replied, have in your mind a truly sublime conception of our knowledge of the things above. And I dare say that if a person were to throw his head back and study the fretted ceiling, you would still think that his mind was the percipient, and not his eyes. And you are very likely right, and I may be a simpleton: but, in my opinion, that knowledge only which is of being and of the unseen can make the soul look upwards, and whether a man gapes at the heavens or blinks on the ground, seeking to learn some particular of sense, I would deny that he can learn, for nothing of that sort is matter of science; his soul is looking downwards, not upwards, whether his way to knowledge is by water or by land, whether he floats, or only lies on his back.

I acknowledge, he said, the justice of your rebuke. Still, I should like to ascertain how astronomy can be learned in any manner more conducive to that knowledge of which we are speaking?

I will tell you, I said: The starry heaven which we behold is wrought upon a visible ground, and therefore, although the fairest and most perfect of visible things, must necessarily be deemed inferior far to the true motions of absolute swiftness and absolute slowness, which are relative to each other, and carry with them that which is contained in them, in the true number and in every true figure. Now, these are to be apprehended by reason and intelligence, but not by sight.

True, he replied.

The spangled heavens should be used as a pattern and with a view to that higher knowledge; their beauty is like the beauty of figures or pictures excellently wrought by the hand of Daedalus, or some other great artist, which we may chance to behold; any geometrician who saw them would appreciate the exquisiteness of their workmanship, but he would never dream of thinking that in them he could find the true equal or the true double, or the truth of any other proportion.

No, he replied, such an idea would be ridiculous.

And will not a true astronomer have the same feeling when he looks at the movements of the stars? Will he not think that heaven and the things in heaven are framed by the Creator of them in the most perfect manner? But he will never imagine that the proportions of night and day, or of both to the month, or of the month to the year, or of the stars to these and to one another, and any other things that are material and visible can also be eternal and subject to no deviation—that would be absurd; and it is equally absurd to take so much pains in investigating their exact truth.

I quite agree, though I never thought of this before.

Then, I said, in astronomy, as in geometry, we should employ problems, and let the heavens alone if we would approach the subject in the right way and so make the natural gift of reason to be of any real use.

That, he said, is a work infinitely beyond our present astronomers.

Yes, I said; and there are many other things which must also have a similar extension given to them, if our legislation is to be of any value. But can you tell me of any other suitable study?

No, he said, not without thinking.

Motion, I said, has many forms, and not one only; two of them are obvious enough even to wits no better than ours; and there are others, as I imagine, which may be left to wiser persons.

But where are the two?

There is a second, I said, which is the counterpart of the one already named.

And what may that be?

The second, I said, would seem relatively to the ears to be what the first is to the eyes; for I conceive that as the eyes are designed to look up at the stars, so are the ears to hear harmonious motions; and these are sister sciences—as the Pythagoreans say, and we, Glaucon, agree with them?

Yes, he replied.

But this, I said, is a laborious study, and therefore we had better go and learn of them; and they will tell us whether there are any other applications of these sciences. At the same time, we must not lose sight of our own higher object.

What is that?

There is a perfection which all knowledge ought to reach, and which our pupils ought also to attain, and not to fall short of, as I was saying that they did in astronomy. For in the science of harmony, as you probably know, the same thing happens. The teachers of harmony compare the sounds and consonances which are heard only, and their labour, like that of the astronomers, is in vain.

Yes, by heaven! he said; and 'tis as good as a play to hear them talking about their condensed notes, as they call them; they put their ears close alongside of the strings like persons catching a sound from their neighbour's wall—one set of them declaring that they distinguish an intermediate note and have found the least interval which should be the unit of measurement; the others insisting that the two sounds have passed into the same—either party setting their ears before their understanding.

You mean, I said, those gentlemen who tease and torture the strings and rack them on the pegs of the instrument: I might carry on the metaphor and speak after their manner of the blows which the plectrum gives, and make accusations against the strings, both of backwardness and forwardness to sound; but this would be tedious, and therefore I will only say that these are not the men, and that I am referring to the Pythagoreans, of whom I was just now proposing to enquire about harmony. For they too are in error, like the astronomers; they investigate the numbers of the harmonies which are heard, but they never attain to problems—that is to say, they never reach the natural harmonies of number, or reflect why some numbers are harmonious and others not.

That, he said, is a thing of more than mortal knowledge.

A thing, I replied, which I would rather call useful; that is, if sought after with a view to the beautiful and good; but if pursued in any other spirit, useless.

Very true, he said.

Now, when all these studies reach the point of inter-communion and connection with one another, and come to be considered in their mutual affinities, then, I think, but not till then, will the pursuit of them have a value for our objects; otherwise there is no profit in them.

I suspect so; but you are speaking, Socrates, of a vast work.

What do you mean? I said; the prelude or what? Do you not know that all this is but the prelude to the actual strain which we have to learn? For you surely would not regard the skilled mathematician as a dialectician?

Assuredly not, he said; I have hardly ever known a mathematician who was capable of reasoning.

But do you imagine that men who are unable to give and take a reason will have the knowledge which we require of them?

Neither can this be supposed.

And so, Glaucon, I said, we have at last arrived at the hymn of dialectic. This is that strain which is of the intellect only, but which the faculty of sight will nevertheless be found to imitate; for sight, as you may remember, was imagined by us after a while to behold the real animals and stars, and last of all the sun himself. And so with dialectic; when a person starts on the discovery of the absolute by the light of reason only, and without any assistance of sense, and perseveres until by pure intelligence he arrives at the perception of the absolute good, he at last finds himself at the end of the intellectual world, as in the case of sight at the end of the visible.

Exactly, he said.

Then this is the progress which you call dialectic?

True.

But the release of the prisoners from chains, and their translation from the shadows to the images and to the light, and the ascent from the underground den to the sun, while in his presence they are vainly trying to look on animals and plants and the light of the sun, but are able to perceive even with their weak eyes the images in the water (which are divine), and are the shadows of true existence (not shadows of images cast by a light of fire, which compared with the sun is only an image)—this power of elevating the highest principle in the soul to the contemplation of that which is best in existence, with which we may compare the raising of that faculty which is the very light of the body to the sight of that which is brightest in the material and visible world—this power is given, as I was saying, by all that study and pursuit of the arts which has been described.

I agree in what you are saying, he replied, which may be hard to believe, yet, from another point of view, is harder still to deny. This, however, is not a theme to be treated of in passing only, but will have to be discussed again and again. And so, whether our conclusion be true or false, let us assume all this, and proceed at once from the prelude or preamble to the chief strain (A play upon the Greek word, which means both 'law' and 'strain.'), and describe that in like manner. Say, then, what is the nature and what are the divisions of dialectic, and what are the paths which lead thither; for these paths will also lead to our final rest.

Dear Glaucon, I said, you will not be able to follow me here, though I would do my best, and you should behold not an image only but the absolute truth, according to my notion. Whether what

I told you would or would not have been a reality I cannot venture to say; but you would have seen something like reality; of that I am confident.

Doubtless, he replied.

But I must also remind you, that the power of dialectic alone can reveal this, and only to one who is a disciple of the previous sciences.

Of that assertion you may be as confident as of the last.

And assuredly no one will argue that there is any other method of comprehending by any regular process all true existence or of ascertaining what each thing is in its own nature; for the arts in general are concerned with the desires or opinions of men, or are cultivated with a view to production and construction, or for the preservation of such productions and constructions; and as to the mathematical sciences which, as we were saying, have some apprehension of true being—geometry and the like—they only dream about being, but never can they behold the waking reality so long as they leave the hypotheses which they use unexamined, and are unable to give an account of them. For when a man knows not his own first principle, and when the conclusion and intermediate steps are also constructed out of he knows not what, how can he imagine that such a fabric of convention can ever become science?

Impossible, he said.

Then dialectic, and dialectic alone, goes directly to the first principle and is the only science which does away with hypotheses in order to make her ground secure; the eye of the soul, which is literally buried in an outlandish slough, is by her gentle aid lifted upwards; and she uses as handmaids and helpers in the work of conversion, the sciences which we have been discussing. Custom terms them sciences, but they ought to have some other name, implying greater clearness than opinion and less clearness than science: and this, in our previous sketch, was called understanding. But why should we dispute about names when we have realities of such importance to consider?

Why indeed, he said, when any name will do which expresses the thought of the mind with clearness?

At any rate, we are satisfied, as before, to have four divisions; two for intellect and two for opinion, and to call the first division science, the second understanding, the third belief, and the fourth perception of shadows, opinion being concerned with becoming, and intellect with being; and so to make a proportion:—

As being is to becoming, so is pure intellect to opinion. And as intellect is to opinion, so is science to belief, and understanding to the perception of shadows.

But let us defer the further correlation and subdivision of the subjects of opinion and of intellect, for it will be a long enquiry, many times longer than this has been.

As far as I understand, he said, I agree.

And do you also agree, I said, in describing the dialectician as one who attains a conception of the essence of each thing? And he who does not possess and is therefore unable to impart this conception, in whatever degree he fails, may in that degree also be said to fail in intelligence? Will you admit so much?

Yes, he said; how can I deny it?

And you would say the same of the conception of the good? Until the person is able to abstract and define rationally the idea of good, and unless he can run the gauntlet of all objections, and is ready to disprove them, not by appeals to opinion, but to absolute truth, never faltering at any step of the argument—unless he can do all this, you would say that he knows neither the idea of good nor any other good; he apprehends only a shadow, if anything at all, which is given by opinion and not by science;—dreaming and slumbering in this life, before he is well awake here, he arrives at the world below, and has his final quietus.

In all that I should most certainly agree with you.

And surely you would not have the children of your ideal State, whom you are nurturing and educating—if the ideal ever becomes a reality—you would not allow the future rulers to be like posts (Literally 'lines,' probably the starting-point of a race-course.), having no reason in them, and yet to be set in authority over the highest matters?

Certainly not.

Then you will make a law that they shall have such an education as will enable them to attain the greatest skill in asking and answering questions?

Yes, he said, you and I together will make it.

Dialectic, then, as you will agree, is the coping-stone of the sciences, and is set over them; no other science can be placed higher—the nature of knowledge can no further go?

I agree, he said.

But to whom we are to assign these studies, and in what way they are to be assigned, are questions which remain to be considered.

Yes, clearly.

You remember, I said, how the rulers were chosen before?

Certainly, he said.

The same natures must still be chosen, and the preference again given to the surest and the bravest, and, if possible, to the fairest; and, having noble and generous tempers, they should also have the natural gifts which will facilitate their education.

And what are these?

Such gifts as keenness and ready powers of acquisition; for the mind more often faints from the severity of study than from the severity of gymnastics: the toil is more entirely the mind's own, and is not shared with the body.

Very true, he replied.

Further, he of whom we are in search should have a good memory, and be an unwearied solid man who is a lover of labour in any line; or he will never be able to endure the great amount of bodily exercise and to go through all the intellectual discipline and study which we require of him.

Certainly, he said; he must have natural gifts.

The mistake at present is, that those who study philosophy have no vocation, and this, as I was before saying, is the reason why she has fallen into disrepute: her true sons should take her by the hand and not bastards.

What do you mean?

In the first place, her votary should not have a lame or halting industry—I mean, that he should not be half industrious and half idle: as, for example, when a man is a lover of gymnastic and hunting, and all other bodily exercises, but a hater rather than a lover of the labour of learning or listening or enquiring. Or the occupation to which he devotes himself may be of an opposite kind, and he may have the other sort of lameness.

Certainly, he said.

And as to truth, I said, is not a soul equally to be deemed halt and lame which hates voluntary falsehood and is extremely indignant at herself and others when they tell lies, but is patient of involuntary falsehood, and does not mind wallowing like a swinish beast in the mire of ignorance, and has no shame at being detected?

To be sure.

And, again, in respect of temperance, courage, magnificence, and every other virtue, should we not carefully distinguish between the true son and the bastard? for where there is no discernment of such qualities states and individuals unconsciously err; and the state makes a ruler, and the individual a friend, of one who, being defective in some part of virtue, is in a figure lame or a bastard.

That is very true, he said.

All these things, then, will have to be carefully considered by us; and if only those whom we introduce to this vast system of education and training are sound in body and mind, justice herself will have nothing to say against us, and we shall be the saviours of the constitution and of the State; but, if our pupils are men of another stamp, the reverse will happen, and we shall pour a still greater flood of ridicule on philosophy than she has to endure at present.

That would not be creditable.

Certainly not, I said; and yet perhaps, in thus turning jest into earnest I am equally ridiculous.

In what respect?

I had forgotten, I said, that we were not serious, and spoke with too much excitement. For when I saw philosophy so undeservedly trampled under foot of men I could not help feeling a sort of indignation at the authors of her disgrace: and my anger made me too vehement.

Indeed! I was listening, and did not think so.

But I, who am the speaker, felt that I was. And now let me remind you that, although in our former selection we chose old men, we must not do so in this. Solon was under a delusion when he said that a man when he grows old may learn many things—for he can no more learn much than he can run much; youth is the time for any extraordinary toil.

Of course.

And, therefore, calculation and geometry and all the other elements of instruction, which are a preparation for dialectic, should be presented to the mind in childhood; not, however, under any notion of forcing our system of education.

Why not?

Because a freeman ought not to be a slave in the acquisition of knowledge of any kind. Bodily exercise, when compulsory, does no harm to the body; but knowledge which is acquired under compulsion obtains no hold on the mind.

Very true.

Then, my good friend, I said, do not use compulsion, but let early education be a sort of amusement; you will then be better able to find out the natural bent.

That is a very rational notion, he said.

Do you remember that the children, too, were to be taken to see the battle on horseback; and that if there were no danger they were to be brought close up and, like young hounds, have a taste of blood given them?

Yes, I remember.

The same practice may be followed, I said, in all these things—labours, lessons, dangers—and he who is most at home in all of them ought to be enrolled in a select number.

At what age?

At the age when the necessary gymnastics are over: the period whether of two or three years which passes in this sort of training is useless for any other purpose; for sleep and exercise are unpropitious to learning; and the trial of who is first in gymnastic exercises is one of the most important tests to which our youth are subjected.

Certainly, he replied.

After that time those who are selected from the class of twenty years old will be promoted to higher honour, and the sciences which they learned without any order in their early education will now be brought together, and they will be able to see the natural relationship of them to one another and to true being.

Yes, he said, that is the only kind of knowledge which takes lasting root.

Yes, I said; and the capacity for such knowledge is the great criterion of dialectical talent: the comprehensive mind is always the dialectical.

I agree with you, he said.

These, I said, are the points which you must consider; and those who have most of this comprehension, and who are most steadfast in their learning, and in their military and other appointed duties, when they have arrived at the age of thirty have to be chosen by you out of the select class, and elevated to higher honour; and you will have to prove them by the help of dialectic, in order to learn which of them is able to give up the use of sight and the other senses, and in company with truth to attain absolute being: And here, my friend, great caution is required.

Why great caution?

Do you not remark, I said, how great is the evil which dialectic has introduced?

What evil? he said.

The students of the art are filled with lawlessness.

Quite true, he said.

Do you think that there is anything so very unnatural or inexcusable in their case? or will you make allowance for them?

In what way make allowance?

I want you, I said, by way of parallel, to imagine a supposititious son who is brought up in great wealth; he is one of a great and numerous family, and has many flatterers. When he grows up to manhood, he learns that his alleged are not his real parents; but who the real are he is unable to discover. Can you guess how he will be likely to behave towards his flatterers and his supposed parents, first of all during the period when he is ignorant of the false relation, and then again when he knows? Or shall I guess for you?

If you please.

Then I should say, that while he is ignorant of the truth he will be likely to honour his father and his mother and his supposed relations more than the flatterers; he will be less inclined to neglect them when in need, or to do or say anything against them; and he will be less willing to disobey them in any important matter.

He will.

But when he has made the discovery, I should imagine that he would diminish his honour and regard for them, and would become more devoted to the flatterers; their influence over him would greatly increase; he would now live after their ways, and openly associate with them, and, unless he were of an unusually good disposition, he would trouble himself no more about his supposed parents or other relations.

Well, all that is very probable. But how is the image applicable to the disciples of philosophy?

In this way: you know that there are certain principles about justice and honour, which were taught us in childhood, and under their parental authority we have been brought up, obeying and honouring them.

That is true.

There are also opposite maxims and habits of pleasure which flatter and attract the soul, but do not influence those of us who have any sense of right, and they continue to obey and honour the maxims of their fathers.

True.

Now, when a man is in this state, and the questioning spirit asks what is fair or honourable, and he answers as the legislator has taught him, and then arguments many and diverse refute his words, until he is driven into believing that nothing is honourable any more than dishonourable, or just and good any more than the reverse, and so of all the notions which he most valued, do you think that he will still honour and obey them as before?

Impossible.

And when he ceases to think them honourable and natural as heretofore, and he fails to discover the true, can he be expected to pursue any life other than that which flatters his desires?

He cannot.

And from being a keeper of the law he is converted into a breaker of it?

Unquestionably.

Now all this is very natural in students of philosophy such as I have described, and also, as I was just now saying, most excusable.

Yes, he said; and, I may add, pitiable.

Therefore, that your feelings may not be moved to pity about our citizens who are now thirty years of age, every care must be taken in introducing them to dialectic.

Certainly.

There is a danger lest they should taste the dear delight too early; for youngsters, as you may have observed, when they first get the taste in their mouths, argue for amusement, and are always contradicting and refuting others in imitation of those who refute them; like puppy-dogs, they rejoice in pulling and tearing at all who come near them.

Yes, he said, there is nothing which they like better.

And when they have made many conquests and received defeats at the hands of many, they violently and speedily get into a way of not believing anything which they believed before, and hence, not only they, but philosophy and all that relates to it is apt to have a bad name with the rest of the world.

Too true, he said.

But when a man begins to get older, he will no longer be guilty of such insanity; he will imitate the dialectician who is seeking for truth, and not the eristic, who is contradicting for the sake of amusement; and the greater moderation of his character will increase instead of diminishing the honour of the pursuit.

Very true, he said.

And did we not make special provision for this, when we said that the disciples of philosophy were to be orderly and steadfast, not, as now, any chance aspirant or intruder?

Very true.

Suppose, I said, the study of philosophy to take the place of gymnastics and to be continued diligently and earnestly and exclusively for twice the number of years which were passed in bodily exercise—will that be enough?

Would you say six or four years? he asked.

Say five years, I replied; at the end of the time they must be sent down again into the den and compelled to hold any military or other office which young men are qualified to hold: in this way they will get their experience of life, and there will be an opportunity of trying whether, when they are drawn all manner of ways by temptation, they will stand firm or flinch.

And how long is this stage of their lives to last?

Fifteen years, I answered; and when they have reached fifty years of age, then let those who still survive and have distinguished themselves in every action of their lives and in every branch of knowledge come at last to their consummation: the time has now arrived at which they must raise the eye of the soul to the universal light which lightens all things, and behold the absolute good; for that is the pattern according to which they are to order the State and the lives of individuals, and the remainder of their own lives also; making philosophy their chief pursuit, but, when their turn comes, toiling also at politics and ruling for the public good, not as though they were performing some heroic action, but simply as a matter of duty; and when they have brought up in each generation others like themselves and left them in their place to be governors of the State, then they will depart to the Islands of the Blest and dwell there; and the city will give them public memorials and sacrifices and honour them, if the Pythian oracle consent, as demigods, but if not, as in any case blessed and divine.

You are a sculptor, Socrates, and have made statues of our governors faultless in beauty.

Yes, I said, Glaucon, and of our governesses too; for you must not suppose that what I have been saying applies to men only and not to women as far as their natures can go.

There you are right, he said, since we have made them to share in all things like the men.

Well, I said, and you would agree (would you not?) that what has been said about the State and the government is not a mere dream, and although difficult not impossible, but only possible in the way which has been supposed; that is to say, when the true philosopher kings are born in a State, one or more of them, despising the honours of this present world which they deem mean and worthless, esteeming above all things right and the honour that springs from right, and regarding justice as the greatest and most necessary of all things, whose ministers they are, and whose principles will be exalted by them when they set in order their own city?

How will they proceed?

They will begin by sending out into the country all the inhabitants of the city who are more than ten years old, and will take possession of their children, who will be unaffected by the habits of their parents; these they will train in their own habits and laws, I mean in the laws which we have given them: and in this way the State and constitution of which we were speaking will soonest and most easily attain happiness, and the nation which has such a constitution will gain most.

Yes, that will be the best way. And I think, Socrates, that you have very well described how, if ever, such a constitution might come into being.

Enough then of the perfect State, and of the man who bears its image—there is no difficulty in seeing how we shall describe him.

There is no difficulty, he replied; and I agree with you in thinking that nothing more need be said.

Questions about "The Allegory of the Cave"

READING AND WRITING TO COMPREHEND

1. **Look up** the term *allegory*. How does this affect how you read this piece?
2. **Create** a difficulty inventory in which you list the elements of this piece that stand in your way of easily reading and grasping it (see Chapter 3 for help with difficult inventories).
3. **Annotate** the text, recognizing that this is a dialogue between Socrates and his student Glaucon, using the says/does approach to see what each participant is saying and doing with his contributions to the dialogue (see Chapter 2 for help with the says/does approach).
4. **Explain** the context. Early in this dialogue, Socrates says to Glaucon, "The truth would be literally nothing but the shadows of the images." What does this mean?
5. **Explain** the context. Later in the dialogue, Socrates says, "Because a freeman ought not to be a slave in the acquisition of knowledge of any kind. Bodily exercise, when compulsory, does no harm to the body; but knowledge which is acquired under compulsion obtains no hold on the mind." What does this mean?
6. **Multimodal Option.** Develop a visual representation of the cave as it is described in this allegory using whatever modes you like. Then, write a short piece about what this model helps you understand about the allegory.

READING AND WRITING TO RESPOND

7. **Respond:** Using your annotations from the says/days approach, write an intellectual response to a quotation about knowledge from this dialogue (see Chapter 3 for help with intellectual responses). Where do you stand on what is said about those who hold knowledge, (i.e. experts) and how they share this knowledge with others?

READING AND WRITING TO APPLY AND REFLECT

8. One way to understand this allegory is to imagine that the puppeteer is using a form of technology—namely the puppets—to help construct a reality for those in the cave. Using your annotations and your answers to the previous questions to help you understand what the allegory says, choose a contemporary technology that you think might also play a role in constructing reality for those living in the world today.
9. **Multimodal Option.** Use the RLW strategy to reread this allegory (see Chapter 2 for help with RLW). Using Plato's piece as a model, develop your own non-print-based dialogue between two people on a subject of your choice. Reflect on what this form and the modes you chose both allow and prohibit you from accomplishing.

Digital Maoism

By Jaron Lanier

This essay considers the rise of what Lanier calls collectives and collectivism. Using examples such as Wikipedia and the once leading social network MySpace, Lanier addresses what this rise means for the individual and for democracy.

Edge

Visit https://www.edge.org/conversation/jaron_lanier-digital-maoism-the-hazards-of-the-new-online-collectivism

Questions about "Digital Maoism"

READING AND WRITING TO COMPREHEND

1. **Define** the terminology. Lanier describes Wikipedia as a form of online collectivism that is different from a representative democracy or meritocracy. What does he mean?

2. **Choose** a reading strategy that you think will help you understand the concept of Meta sites. Reread the relevant sections of this text using this strategy to help you understand what Meta sites are and why Lanier spends so much time talking about these.

3. **Consider** the title of the piece: What is Maoism and what does it have to do with the subject of this piece?

READING AND WRITING TO RESPOND

4. **Write** an intellectual response to the piece that addresses Lanier's concerns from a contemporary perspective (see Chapter 3 for help with intellectual responses). In 2007 when this piece was published, Lanier indicated his concerns about "empowering the hive mind." To what extent has the hive mind been empowered since this was written?

READING AND WRITING TO APPLY AND REFLECT

5. **Reread** the piece using a reading strategy that allows you to understand what Lanier means by the phrase, "humanistic and practical," which he uses in his conclusion to describe how to "maximize the value of the collective on the Web without turning ourselves into idiots." Then, **consider** whether this "way" currently exists in practice. If yes, **describe** how and where. If no, **describe** why not and imagine a humanistic and practical way to maximize the value of the collective on the web.

The Rise of Crowdsourcing

By Jeff Howe

This essay explores the open source software movement, as well its responsibility for the rise of what Howe calls "crowdsourcing." Exploring this phenomenon, Howe raises questions about new labor models and how these will affect understandings of expertise.

You will be required to purchase a subscription after you visit *Wired* a certain number of times. Keep this in mind as you are working with this reading.

Visit https://www.wired.com/2006/06/crowds/

Questions about "The Rise of Crowdsourcing"

READING AND WRITING TO COMPREHEND

1. **Read** this piece using a reading strategy of your choice to help you understand the difference Howe is pointing to between outsourcing and crowdsourcing. Why does this difference matter?
2. **Complete a rhetorical reading** of the piece with an eye toward the evidence and kind of rhetorical appeals that Howe uses to make his claims about crowdsourcing. What kind of evidence is used? Which rhetorical appeals does Howe use (see Chapter 2 for help with rhetorical appeals and rhetorical reading, more generally)?
3. What is the Turk and what does it have to do with Howe's argument?

READING AND WRITING TO RESPOND

4. **Write** an intellectual response to the piece in which you consider the implications of Howe's argument beyond those he outlines in his piece (see Chapter 3 for help with intellectual responses).

READING AND WRITING TO APPLY AND REFLECT

5. Toward the beginning of his essay, Howe notes that the "open source software movement proved that a network of passionate, geeky volunteers could write code just as well as the highly paid developers at Microsoft or Sun Microsystems." Do some preliminary research about what it means for something to be open source. Where else is this term used? How can understanding what the open source software movement is help you to understand other things designated as "open source," such as this very textbook?

It Should Happen to You

By Ben McGrath

This essay explores the creation of YouTube in 2005, as well as some of the people who found fame on YouTube while the platform was still in its infancy. The snapshots that McGrath provides into these YouTube stars' lives raise questions about fame, entertainment, talent, and art in a capitalist and democratic society.

THE NEW YORKER

You will be required to purchase a subscription after you visit *The New Yorker* a certain number of times. Keep this in mind as you are working with this reading.

Visit https://www.newyorker.com/magazine/2006/10/16/it-should-happen-to-you

Questions about "It Should Happen to You"

READING AND WRITING TO COMPREHEND

1. **Rhetorically read** "It Should Happen to You" with particular attention to its purpose. What do you think the author's purpose is in writing this piece? How do you know?

2. The CEO of YouTube is quoted in this essay saying that YouTube wanted to "democratize the entertainment process." Yet, McGrath, the author, describes Crispin Glover as "warning [Stevie Ryan/Little Loca] against the inevitable corruption of

her utopian Internet democracy." How do you make sense of these potentially competing ideas about YouTube?

READING AND WRITING TO RESPOND

3. **Rhetorically read** "It Should Happen to You" with particular attention to McGrath's argument. Then, write an intellectual response to this argument (see Chapter 3 for help with intellectual responses).

READING AND WRITING TO APPLY AND REFLECT

4. While reading this essay, we find out it was written just ten months after YouTube's launch in 2005. Return to your annotations in order to better understand what YouTube was like at this time. Then, spend some time perusing the YouTube of today. To what extent has it changed? *So What*? To what extent do McGrath's claims and the others he presents in his piece still apply?

5. **Multimodal Option:** Develop your own YouTube video in which you communicate how the YouTube of today is different from how McGrath describes YouTube. Then, write a short reflection on how developing a visual composition affected what you could say and how you could communicate your points.

LONG WRITING ASSIGNMENTS BASED ON READINGS IN CHAPTER 8: EXPERTISE AND TECHNOLOGY

1. If you have not done so yet, re-read "The Allegory of the Cave" using the RLW strategy. Then, **develop** your own allegory on a subject of your choice. Use what you can **infer** about allegories from Plato's piece, as well as from the definition of an allegory. Then, **write** a short reflection about the rhetorical choices you made while writing this piece and the extent to which they draw on those in "The Allegory of the Cave."

2. **Multimodal Option.** Develop your own allegory on a subject of your choice using multiple modes. Then, write a short reflection about the rhetorical choices you made while composing the piece and the extent to which they draw on those in "The Allegory of the Cave."

3. The selections in this chapter examine the role of individual or independent thought within a larger culture whether that culture is the cave in Plato's allegory, on Wikipedia, or on YouTube. Choose two or three of these selections and develop an academic argument that addresses why the individual is important to these discussions about technology (see Chapter 4 for help with developing an academic argument). What is at stake for individuals? Look back at the annotations you already have on the texts to determine how helpful those are. It is likely that you will need to reread the selections by applying a reading strategy that you think will be most effective for completing this particular assignment.

4. The selections in this chapter were written at least a decade ago. Using one of the author's arguments as a lens, develop an essay in which you explore a current technology or a handful of related, current technologies in order to update the author's take on the technology. What would the author notice about your chosen technology? What observations might the author make? What position might the author take in relation to its use(s)? Look back at the annotations you already have on the texts to determine how helpful those are. It is likely that you will need to reread the selections by applying a reading strategy that you think will be most effective for completing this particular assignment.

5. **Multimodal Option.** Explore a current technology or a handful of related, current technologies in order to discover what an author of one of the texts in this chapter might say about these. In other words, extend the author's argument so that it addresses a current technology. What would the author notice about your chosen technology? What observations might the author make? What position might the author take in relation to its use(s)? Use the very form of technology that you have chosen in order to extend the author's argument so that it addresses this technology.

6. Each selection in this chapter explores the concept of expertise in some way. Choose three of these selections and develop a synthesis paper in which you consider how their arguments about expertise relate to each other (see Chapter 3 for help with writing a synthesis). What would one author say to another? Where do their ideas about expertise converge and diverge? *So what?* Look back at the annotations you already have on the texts to determine how helpful those are. It is likely that you will need to reread the selections by applying a reading strategy that you think will be most effective for completing this particular assignment.

REFLECTING ON YOUR READING STRATEGIES AND ANNOTATIONS

Consider the different reading strategies you applied while reading the selections in this chapter. Which were most useful for understanding the text? For writing a summary? For figuring out what you think? For responding to the text? For imitating an author's style? Anticipate future uses of these reading strategies in this class, in other classes, and in other contexts. Also, consider previous courses and contexts in which these strategies would have been helpful.

Chapter 9. Gender and Technology

Although the subjects of this chapter—gender and technology—may seem at first glance an odd pair, there are a number of ways to explore the relationship between gender and technology; the selections within this chapter represent some of those ways. The opening piece, a research essay written by then University of Connecticut undergraduate student Sarah Davis, explores the role that music and music videos play in perpetuating gender stereotypes, as well as rape culture, which Davis argues, grows out of these stereotypes. Poet Stacey Waite's piece, "On the Occasion of Being Mistaken for a Man by Security Personnel at Newark International Airport," includes a speaker reflecting on how the screening technologies at airports that we have come to take for granted raise vexing questions about one's identity and its relationship to one's body. Lal Zimman's blog entry "Facebook, The Gender Binary, and Third Person" explores how Facebook has taken the lead in gendered language activism while Nussbaum's "Mothers Anonymous" explores UrbanBaby, a New-York based website with an anonymous message-board on which mothers share their darkest fears and biggest secrets about marriage and mothering. Each selection approaches gender through some form of technology, providing ample opportunities for readers to explore how technology is raising new questions about gender, answering others, and underscoring age-old questions.

PRIOR TO READING EACH SELECTION IN THIS CHAPTER

Look at the questions after each reading. What are you expected to do after reading this selection? In other words, what are your purposes for reading? Although you will be asked to apply particular reading strategies in order to complete some of the tasks, others will leave the choice of strategy up to you. Refer to the descriptions of the reading strategies in Chapter 2 and decide which will be most useful in helping you accomplish those tasks. Remember that you will be reading each selection multiple times and, therefore, will have additional opportunities to apply different reading strategies.

READINGS

The "Blurred Lines" Effect: Popular Music and the Perpetuation of Rape Culture

By Sarah Davis

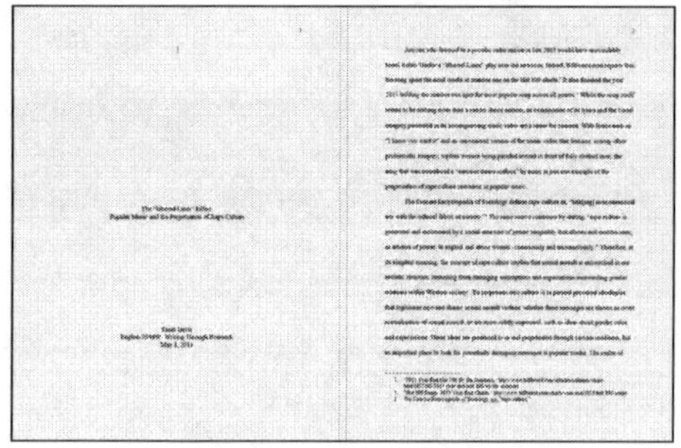

Submitted for English 2049W: Writing Through Research, University of Connecticut, May 1, 2014

Anyone who listened to a popular radio station in late 2013 would have unavoidably heard Robin Thicke's "Blurred Lines" play over the airwaves. Indeed, Billboard.com reports that the song spent the most weeks at number one on the Hot 100 charts.[1] It also finished the year 2013 holding the number two spot for most popular song across all genres.[2] While the song itself seems to be nothing more than a catchy dance anthem, an examination of its lyrics and the visual imagery presented in its accompanying music video are a cause for concern. With lyrics such as "I know you want it" and an uncensored version of the music video that features, among other problematic imagery, topless women being paraded around in front of fully clothed men, the song that was considered a "summer dance anthem" by many is just one example of the perpetuation of rape culture prevalent in popular music.

The Concise Encyclopedia of Sociology defines rape culture as, "link[ing] nonconsensual sex with the cultural fabric of society."[3] The same source continues by stating, "rape culture is generated and maintained by a social structure of gender inequality that allows and enables men, as arbiters of power, to exploit and abuse women—consciously and unconsciously." Therefore, at its simplest meaning, the concept of rape culture implies that sexual assault is entrenched in our societal structure, stemming from damaging assumptions and expectations surrounding gender relations within Western society. To perpetuate rape culture is to present prevalent ideologies that legitimize rape and shame sexual assault victims, whether these messages are shown as overt normalization of sexual assault, or are more subtly-expressed, such as ideas about gender roles and expectations. These ideas are presented to us and perpetuated through various mediums, but an important place to

1 "2013 Year-End Hot 100 By the Numbers," http://www.billboard.com/articles/columns/chart-beat/5827382/2013-year-end-hot–100-by-the-numbers

2 "Hot 100 Songs: 2013 Year-End Charts," http://www.billboard.com/charts/year-end/2013/hot–100-songs

3 *The Concise Encyclopedia of Sociology, s.v. "rape culture."*

look for potentially damaging messages is popular media. The realm of television, movies, music, and music videos provides an excellent channel for unsafe ideas about gender relations to reach the public. For one, popular media is an inescapable phenomenon in today's technologically advanced, interconnected world. One cannot simply get away from messages in the media; from the newsstand to the internet to radio stations, we are constantly being shown messages about sexuality and relationships. Because of this constant immersion in media, it is easy to unconsciously internalize potentially harmful messages; messages that help perpetuate rape culture and make the world a more dangerous place for the vulnerable.

The implications of rape culture are alarming. As of April 2014, the Rape, Abuse & Incest National Network (RAINN) listed some startling statistics on its website. "Every two minutes, another American is sexually assaulted . . . each year, there are about 237,868 victims of sexual assault," the organization reports.[4] Additionally, nearly half of victims are under the age of eighteen.[5] The statistics also show that in 93% of juvenile rapes, the attacker is someone the victim knows.[6] This implies that the typical rapist is not a criminal hiding in the bushes, but rather someone the victim knows and trusts more than a stranger. Rape culture can play a central role in rape reporting. Rape is the most underreported crime in the country, with 60% of rapes going unreported to law enforcement.[7] It is perhaps easy to correlate this astounding lack of reports with the prevalence of rape culture. If sexual assault is normalized through the prevailing attitudes expressed in the media, it is only logical to suggest that many victims do not realize that they have been sexually assaulted because they have been told that such behavior is normal and expected. Therein lies the problem, especially because victims of sexual assault, whether reported are not, are thirteen times more likely to abuse alcohol, twenty-six times more likely to abuse drugs, and are four times more likely to contemplate suicide than non-victims.[8] If rape culture is being perpetuated through mass media, a victim is arguably less likely to report a sexual assault, which makes them less likely to seek support. This complicates the healing process and puts strain on their self-image and mental health, as well as their relationships with others. It is only logical that in order to reduce the rate of sexual assault, society needs to closely examine the culture it presents that normalizes this crime. One way to do this is to examine the way in which mass media encourages potentially dangerous ideas.

With all of the potentially dangerous messages sent through the media as a whole, why focus on music and music videos? Aren't movies and television shows equally as responsible for presenting misogynistic messages? Although movies and television shows should be considered in regards to

4 "Statistics." RAINN, accessed April 29, 2014, https://www.rainn.org/statistics

5 Ibid

6 Ibid

7 Ibid

8 Ibid

their potential for damaging or dangerous ideas, a 2009 policy statement released by the American Academy of Pediatrics highlights why music is a particularly successful medium for transmitting messages regarding sexuality. "Music . . . provide[s] a background for romance and serve[s] as the basis for establishing relationships in diverse settings . . . adolescents use music in their process of identity formation and their music preference provides them a means to achieve group identity and integration into the youth culture."[9] Doesn't television provide these same functions? According to the Academy, music may be more successful than television at existing as a model for relationships. It is impossible to escape popular music, as its presence is almost everywhere; it is used as background noise in supermarkets and malls, and as technology advances, it is often more easily accessible through downloads and internet radio.[10] Unlike television, one does not have to consciously choose to access music in order to absorb the message being transmitted. The Academy also suggests that music videos are an even bigger cause for concern, as they mix two popular forms of media, meaning that suggestive lyrics are accompanied by visual imagery that brings a potentially harmful message even further into the psyche of an individual who is beginning to take cues about "normal" relationships from any source they can.[11] It is with these ideas in mind that one can look to popular music for possibly harmful messages about women and female sexuality.

What does this have to do with rape culture? As noted previously, a rape culture is one in which sexual assault is normalized through the prevailing social structure. This social structure relies on the widespread prevalence of harmful messages that trivialize sexual assault and present it as a logical or expected part of society. These kinds of messages also make life more difficult for victims of sexual assault, who will often find themselves at the mercy of a social structure that blames them for their own rape. Messages need not be overt to be dangerous. Even underlying psychological messages about gender roles and what is expected behavior in relationships can support problematic ideologies and maintain rape culture.

A 1980 study by Martha R. Burt is worth mentioning, as it is cross referenced throughout many of the more recent studies cited here. Burt's study looked at cultural attitudes about various myths about rape and examined them in concurrence with other beliefs about gender roles and interpersonal violence.[12] Some of the rape myths used in Burt's study include ideas that a generally promiscuous woman is the "typical" rape victim, that a woman who dresses in a provocative manner is asking to be raped, and, perhaps most disturbing, that all women have an unconscious desire to

---

9 American Academy of Pediatrics. *Policy Statement—Impact of Music, Music Lyrics, and Music Videos on Children and Youth.* (2009).

10 American Academy of Pediatrics, 1489.

11 American Academy of Pediatrics, 1490.

12 Martha R. Burt, "Cultural Myths and Support for Rape," *Journal of Personality and Social Psychology 38 (1980): 217.*

be sexually assaulted.[13] Burt examined these myths in concurrence with other beliefs about gender roles, such as the "proper" roles of men and women in relationships and ideas about female sexual promiscuity in general. The results of the study were disturbing, in that they indicated a prevalent acceptance of myths surrounding rape:

> Rape attitudes are strongly connected to other deeply held and pervasive attitudes such as sex role stereotyping, distrust of the opposite sex (adversarial sexual beliefs), and acceptance of interpersonal violence. When over half of the sampled individuals agree with statements such as "A woman who goes to the home or apartment of a man on the first date implies she is willing to have sex" and "In the majority of rapes, the victim was promiscuous or had a bad reputation," . . . the world is indeed not a safe place for rape victims.[14]

What use is a thirty-four year old study to us in today's enlightened and technologically advanced culture? Haven't we advanced beyond such antiquated beliefs about female sexuality and gender roles? The answer is that we unfortunately have not. With explicit sexual content becoming more widespread across all forms of media and the new ease of access to music videos through streaming websites such as YouTube and Vevo, there is more potential for problematic messages to filter through.[15] This means more opportunities for young people to absorb harmful ideas about relationships and sexuality.

What effects does sexual imagery have on perceptions of female sexuality? After all, aren't people aware that imagery in music videos is just a form of storytelling? A study by Kistler and Lee (2009) sought to determine this by examining the effects exposure to sexual hip-hop videos had on college students' acceptance of various rape myths. Researchers exposed college students to music videos with either low or high sexual content and then examined the subjects' acceptance of some of the rape myths previously examined by Burt. The male students exposed to highly sexual music videos subsequently expressed more acceptance of rape myths and objectification of women.[16] Researchers believe that the lavish and powerful presentations of the male artists in the music video served as cues for male participants, maintaining the idea that women exist solely for the entertainment and sexual fulfillment of men, and therefore, coercing women into sexual activity is acceptable, even expected.[17] It is this expectation of sexual coercion as a normal part of gender interaction that sup-

---

13 Ibid, 223.

14 Ibid, 229.

15 *American Academy of Pediatrics, 1489.*

16 Michelle Kistler and Moon J. Lee, "Does Exposure to Sexual Hip-Hop Music Videos Influence the Sexual Attitudes of College Students?" *Mass Communication and Society 13 (2009): 82.*

17 Ibid, 83.

ports the idea of rape culture. Obviously, not every young male adolescent who is exposed to such sexual imagery is going to become a serial rapist, but the potential consequences of such exposure cannot be ignored.

It is not only imagery in music videos that contributes to potentially dangerous ideas. In addition to the Kistler and Lee study, a 2006 study by Bretthauer et al. sought to examine the prevalent messages in popular music, and found disturbing trends in the prevalence of misogynistic themes in lyrics across several genres, including pop and rock as well as hip-hop. From lyrical analysis of songs chosen from the Billboard Hot 100 Charts, researchers identified themes of men and power, sex as top priority for males, objectification of women, and sexual violence occurring across genres.[18] Some of the lyrics analyzed presented "males ordering females . . . the motivation behind the males' demands often involved obtaining sexual pleasure from women."[19] Another subtheme present was male artists presenting women as "something to be won," with the concept of pursuing a woman as that of a game.[20] Both of these themes play very well into the concept of rape culture. When male artists are seen as powerful figures who expect their demands, especially sexual ones, to be met without question, it supports the idea that a woman cannot rightfully turn down sexual advances without disrupting normal power relations. This falls in line with the results of the Kistler and Lee study, in which male artists presented themselves in ways that asserted their apparent power over women, reinforcing the participants' acceptance of male dominance. In addition, the idea of "winning" a woman results in the misguided belief that all women initially reject a man's advances, but those rejections may soon be overcome by persistent attention. This is especially problematic, as adolescents receive the message that a woman who rejects sexual advances is only "playing hard to get." A denial of consent, therefore, is not taken seriously, which can lead to sexual assault. The main issue here is that these ideas are presented as normal "rules" for relationships. Adolescents hear and absorb these messages and possibly internalize harmful messages about what is expected of them in the world of sexual relationships. This can lead to false ideas about what contributes unhealthy relationships and can place many teenagers and young adults in precarious situations.

One powerful result of the Kistler and Lee study illustrated that it is not only male artists who participate in the perpetuation of harmful gender expectations. Researchers examined and analyzed lyrics performed by female artists alongside male artists and found disturbing trends even in the lyrics performed by female artists. "A number of female artists adhered to "appropriate" gender roles by fulfilling the male's demands and by functioning as an object possessed by the

---

18 Brook Bretthauer et al., "A Feminist Analysis of Popular Music: Power Over, Objectification Of, and Violence Against Women," *Journal of Feminist Family Therapy 18 (2006): 29.*

19 Ibid, 38.

20 Ibid, 39.

male . . . in general female artists communicated messages that they were not inherently valuable and did not deserve respect."[21] This is incredibly problematic in more than one way. Adolescent females learn through the example of female artists that abuse is part of a healthy relationship. If they are told that violence, objectification, and lack of respect are normal, they are less likely to try to leave a damaging relationship, which can take a heavy toll on their own self-concept, and possibly affect their relationships in the future.

Objectification may seem a somewhat less harmful concept than overt sexual violence, but research illustrates the fallacy of such a claim. A study by Loughnan et al. (2013) revealed that undergraduate students at a British university showed less "moral concern" for a sexualized fictional victim versus a non-sexualized one.[22] As noted by Burt and others, a commonly accepted rape myth is that women desire to be sexually assaulted and women can "ask" for rape by dressing or acting in a certain way. The Loughnan study reinforced this idea, as participants assigned more blame to a sexualized victim: "compared with nonobjectified women, the objectified were perceived to be more responsible for being raped."[23] An unsavory consequence of this is that even seemingly "harmless" objectification can result in negative views of rape victims. The practice of blaming a victim for their sexual assault means that support systems meant to help victims (such as law enforcement and medical personnel) could be inadequate in fulfilling that duty.[24] It also implies that victims will continue to needlessly suffer following their assault when faced with an onslaught of social stigma and misdirected blame. When sexual assault is normalized through sexual content in popular media and victims are blamed for their assaults, rape culture continues to flourish.

This is precisely where the issue lies in popular songs such as "Blurred Lines." Though there are numerous examples of songs with lyrics suggestive of rape culture, further exploration would require more than can reasonably fit here. It is with this in mind that I chose to focus on the lyrical content and music video imagery of this song alone.

Before delving into the actual lyrics of the song, one must understand where artist Robin Thicke's mindset sits on the concept of relationships. In an interview that's been quoted numerous times throughout the media, when asked about the song and its accompanying video, Thicke stated, "People say, 'Hey, do you think this is degrading to women?' I'm like, 'Of course it is. What a pleasure it is to degrade a woman.'"[25] Upon examining the lyrics of the song and viewing the video, one has to acknowledge that Thicke certainly made his view clear, even if he disagrees that

21 Ibid, 44.

22 Steve Loughnan et al., "Sexual Objectification Increases Rape Victim Blame and Decreases Perceived Suffering." *Psychology of Women Quarterly, 37 (2013): 455.*

23 Ibid

24 Ibid, 490.

25 "Robin Thicke's Blurred Vision: A Critique of a Rape Anthem in Two Parts." Last updated August 4, 2013.

the song is a "rape anthem" and even attempts to argue that it is, instead a "feminist anthem."[26] That Thicke does not seem to see the incredibly problematic aspects of his work illustrates how deeply rape culture is entrenched in society.

A number of problematic lyrics run throughout the song, either celebrating objectification of women or making references to nonconsensual sexual activity. In the first pre-chorus, Thicke reinforces the idea of women as less-than-human as he sings: "now he was close, tried to domesticate you / but you're an animal, baby, it's in your nature."[27] In addition to this, further in the lyrics the concept of women existing solely for male entertainment: "When you got them jeans on . . . you the hottest [expletive] in this place." The music video reinforces this constant objectification, with the male artists repeatedly making glances at the bodies of the female models as they walk past. In one particular scene, a topless female model parades past Thicke as he points after her and smirks at the camera.[28] Soon after this, the same model walks quickly past Thicke in the opposite direction, and he follows her around in a manner similar to the actions of a man pursuing an unwilling woman in a dance club. Upon viewing the video in its entirety, one cannot help but notice that the female models are clearly intended as props, parading past the male artists in the background and posing with emotionless expressions atop bicycles. The choice of wardrobe must also be taken into question. The male artists such as T.I. and Thicke himself are dressed in suits, clothing items for decades associated with power and prestige. The female models, however, are, for the most part, clothed in minimal underwear with their bare chests completely exposed. It is clear who is meant to be in charge here, and it is not the half-naked women. As expressed in the results of the Kistler and Lee study, male artists having power over the women in their music videos can have damaging effects on the sexual attitudes of male college students. This means that scenarios of power and dominance such as the one expressed in Thicke's video can negatively impact male acceptance of sexual assault, thereby perpetuating rape culture.

The main issue with "Blurred Lines," however, is not its objectification of the female models. Though this is something that absolutely needs to be addressed, especially in the wake of the Loughnan study regarding objectification and victim-blaming, the bigger issue here lies in the incredibly problematic lyrical content; content that reinforces and helps to maintain rape culture and the myths associated with it. The single most repeated lyric in "Blurred Lines" is "I know you want it;" in fact, Thicke repeats this line a total of *eighteen times throughout the entirety of the song.*[29] Accompanying this assertion is also a series of lyrics including, "the way you grab me / must wanna get nasty" and Thicke asserting that he "hates these blurred lines." What are the blurred

26 Ibid.

27 AZLyrics, "Robin Thicke Lyrics—Blurred Lines."

28 "Robin Thicke—Blurred Lines (Unrated Version)..." YouTube video.

29 AZLyrics

lines that he is referring to? Music is, as always, open to interpretation, but considering the other lyrics in the song, particularly the declaration that Thicke "knows" the woman "wants it," one can interpret that he means he hates the supposed "gray area" between sexual consent and rape. Even if this is not Thicke's intention, the fact that one can interpret the meaning as such means that he is a participant in the perpetuation of rape culture, whether he believes so or not. Many of the lyrics expressed fall in line with common rape myths. For example, a commonly held belief regarding rape implies that when woman dances in any suggestive manner with a man, the man is able to assume consent to sexual activity. ("The way you grab me / must wanna get nasty"). Another equally common belief is that a woman turns down initial sexual advances only to appear pure, but she will eventually acquiesce after persistent attention ("I know you want it / But you're a good girl"). Instead of asking the woman, Thicke's lyrics indicate a false assumption of consent based on rape myths. Instead of destroying the foundation of rape myths that place women in precarious situations and blame them for being raped, Thicke's lyrics reinforce them, thereby perpetuating rape culture. When rape culture is allowed to flourish, there are real consequences, as illustrated through real-life context.

There are numerous ventures and online projects that allow sexual assault survivors the opportunity to express their feelings in supportive environments. Project Unbreakable is one of these outlets. A photography-based venture that gives sexual assault survivors of any gender an outlet for their feelings in the hope that this can help them heal, the project involves survivors being photographed holding hand-lettered signs featuring quotations from their attackers, their families, or themselves regarding their sexual assault. The project received more attention in the online social justice community after sociological blogging website *TheSocietyPages.org* featured a story that illustrated with terrible clarity the intersection of rape culture and popular music.[30] Entitled "From the Mouths of Rapists: The Lyrics to Robin Thicke's Blurred Lines," this particular story features participants in Project Unbreakable whose attackers' words are eerily reminiscent of the lyrics from Thicke's hit song. Of the signature lyric, the story reports: "Thicke sings "I know you want it," a phrase that many sexual assault survivors report their rapists saying to justify their actions, *as demonstrated over and over in the Project Unbreakable testimonials*."[31] [italics added] Though other testimonials weren't as directly linked, photos of quotations such as, "*It wasn't rape; you were being such a tease*" and "*we both know you don't really mean it when you say no*" *illustrate that Thicke's lyrics come dangerously close to reinforcing the patriarchal power structure that* normalizes rape and therefore placing more stigma on sexual assault survivors. The fact that some

30 "From the Mouths of Rapists: The Lyrics to Robin Thicke's Blurred Lines," *TheSocietyPages.org*, Accessed April 10, 2014 http://thesocietypages.org/socimages/2013/09/17/from-the-mouths-of-rapists-the-lyrics-of-robin-thickes-blurred-lines-and-real-life-rape/

31 Ibid.

of the lyrics from the song are close in interpretation to the words of actual rapists should be a cause for concern. Unfortunately, "Blurred Lines" is not the only problematic content to be let off the hook because it's just a catchy song or it's just good artistry. Everyone loves a catchy song, and this is why artists are allowed to get away with potentially harmful messages. Individuals sing along to the lyrics in their car or at the gym without fully realizing the seriousness of what is being said. Rape culture is also a cycle; we have a hard time recognizing when something perpetuates rape culture because we are constantly immersed in rape culture. Therefore, problematic attitudes expressed through the media are accepted as normal or logical.

The media we are shown and consume on a daily basis has an immediate impact on our ideologies and the way we shape our interactions with others. Adolescents are especially vulnerable to this shaping as they are just beginning to engage in romantic and sexual relationships. Young adults often look to their favorite artists and celebrities for cues about what constitutes a normal relationship. By giving music that perpetuates rape culture a free pass, we are explicitly telling rape victims that their concerns are not valid, that their experiences were to be expected, that their pain is not real. We are also teaching frightening lessons to adolescents. Males are told that sexual coercion is acceptable, and that a man has the right to demand sexual activity from a woman, even if no explicit consent is given. In turn, females are told that sexual violence is to be expected, and that a short skirt or a low cut tank top is asking for rape. In order to dismantle rape culture, we need to question music and other media that presents ideas supportive of such a culture. By dismantling rape culture, we can in turn make the world a safer place for those whom the media paints as inferior victims, and empower both men and women to engage in only mutually respectful relationships.

Bibliography

American Academy of Pediatrics. *Policy Statement—Impact of Music, Music Lyrics, and Music Videos on Children and Youth.*(2009) doi:10.1542/peds.2009-2145.

AZLyrics. "Robin Thicke Lyrics—Blurred Lines." http://www.azlyrics.com/lyrics/robinthicke/blurredlines.html.

Bretthauer, Brook, Toni Schindler Zimmerman, and James H. Banning. "A Feminist Analysis of Popular Music: Power Over, Objectification of, and Violence Against Women." *Journal of Feminist Family Therapy* 18 (2006): 29–50, doi:10.1300/J086v18n04_02.

Burt, Martha R., "Cultural Myths and Support for Rape," *Journal of Personality and Social Psychology* 38 (1980): 217–230.

Johnson, Jimmy. "Robin Thicke's Blurred Vision: A Critique of a Rape Anthem in Two Parts." *Truth-Out.org.* http://www.truth-out.org/opinion/item/17847robin-thickes-blurred-vision-a-critique-of-a-rape-anthem-in-two-parts/

Kistler, Michelle E. and Moon J. Lee. "Does Exposure to Sexual Hip-Hop Music Videos Influence the Sexual Attitudes of College Students?" *Mass Communication and Society* 13 (2009): 67–86, doi:10.1080/15205430902865336.

Koehler, Sezin. "From the Mouths of Rapists: The Lyrics to Robin Thicke's Blurred Lines." *TheSocietyPages.org*. http://thesocietypages.org/socimages/2013/09/17/from-the-mouths-of-rapists-the-lyrics-of-robin-thickes-blurred-lines-and-real-life-rape/.

Loughnan, Steve, Afroditi Pina, Eduardo A. Vasquez and Elisa Puvia. "Sexual Objectification Increases Rape Victim Blame and Decreases Perceived Suffering." *Psychology of Women Quarterly* 37 (2013): 455–461, doi:10.1177/0361684313485718.

"Robin Thicke—Blurred Lines (Unrated Version) ft. T.I., Pharell." YouTube video, 4:31, posted by "RobinThickeVEVO," March 28, 2013 https://www.youtube.com/watch?v=zwT6DZCQi9k.

Williams, Joyce E., *The Concise Encyclopedia of Sociology*, s.v. "Rape Culture." Oxford: Blackwell Publishing Ltd., 2011.

Questions about "The 'Blurred Lines' Effect: Popular Music and the Perpetuation of Rape Culture"

READING AND WRITING TO COMPREHEND

1. **Analyze**. What does Davis mean when she writes "When sexual assault is normalized through sexual content in popular media and victims are blamed for their assaults, rape culture continues to flourish?"

2. **Rhetorically read** Davis' essay with a particular eye toward her argument and evidence. What is her argument and what are the types of evidence she uses to support it?

3. **Consider**. Where do you see Davis using rhetorical appeals in her essay? How do these work together to create the overall effect of the essay?

READING AND WRITING TO RESPOND

4. **View** the video "Blurred Lines" on the internet (via YouTube or another site). Write an intellectual response in which you focus primarily on how this video affects your reading of Davis' printed essay, which cites lyrics and describes the video, but not does link to the video (see Chapter 3 for help with intellectual responses). In other words, to what extent does experiencing the text visually change your experience of Davis' essay? *So what?*

READING AND WRITING TO APPLY AND REFLECT

5. **Reread** Davis' essay twice in order to apply the Believing/Doubting Game reading strategy. Referring to your annotations from these readings, write a letter to a specific audience of your choice that supports (i.e. "believes") Davis' argument. You may choose to write to a friend, a parent, a professor, or even Robin Thicke, the singer of "Blurred Lines."

6. **Refer** to your annotations indicating your "doubts," then **write** a letter to a specific audience of your choice (see question 5 for some options) explaining these doubts. Now that you have written both letters, **consider** whether one of the letters reveals what you really think. How can you tell?

On the Occasion of Being Mistaken for a Man by Security Personnel at Newark International Airport

By Stacey Waite

This poem, like many others Waite has written, explores the relationships among one's gender, body, and sex. In this particular poem, questions surrounding these relationships emerge when the speaker's body is mistaken or misread for something it is not.

In Waite, Stacey. *Butch Geography*. Tupelo Press, 2013.

It's like being born again, these metal detectors
are like traveling through the womb, the buzz
goes off to indicate the birth of trouble.
And the gender of trouble matters because
when a woman goes through, Jimmy yells,
"Female Search" and a large woman appears
from behind her security table. So when I walk through
and my wallet chain sets off the womb alert,
I wait. I wait for "Female Search" like I wait for the bus,
that hopeful and expecting look. But Jimmy takes me

himself. Jimmy slides his hands down the length
of my thighs, he pats his palm stiffly against my crotch.
He asks me to remove my boots and jacket.
And so I do. And at first, the woman in me goes unnoticed.
But when I hold my arms straight out
and he traces the outline of my underarms, he makes
that face, the face I've seen before,
the "holy-shit-it's-a-woman" face,
the "pretend-you-don't-notice-the-tits" face.
Jimmy's hands change from a tender sweep
to a kind of wiping, like he's trying to rid my body
of the afterbirth, he is preparing to peel off the skin of my body
as he would the apple he brings to work for break time.
Jimmy stares hard at the metal detector,
with a kind of respect like the arch of it became holy,
transformed me on my walk through.
Jimmy is nervous for the following reasons:
he has just felt the crotch and chest of a woman who he thought was a man,
he can not decide which way he liked her best,
his supervisor might notice he has not yelled "Female Search"
which he knows is grounds for some sort of lawsuit,
he's angry, his blue uniform makes him angry
so that when he is patting her down now, he does it with force,
he wants her to feel he is stronger than she is,
he wants the metal detector to stop being a gender change machine
from which this woman, who is also me, emerges,
unties her boots slowly, follows all his directions.
And when Jimmy is done, he nods. He wants me
to keep him secret, to pretend neither of us had ever been born.

Questions about "On the Occasion of Being Mistaken for a Man by Security Personnel at Newark International Airport"

READING AND WRITING TO COMPREHEND

1. **Apply** and **analyze**. Which reading strategy do you think will best help you understand this poem? Test out your hypothesis and read the poem using that strategy. Then try two more strategies. Which is most productive? Why?

2. **Develop** a difficulty inventory listing. Now that you have read the poem at least three times, are there still elements that you don't understand? Develop a difficulty inventory listing those remaining elements (see Chapter 3 for help with difficulty inventories).

3. **Trace** the speaker's use of pronouns in the poem. Where does the speaker use "I," "my," and "me," and where does the speaker use "her?" *So what?*

READING AND WRITING TO RESPOND

4. **Write** an intellectual response that focuses specifically on the first few lines of the poem in which Waite describes the "birth of trouble" and the "gender of trouble." One way to read this opening is as an allusion to philosopher Judith Butler's 1990 groundbreaking book *Gender Trouble: Feminism and the Subversion of Identity.* Do some research on Butler and her book. Using the "reading and evaluating online sources" strategy to annotate your sources, describe the extent to which recognizing this allusion helps you to understand what is being addressed in the poem.

READING AND WRITING TO APPLY AND REFLECT

5. **Reflect** on how you as a reader approach poetry. What have you been taught to look for when you read poetry? What was your experience like reading this poem using the strategies in this textbook? How was reading this poem different from reading the first selection in this chapter or other prose (non-poetry) selections?

Facebook, the Gender Binary, and Third-Person Pronouns

By Lal Zimman

This blog post posits that Facebook is a pioneer in moving beyond what Zimman calls the "gender binary." Although not as powerful as other institutions such as schools, Zimman maintains that Facebook's cultural cachet can go a long way toward important social change by helping us recognize how our cur-

rent binary-driven linguistic practices do not adequately represent the complexities of gender and sexuality.

Oxford University Press Blog, September 23rd 2014.
Visit http://blog.oup.com/2014/09/facebook-gender-binary-third-person-pronouns/

The death rattle of the gender binary has been ringing for decades now, leaving us to wonder when it will take its last gasp. In this third decade of third wave feminism and the queer critique, dismantling the binary remains a critical task in the gender revolution. Language is among the most socially pervasive tools through which culture is negotiated, but in a language like English, with its minimal linguistic marking of gender, it can be difficult to find concrete signs that linguistic structures are changing to reflect new ways of thinking about the gender binary rather than simply repackaging old ideas.

Sign from Genderblur at Twin Cities Pride 2003. Photo by Transguyjay. CC BY-NC 2.0 via Flickr.

One direction we might look, though, is toward the gendering of third person pronouns, which is what led me to write this post about pronouns on Facebook. Yes, Facebook. The social media giant may not be your first thought when it comes to feminist language activism, but this year's shift in the way Facebook categorizes gender is among the most widely-felt signs of a sea change in institutional attitudes about gendered third person pronouns. Although Facebook does not have the same force as the educational system, governments, or traditional print media, it carries its own linguistic cachet established through its corporate authority, its place in the cultural negotiation of coolness and social connection, and its near inescapable presence in everyday life.

In response to long-standing calls from transgender and gender non-conforming users to broaden its approach to gender, Facebook announced earlier this year that it would offer a new set of options. Rather than limiting members of the site to the selection of female or male, an extensive list of gender identities is offered, along with the option of a custom entry, including labels like *agender, bigender, gender fluid, gender non-conforming, trans person, two-spirit, transgender (wo)man and cisgender* (i.e. non-transgender) *(wo)man.*

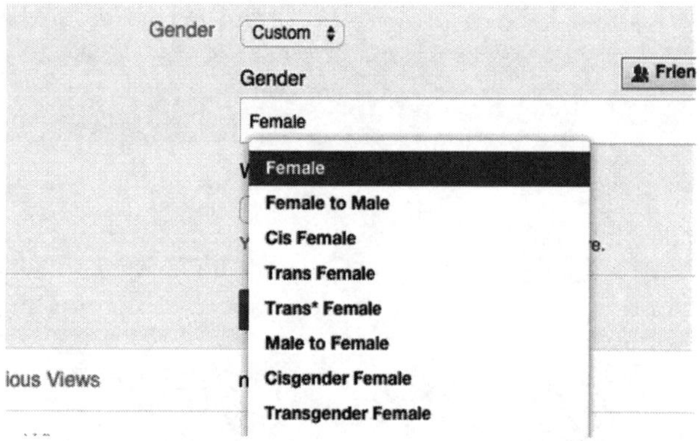

Screenshot courtesy of Lal Zimman.

With all of the potential complexity afforded by these categories, Facebook couldn't rely on a simple algorithm of assigning gendered pronouns for those occasions on which the website generates a third person reference to the user (e.g. "Wish ___ a happy birthday!"). Instead, it asks which set of pronouns a user prefers among three options: *he/him/his, she/her/hers,* or *they/them/theirs.* As a result, there are two important ways that Facebook's reconsideration of its gender classification system goes beyond the listing of additional gender categories. The first is the more obvious of the two: offering singular they as an option for those who prefer gender neutral reference forms. The other is simply the practice of asking for a pronoun preference rather than deriving it from gender or sex.

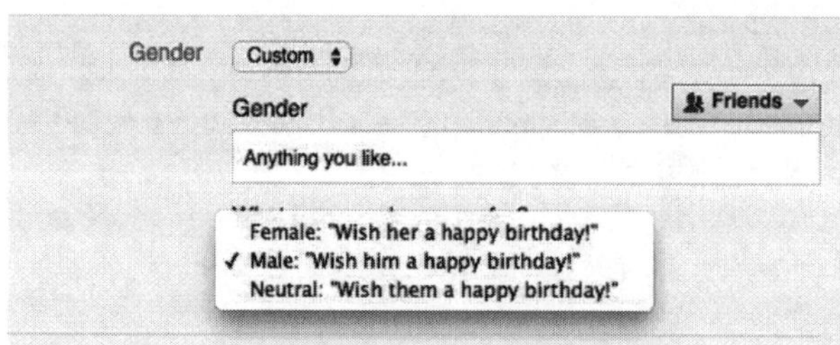

Screenshot courtesy of Lal Zimman

Sanctioning the use of singular they as a gender neutral pronoun counters the centuries-old grammarian's complaint that they can only be used in reference to plural third person referents.

Proponents of singular they, however, point out that the pronoun has been used by some of the English-speaking world's finest writers and that it was in wide-spread use even before blatantly misogynistic language policies determined that he should be the gender-neutral pronoun in official texts of the British government. More recently, an additional source of support for singular *they* has arisen: for those who do not wish to be slotted into one side of the gender binary or the other, *they* is perhaps the most intuitive way to avoid gendered third-person pronouns because of its already familiar presence in most dialects of English. (Other options include innovative pronouns like *ze/hir/hirs* or *ey/em/em's*.) In this case, a speaker must choose between upholding grammatical conventions and affirming someone's identity.

THE PRESCRIPTIVE GRAMMARIAN'S PERSONAL PRONOUN SYSTEM				
	NUMBER			
		SINGULAR		PLURAL
PERSON	1st	I		WE
	2nd	YOU		
	3rd	SHE	HE	THEY

Courtesy of Lal Zimman.

But wait, you might ask – don't we need a distinction between singular and plural they? How are we supposed to know when someone is talking about a single person and when they're talking about a group? Though my post isn't necessarily meant to defend the use of singular they in reference to specific individuals (an argument others have made quite extensively), this point is worth addressing briefly if only to dispel the notion that the standard pronoun system is logical while deviations are somehow logically flawed. As the pronoun charts included here illustrate, there is already a major gap in the standard English pronoun system when compared to many other languages: a distinction between singular and plural you. Somehow we get by, however, relying on context and sometimes asking for clarification. Could we do the same with they?

The second pronoun-related change Facebook has made—asking for preferred pronouns rather than determining them based on gender category – is a more fundamental challenge to the normative take on assigning pronouns. According to conventional wisdom, a speaker will select whether to use she or he based on certain types of information about the person being referred to: how their bodily sex is perceived, how they present their gender, and in some cases other contextual factors like their name. To be uncertain about which gendered pronoun to use can be a source of great anxiety, exemplified by cultural artifacts like Saturday Night Live's androgynous character from the 1990s known only as Pat. No one ever asks Pat about their gender because to do so would presumably be a grave insult, as Pat apparently has no idea that they have an androgynous appearance (were you able to follow me, despite the singular they's?).

A NON-BINARY PERSONAL PRONOUN SYSTEM			
		NUMBER	
		SINGULAR	PLURAL
PERSON	1st	I	WE
	2nd	YOU	
	3rd	SHE / HE / ZE / EY / PER …	THEY

Courtesy of Lal Zimman.

But transgender and queer communities are increasingly turning this logic on its head. Rather than risk being "mis-pronouned," as community members sometimes call it, it is becoming the norm for introductions in many trans and queer contexts to include pronouns preferences along with names. For instance, my name is Lal and I prefer he/him/his pronouns. (Even the custom of calling these "male" pronouns has been critiqued on the basis that one needn't identify as male in order to prefer he/him/his pronouns.) The goal behind this move is to remove the tension of uncertainty and to avoid potential offense or embarrassment before it takes place. But this is not just a practice for transgender and gender non-conforming people; the ideal is that no one's pronoun preferences be taken for granted. Instead of determining pronouns according to appearance, they become a matter of open negotiation in which one can demonstrate an interest in using language that feel maximally respectful to others.

Facebook's adoption of this new approach to pronouns, despite prescriptive grammarians' objections, suggests that the acceptance and use of singular they is expanding. More than that, it furthers the normalization of self-selected pronouns since even those who are totally unfamiliar with the use of singular they as a preferred pronoun, or the very idea of pronoun preferences, may be faced with unexpected pronouns in their daily newsfeeds.

For those of us at academic institutions with sizable transgender and gender non-conforming communities, the practices discussed here may already be underway on campus. During my time teaching at Reed College, for instance, I found students to be enthusiastic about including pronoun preferences in our beginning-of-semester introductions even in classes where everyone's pronoun preferences aligned with normative expectations.

My goal here isn't to argue that the gender binary is dissolving in the face of new pronoun practices. Indeed, linguistic negotiations of gender and sexual binaries are far too complex to draw such a simple conclusion. However, what I do want to suggest is that we are in the midst of some kind of shift in the way pronouns are used and understood among speakers of English. Describing a more fully complete change of this sort, linguistic anthropologist Michael Silverstein has explained how religious and political ideology among speakers of Early Modern English resulted in a collapse of the second person pronouns thou (singular, informal) and you (plural, formal). In the present case, rapidly changing ideologies about the gender binary may be pushing us toward a different organization of third person pronouns of the sort illustrated by the non-binary pronoun chart on the previous page.

The effect of Facebook on linguistic practice more broadly has yet to be fully uncovered, but its capital-driven flexibility and omnipresence in contemporary social life suggests that it may be a powerful tool in ideologically-driven language change.

Headline image credit: People and gender. CCo via Pixabay.

Lal Zimman is the co-editor of Queer Excursions: Retheorizing Binaries in Language, Gender, and Sexuality with Jenny Davis and Joshua Raclaw. Lal Zimman is a Visiting Assistant Professor at Reed College. His research, which brings together ethnographic, sociophonetic, and discourse analytic frameworks, deals with the relationship between gender, sexuality, and embodiment in the linguistic practices of transgender and LGBQ communities.

Questions about "Facebook, the Gender Binary, and Third-Person Pronouns"

READING AND WRITING TO COMPREHEND

1. In his blog entry, Zimman writes, "Language is among the most socially pervasive tools through which culture is negotiated, but in a language like English, with its minimal linguistic marking of gender, it can be difficult to find concrete signs that linguistic structures are changing to reflect new ways of thinking about the gender binary rather than simply repackaging old idea." What does this mean?

2. Zimman concludes with the following: "The effect of Facebook on linguistic practice more broadly has yet to be fully uncovered, but its capital-driven flexibility and omnipresence in contemporary social life suggests that it may be a powerful tool in ideologically-driven language change." What does Zimman mean by the terms "capital-driven flexibility," "omnipresence," and "ideologically-driven?"

3. How do the images in Zimman's blog entry connect to the printed text? How would you describe the relationship? For example, do the images highlight Zimman's argument? Help develop his ideas? Represent the voices of others who might disagree with him?

READING AND WRITING TO RESPOND

4. In this blog entry, Zimman writes that the movement to introduce one's preferred pronouns alongside one's name is becoming more common and is based on the notion that "no one's pronoun preference should be taken for granted." Write an intellectual response in which you describe what you think of this as a widespread practice. Do you engage in it? Do you know others who do? *So what*? (see Chapter 3 for help with intellectual responses).

READING AND WRITING TO APPLY AND REFLECT

5. Although not as powerful as the education system or government, Zimman argues that Facebook still wields a great deal of power in part because of its "inescapable presence in everyday life." Beyond its potential power to affect the use of pronouns, where else do you see Facebook exercising its power? Choose one example and explore the implications of this, as Zimman does with Facebook's power to affect language.

Mothers Anonymous

By Emily Nussbaum

NEW YORK

This essay explores UrbanBaby, a New York–based website with an anonymous message-board on which women comment about parenting. As Nussbaum recounts, though, the forum offers a space in which women often confess their deepest and darkest feelings about their children, their spouses, and about mothering.

Visit http://nymag.com/news/features/17668/

Questions about "Mothers Anonymous"

READING AND WRITING TO COMPREHEND

1. **Rhetorically read and annotate** "Mothers Anonymous" with specific attention to Nussbaum's argument and the types of evidence she uses to make this argument (see Chapter 3 for help with rhetorical reading).
2. **Consider**. Nussbaum spends some time talking about how many of the women who post on UrbanBaby's message-board seem nostalgic for certain eras. What does nostalgia have to do with Nussbaum's argument?
3. **Infer**. Readers can imagine that not all of the posts from UrbanBaby's message-board are represented in this piece. Why do you think Nussbaum chose to focus on the posts she does? So what?

READING AND WRITING TO RESPOND

4. Using your annotations, **write** an intellectual response in which you address how important you think anonymity is to UrbanBaby's message-board (see Chapter 4 for help with intellectual responses).

READING AND WRITING TO APPLY AND REFLECT

5. Using your intellectual response, as well as your answers to questions 1–3, come up with an example of something that depends on anonymity. You may choose chatrooms or similar spaces on the internet or something that is not associated with technology at all such as groups like Alcoholics Anonymous or anonymous comment cards distributed at restaurants. What role does anonymity play in your chosen example? How important is it? So what?

LONG WRITING ASSIGNMENTS BASED ON READINGS IN CHAPTER 9: GENDER AND TECHNOLOGY

1. **Multimodal Option.** Using Sarah Davis' essay "The 'Blurred Lines' Effect: Popular Music and the Perpetuation of Rape Culture" as a starting point, develop a multimodal project that "remixes" her essay to include elements that are not print-based. In other words, re-present her essay through multimodal means that help to underscore her argument. Then, write a reflection that addresses the choices you made as you developed your multimodal project. Address how you think your use of multimodal components make her argument that much stronger.

2. **Reread** and **consider** Sarah Davis' essay "The 'Blurred Lines' Effect: Popular Music and the Perpetuation of Rape Culture" using the RLW strategy. Then, choose a song or other artifact and **develop** an argument that draws on sources (as does Davis' essay) to expose some aspect of it (see Chapter 4 for help with writing academic arguments) not readily visible. Finally, **write** a reflection that addresses the decisions you made in writing your essay and how they relate to what you noticed about Davis' essay. Which elements and techniques from Davis' essay did you find helpful in developing your own essay and which did you choose not to include. Why?

3. **Develop** an argument. Using the selections from this chapter and your annotations on these selections, develop an argument about what a specific technology or set of related technologies are contributing to discussions of gender. How is this technology adding to the discussion? *So what?* Look back at the annotations you already have on the texts to determine how helpful those are. It is likely that you will need to reread the selections by applying a reading strategy that you think will be most effective for completing this particular assignment.

4. **Multimodal Option.** Develop a multimodal project that develops an argument about what a specific technology or set of related technologies are contributing to discussions of gender. How is this technology adding to the discussion? *So what?*

5. *Rebellious Magazine for Women* introduces Stacey Waite's poem "On the Occasion of Being Mistaken for a Man by Security Personnel at Newark International Airport" as follows: "Stacey Waite's poetry rebels against and with identity, against and with the body. Waite's poetry rebels against how outsiders perceive both as working together or against one another." **Develop** this idea further by returning to Waite's poem and locating evidence to support this interpretation. How does the poem help

you understand what it means to "rebel against and with identity, against and with the body?," as well as "how outsiders perceive both as working together or against one another?" Are there moments in the poem that might challenge this interpretation? Look back at the annotations you already have on the poem to determine how helpful those are. It is likely that you will need to reread the poem by applying a reading strategy that you think will be most effective for completing this particular assignment.

REFLECTING ON YOUR READING STRATEGIES AND ANNOTATIONS

Consider the different reading strategies you applied while reading the selections in this chapter. Which were most useful for understanding the text? For reading poetry? For figuring out what you think? For responding to the text? Anticipate future uses of these reading strategies in this class, in other classes, and in other contexts. Also, consider previous courses and contexts in which these strategies would have been helpful.

Chapter 10. The Environment and Technology

This chapter contains selections that explore the relationship between the environment and technology or—to be more precise—technologies. Opening with an opinion piece by environmentalist Wendell Berry that accuses Americans of being too lax about the country's conservation efforts, this chapter includes a range of perspectives on the issue of environmentalism, all of which address—to varying degrees—the role that technology might play when it comes to both understanding environmental issues and addressing them. Like Berry's piece, Derrick Jensen's more contemporary "Forget Shorter Showers" makes similar claims about the need for Americans to be more aggressive in the fight to save the environment. Moreover, Jensen also addresses (what Jensen sees as) the misnomer of "green technology." Finally, Amelia Urry and James W. Cortada's selections address the relationship between technology and the environment most directly as they consider the role of technology in national parks and on farms, respectively.

PRIOR TO READING EACH SELECTION IN THIS CHAPTER

Look at the questions after each reading. What are you expected to do after reading this selection? In other words, what are your purposes for reading? Although you will be asked to apply particular reading strategies in order to complete some of the tasks, others will leave the choice of strategy up to you. Refer to the descriptions of the reading strategies in Chapter 2 and decide which will be most useful in helping you accomplish those tasks. Remember that you will be reading each selection multiple times and, therefore, will have additional opportunities to apply different reading strategies.

READINGS

Environmentalists Have Given Up Too Much by Not Being Radical Enough

By Wendell Berry

This article explores conservation efforts in the United States. Berry outlines the problems with the current way in which conservation is addressed and offers recommendations for what he sees as more productive approaches.

Published October 21, 2004, at Grist.org.
Visit http://grist.org/article/berry/

We are destroying our country—I mean our country itself, our land. This is a terrible thing to know, but it is not a reason for despair unless we decide to continue the destruction. If we decide to continue the destruction, that will not be because we have no other choice. This destruction is not necessary. It is not inevitable, except that by our submissiveness we make it so.

We Americans are not usually thought to be a submissive people, but of course we are. Why else would we allow our country to be destroyed? Why else would we be rewarding its destroyers? Why else would we all—by proxies we have given to greedy corporations and corrupt politicians—be participating in its destruction? Most of us are still too sane to piss in our own cistern, but we allow others to do so and we reward them for it. We reward them so well, in fact, that those who piss in our cistern are wealthier than the rest of us.

How do we submit? By not being radical enough. Or by not being thorough enough, which is the same thing.

Protection to the People

Since the beginning of the conservation effort in our country, conservationists have too often believed that we could protect the land without protecting the people. This has begun to change, but for a while yet we will have to reckon with the old assumption that we can preserve the natural world by protecting wilderness areas while we neglect or destroy the economic landscapes—the farms and ranches and working forests—and the people who use them. That assumption is understandable in view of the worsening threats to wilderness areas, but it is wrong. If conservationists hope to save even the wild lands and wild creatures, they are going to have to address issues of economy, which is to say issues of the health of the landscapes and the towns and cities where we do our work, and the quality of that work, and the well-being of the people who do the work.

Governments seem to be making the opposite error, believing that the people can be adequately protected without protecting the land. And here I am not talking about parties or party doctrines, but about the dominant political assumption. Sooner or later, governments will have to recognize that if the land does not prosper, nothing else can prosper for very long. We can have no industry or trade or wealth or security if we don't uphold the health of the land and the people and the people's work.

It is merely a fact that the land, here and everywhere, is suffering. We have the "dead zone" in the Gulf of Mexico and undrinkable water to attest to the toxicity of our agriculture. We know that we are carelessly and wastefully logging our forests. We know that soil erosion, air and water pollution, urban sprawl, the proliferation of highways and garbage are making our lives always less pleasant, less healthful, less sustainable, and our dwelling places more ugly.

Nearly 40 years ago, my state of Kentucky, like other coal-producing states, began an effort to regulate strip mining. While that effort has continued, and has imposed certain requirements of "reclamation," strip mining has become steadily more destructive of the land and the land's future. We are now permitting the destruction of entire mountains and entire watersheds. No war, so far, has done such extensive or such permanent damage. If we know that coal is an exhaustible resource, whereas the forests over it are with proper use inexhaustible, and that strip mining destroys the forest virtually forever, how can we permit this destruction? If we honor at all that fragile creature the topsoil, so long in the making, so miraculously made, so indispensable to all life, how can we destroy it? If we believe, as so many of us profess to do, that the earth is God's property and is full of His glory, how can we do harm to any part of it?

In Kentucky, as in other unfortunate states, and again at great public cost, we have allowed—in fact we have officially encouraged—the establishment of the confined animal-feeding industry, which exploits and abuses everything involved: the land, the people, the animals, and the consumers. If we love our country, as so many of us profess to do, how can we so desecrate it?

But the economic damage is not confined just to our farms and forests. For the sake of "job creation," in Kentucky, and in other backward states, we have lavished public money on corporations that come in and stay only so long as they can exploit people here more cheaply than elsewhere. The general purpose of the present economy is to exploit, not to foster or conserve.

Look carefully, if you doubt me, at the centers of the larger towns in virtually every part of our country. You will find that they are economically dead or dying. Good buildings that used to house needful, useful, locally owned small businesses of all kinds are now empty or have evolved into junk stores or antique shops. But look at the houses, the churches, the commercial buildings, the courthouse, and you will see that more often than not they are comely and well made. And then go look at the corporate outskirts: the chain stores, the fast-food joints, the food-and-fuel stores that no longer can be called service stations, the motels. Try to find something comely or well made there.

What is the difference? The difference is that the old town centers were built by people who were proud of their place and who realized a particular value in living there. The old buildings look good because they were built by people who respected themselves and wanted the respect of their neighbors. The corporate outskirts, on the contrary, were built by people who manifestly take no pride in the place, see no value in lives lived there, and recognize no neighbors. The only value they see in the place is the money that can be siphoned out of it to more fortunate places—that is, to the wealthier suburbs of the larger cities.

Can we actually suppose that we are wasting, polluting, and making ugly this beautiful land for the sake of patriotism and the love of God? Perhaps some of us would like to think so, but in fact this destruction is taking place because we have allowed ourselves to believe, and to live, a mated pair of economic lies: that nothing has a value that is not assigned to it by the market; and that the economic life of our communities can safely be handed over to the great corporations.

We citizens have a large responsibility for our delusion and our destructiveness, and I don't want to minimize that. But I don't want to minimize, either, the large responsibility that is borne by government.

The Dissent of the Governed

It is commonly understood that governments are instituted to provide certain protections that citizens individually cannot provide for themselves. But governments have tended to assume that this responsibility can be fulfilled mainly by the police and the military. They have used their regulatory powers reluctantly and often poorly. Our governments have only occasionally recognized the need of land and people to be protected against economic violence. It is true that economic violence is not always as swift, and is rarely as bloody, as the violence of war, but it can be devastating nonetheless. Acts of economic aggression can destroy a landscape or a community or the center of a town or city, and they routinely do so.

Such damage is justified by its corporate perpetrators and their political abettors in the name of the "free market" and "free enterprise," but this is a freedom that makes greed the dominant economic virtue, and it destroys the freedom of other people along with their communities and livelihoods. There are such things as economic weapons of massive destruction. We have allowed them to be used against us, not just by public submission and regulatory malfeasance, but also by public subsidies, incentives, and sufferances impossible to justify.

We have failed to acknowledge this threat and to act in our own defense. As a result, our once-beautiful and bountiful countryside has long been a colony of the coal, timber, and agribusiness corporations, yielding an immense wealth of energy and raw materials at an immense cost to our land and our land's people. Because of that failure also, our towns and cities have been gutted by the likes of Wal-Mart, which have had the permitted luxury of destroying locally owned small businesses by means of volume discounts.

Because as individuals or even as communities we cannot protect ourselves against these aggressions, we need our state and national governments to protect us. As the poor deserve as much justice from our courts as the rich, so the small farmer and the small merchant deserve the same economic justice, the same freedom in the market, as big farmers and chain stores. They should not suffer ruin merely because their rich competitors can afford (for a while) to undersell them.

Furthermore, to permit the smaller enterprises always to be ruined by false advantages, either at home or in the global economy, is ultimately to destroy local, regional, and even national capabilities of producing vital supplies such as food and textiles. It is impossible to understand, let alone justify, a government's willingness to allow the human sources of necessary goods to be destroyed by the "freedom" of this corporate anarchy. It is equally impossible to understand how a government can permit, and even subsidize, the destruction of the land and the land's productivity. Somehow we have lost or discarded any controlling sense of the interdependence of the earth and the human capacity to use it well. The governmental obligation to protect these economic resources, inseparably human and natural, is the same as the obligation to protect us from hunger or from foreign invaders. In result, there is no difference between a domestic threat to the sources of our life and a foreign one.

It appears that we have fallen into the habit of compromising on issues that should not, and in fact cannot, be compromised. I have an idea that a large number of us, including even a large number of politicians, believe that it is wrong to destroy the earth. But we have powerful political opponents who insist that an earth-destroying economy is justified by freedom and profit. And so we compromise by agreeing to permit the destruction only of parts of the earth, or to permit the earth to be destroyed a little at a time—like the famous three-legged pig that was too well-loved to be slaughtered all at once.

The logic of this sort of compromising is clear, and it is clearly fatal. If we continue to be economically dependent on destroying parts of the earth, then eventually we will destroy it all.

Hope Notes

So long a complaint accumulates a debt to hope, and I would like to end with hope. To do so I need only repeat something I said at the beginning: Our destructiveness has not been, and it is not, inevitable. People who use that excuse are morally incompetent, they are cowardly, and they are lazy. Humans don't have to live by destroying the sources of their life. People can change; they can learn to do better. All of us, regardless of party, can be moved by love of our land to rise above the greed and contempt of our land's exploiters. This of course leads to practical problems, and I will offer a short list of practical suggestions.

We have got to learn better to respect ourselves and our dwelling places. We need to quit thinking of rural America as a colony. Too much of the economic history of our land has been that of the export of fuel, food, and raw materials that have been destructively and too cheaply produced. We must reaffirm the economic value of good stewardship and good work. For that we will need better accounting than we have had so far.

We need to reconsider the idea of solving our economic problems by "bringing in industry." Every state government appears to be scheming to lure in a large corporation from somewhere else by "tax incentives" and other squanderings of the people's money. We ought to suspend that practice until we are sure that in every state we have made the most and the best of what is already there. We need to build the local economies of our communities and regions by adding value to local products and marketing them locally before we seek markets elsewhere.

We need to confront honestly the issue of scale. Bigness has a charm and a drama that are seductive, especially to politicians and financiers; but bigness promotes greed, indifference, and damage, and often bigness is not necessary. You may need a large corporation to run an airline or to manufacture cars, but you don't need a large corporation to raise a chicken or a hog. You don't need a large corporation to process local food or local timber and market it locally.

And, finally, we need to give an absolute priority to caring well for our land—for every bit of it. There should be no compromise with the destruction of the land or of anything else that we cannot replace. We have been too tolerant of politicians who, entrusted with our country's defense, become the agents of our country's destroyers, compromising on its ruin.

And so I will end this by quoting my fellow Kentuckian, a great patriot and an indomitable foe of strip-mining, Joe Begley of Blackey: "Compromise, hell!"

Questions about "Environmentalists Have Given Up Too Much by Not Being Radical Enough"

READING AND WRITING TO COMPREHEND

1. **Analyze** the quote. What does Berry mean when he writes, "This destruction is not necessary. It is not inevitable, except that by our submissiveness we make it so?"
2. **Understand** the rhetorical appeals. What kind of rhetorical appeal(s) does Berry use. How do they affect you as a reader? (For help with rhetorical appeals see Chapter 2.)
3. **Analyze** the conclusion. What do you make of the quote Berry uses to conclude his piece? How does this work as a conclusion to his argument?

READING AND WRITING TO RESPOND

4. **Write** an intellectual response. Berry's piece is an op-ed, which is short for "opinion editorial." Annotate the piece using the RLW strategy to help you notice Berry's techniques. Based on your annotations, write an intellectual response that details what you believe to be the characteristics of an op-ed and how these separate it from other genres. What seem to be the defining features? What does this genre allow and what might it prohibit?

READING AND WRITING TO APPLY AND REFLECT

5. **Compose** a reflection. Use your RLW annotations about Berry's techniques as well as your answers to the previous questions to write your own an op-ed on any subject.

Then, write a reflection describing your choices. Which techniques, including the kind of rhetorical appeals Berry uses, did you choose to imitate? Why? Which did you decide against imitating? Why?

Forget Shorter Showers

By Derrick Jensen

ORION MAGAZINE

Orion Magazine > Articles > Columns > Upping the Stakes > Forget Shorter Showers

Forget Shorter Showers

by DERRICK JENSEN

WOULD ANY SANE PERSON think dumpster diving would have stopped Hitler, or that composting would have ended slavery or brought about the eight-hour workday, or that chopping wood and carrying water would have gotten people out of Tsarist prisons, or that dancing naked around a fire would have helped put in place the Voting Rights Act of 1957 or the Civil Rights Act of 1964? Then why now, with all the world at stake, do so many people retreat into these entirely personal "solutions"?

This essay contends that current efforts to address large environmental issues are misguided. In place of these insufficient responses, Jensen recommends what he imagines are more far-reaching and sustainable solutions.

Visit https://orionmagazine.org/article/forget-shorter-showers/

WOULD ANY SANE PERSON think dumpster diving would have stopped Hitler, or that composting would have ended slavery or brought about the eight-hour workday, or that chopping wood and carrying water would have gotten people out of Tsarist prisons, or that dancing naked around a fire would have helped put in place the Voting Rights Act of 1957 or the Civil Rights Act of 1964? Then why now, with all the world at stake, do so many people retreat into these entirely personal "solutions"?

Part of the problem is that we've been victims of a campaign of systematic misdirection. Consumer culture and the capitalist mindset have taught us to substitute acts of personal consumption (or enlightenment) for organized political resistance. *An Inconvenient Truth* helped raise consciousness about global warming. But did you notice that all of the solutions presented had to do with personal consumption—changing light bulbs, inflating tires, driving half as much—and had nothing to do with shifting power away from corporations, or stopping the growth economy that is destroying the planet? Even if every person in the United States did everything the movie suggested, U.S. carbon emissions would fall by only 22 percent. Scientific consensus is that emissions must be reduced by at least 75 percent worldwide.

Or let's talk water. We so often hear that the world is running out of water. People are dying from lack of water. Rivers are dewatered from lack of water. Because of this we need to take shorter showers. See the disconnect? *Because I take showers, I'm responsible for drawing down aquifers?* Well, no. More than 90 percent of the water used by humans is used by agriculture and industry. The remaining 10 percent is split between municipalities and actual living breathing individual humans. Collectively, municipal golf courses use as much water as municipal human beings. People (both human people and fish people) aren't dying because the world is running out of water. They're dying because the water is being stolen.

Or let's talk energy. Kirkpatrick Sale summarized it well: "For the past 15 years the story has been the same every year: individual consumption—residential, by private car, and so on—is never more than about a quarter of all consumption; the vast majority is commercial, industrial, corporate, by agribusiness and government [he forgot military]. So, even if we all took up cycling and wood stoves it would have a negligible impact on energy use, global warming and atmospheric pollution."

Or let's talk waste. In 2005, per-capita municipal waste production (basically everything that's put out at the curb) in the U.S. was about 1,660 pounds. Let's say you're a die-hard simple-living activist, and you reduce this to zero. You recycle everything. You bring cloth bags shopping. You fix your toaster. Your toes poke out of old tennis shoes. You're not done yet, though. Since municipal waste includes not just residential waste, but also waste from government offices and businesses, you march to those offices, waste reduction pamphlets in hand, and convince them to cut down on their waste enough to eliminate your share of it. Uh, I've got some bad news. Municipal waste accounts for only 3 percent of total waste production in the United States.

I want to be clear. I'm not saying we shouldn't live simply. I live reasonably simply myself, but I don't pretend that not buying much (or not driving much, or not having kids) is a powerful political act, or that it's deeply revolutionary. It's not. Personal change doesn't equal social change.

So how, then, and especially with all the world at stake, have we come to accept these utterly insufficient responses? I think part of it is that we're in a double bind. A double bind is where you're given multiple options, but no matter what option you choose, you lose, and withdrawal is not an option. At this point, it should be pretty easy to recognize that every action involving the industrial economy is destructive (and we shouldn't pretend that solar photovoltaics, for example, exempt us from this: they still require mining and transportation infrastructures at every point in the production processes; the same can be said for every other so-called green technology). So if we choose option one—if we avidly participate in the industrial economy—we may in the short term think we win because we may accumulate wealth, the marker of "success" in this culture. But we lose, because in doing so we give up our empathy, our animal humanity. And we really lose because industrial civilization is killing the planet, which means everyone loses. If we choose the "alternative" option of living more simply, thus causing less harm, but still not stopping the industrial economy from killing the planet, we may in the short term think we win because we get to feel pure, and we didn't even have to give up all of our empathy (just enough to justify not stopping the horrors), but once again we really lose because industrial civilization is still killing the planet, which means everyone still loses. The third option, acting decisively to stop the industrial economy, is very scary for a number of reasons, including but not restricted to the fact that we'd lose some of the luxuries (like electricity) to which we've grown accustomed, and the fact that those in power might try to kill us if we seriously impede their ability to exploit the world—none of which alters the fact that it's a better option than a dead planet. Any option is a better option than a dead planet.

Besides being ineffective at causing the sorts of changes necessary to stop this culture from killing the planet, there are at least four other problems with perceiving simple living as a political act (as opposed to living simply because that's what you want to do). The first is that it's predicated on the flawed notion that humans inevitably harm their landbase. Simple living as a political act consists solely of harm reduction, ignoring the fact that humans can help the Earth as well as harm it. We can rehabilitate streams, we can get rid of noxious invasives, we can remove dams, we can disrupt a political system tilted toward the rich as well as an extractive economic system, we can destroy the industrial economy that is destroying the real, physical world.

The second problem—and this is another big one—is that it incorrectly assigns blame to the individual (and most especially to individuals who are particularly powerless) instead of to those who actually wield power in this system and to the system itself. Kirkpatrick Sale again: "The whole individualist what-you-can-do-to-save-the-earth guilt trip is a myth. We, as individuals, are not creating the crises, and we can't solve them."

The third problem is that it accepts capitalism's redefinition of us from citizens to consumers. By accepting this redefinition, we reduce our potential forms of resistance to consuming and not consuming. Citizens have a much wider range of available resistance tactics, including voting, not voting, running for office, pamphleting, boycotting, organizing, lobbying, protesting, and, when a government becomes destructive of life, liberty, and the pursuit of happiness, we have the right to alter or abolish it.

The fourth problem is that the endpoint of the logic behind simple living as a political act is suicide. If every act within an industrial economy is destructive, and if we want to stop this destruction, and if we are unwilling (or unable) to question (much less destroy) the intellectual, moral, economic, and physical infrastructures that cause every act within an industrial economy to be destructive, then we can easily come to believe that we will cause the least destruction possible if we are dead.

The good news is that there are other options. We can follow the examples of brave activists who lived through the difficult times I mentioned—Nazi Germany, Tsarist Russia, antebellum United States—who did far more than manifest a form of moral purity; they actively opposed the injustices that surrounded them. We can follow the example of those who remembered that the role of an activist is not to navigate systems of oppressive power with as much integrity as possible, but rather to confront and take down those systems.

Derrick Jensen is the author of *Thought to Exist in the Wild, Songs of the Dead, Endgame, Dreams,* and other books. In 2008, he was named one of Utne Reader's "50 Visionaries Who Are Changing Your World." His *Orion* column is called "Upping the Stakes."

Questions about "Forget Shorter Showers"

READING AND WRITING TO COMPREHEND

1. **Analyze the quote.** In "Forget Shorter Showers," Jensen writes that people retreat into entirely personal "solutions" in part because "we've been victims of a campaign of systematic misdirection." What does he mean?

2. **Rhetorically read** Jensen's piece with specific attention to his argument. What is he arguing?

3. **Connect.** What does Jensen mean when he writes that "personal change doesn't equal social change?" How does this statement connect to his argument?

READING AND WRITING TO RESPOND

4. **Write** an intellectual response. Using your annotations and your answers to the previous questions, write an intellectual response to Jensen's argument (see Chapter 3 for help with intellectual responses).

READING AND WRITING TO APPLY AND REFLECT

5. **Reread** Jensen's text twice in order to apply the Believing/Doubting Game reading strategy. Referring to your annotations from these readings, **write** a letter to a specific audience of your choice that supports (i.e. "believes") Jensen's argument. You may choose to write to a friend, a parent, or a professor, for example. (see Chapter 2 for help with the Believing/Doubting Game strategy).

6. **Refer** to your annotations indicating your "doubts," then **write** a letter to the author, Jensen, explaining these doubts. Now, **revisit** your two letters. How do they compare to each other? To the intellectual response you wrote in #4? *So what?*

If You Think Technology Has No Place In the National Parks, Think Again

By Amelia Urry

This essay addresses the benefits of using technology in national parks. Urry considers how devices such as smart phones, cameras, sensors, and microphones, among others, are being put to good use across the country's national parks and, moreover, how inviting electronic devices into parks may, in fact, increase the number and kinds of people who visit parks annually.

Published August 25, 2016, at Grist.org.

Visit http://grist.org/business-technology/if-you-think-technology-has-no-place-in-the-national-parks-think-again/

grist BRIEFLY GRIST 50 VIDEO SECTIONS NEWSLETTERS DONATE MORE

Shutterstock

HUMAN/NATURE

If you think technology has no place in the national parks, think again

By Amelia Urry on Aug 25, 2016

Share Tweet

On their 100th anniversary, Grist is exploring America's national parks and the humans who use them. See the full series.

It's easy to blame it all on the cellphone tower. It's right there, ruining the postcard-perfect shot you line up on your smartphone screen on your visit to Old Faithful.

It's easy to blame it all on the cellphone tower. It's right there, ruining the postcard-perfect shot you line up on your smartphone screen on your visit to Old Faithful.

Cellphone coverage and wireless internet are seeping into the parts of the country we like to think of as one-hundred-percent-natural, frozen in pre-industrial time. Of the 412 parks and monuments administered by the National Park Service, none is more iconic than Yellowstone National Park. Yet half of this bison- and bear-filled wilderness has cellphone reception, and there has been talk of running a high-speed fiber optic cable to the park through the Tetons.

"The question is not whether technology is good or bad, or appropriate or inappropriate—it's all those things," says Gary Machlis, science advisor to the director of the National Park Service. "It can do amazing things, and it can cause unintended consequences and harm. What we've gotta do is be very thoughtful."

As the National Park Service marks its 100th trip around the sun, it faces an all-you-can-eat buffet of challenges from the fickle attention of an increasingly urbanized population to the titanic threat of climate change. Whether it's drones or data plans, the technologies that are increasingly fundamental to the way we live will become a bigger and bigger part of all life on Earth. That means our parks are changing, whether we like it or not.

All that connectivity brings more than just think-pieces about the shenanigans of screen-addicted tourists (and there are plenty of those). We're also getting unprecedented access to some of the wildest places in America, for more Americans than ever before. We have better data for scientists and new vistas for would-be visitors—and all that means a better shot at protecting these places for another hundred years.

Streams, Live

I'd bet I'm in the majority of the American population when I say that I've never seen a bear. At least, not in the wild—but that distinction might turn out to mean less than you'd guess.

This summer, 2 million people tuned in to watch the grizzly bears of Katmai National Park standing knee-deep in the gushing glacial Brooks River, scooping up salmon with the lazy enthusiasm of a Thanksgiving guest going in for a third helping of mashed potatoes. Some veteran viewers, many of whom have never been closer to a grizzly than the livestream on their computer monitor, can recognize the individual bears that return year after year to the river as the salmon do. On message boards and in live chats with park rangers, they share screenshots and guess at the identity of this or that bear lumbering through the stream, trying to predict when a venerable grizzly named Otis will show up this year.

Jeffrey Skibins, a professor of conservation and park management at Kansas State University, is interested in the huge fandom these bears have accumulated online. Skibins was surprised when he learned just how popular the Katmai bear cams, hosted by the nonprofit explore.org, were. So he teamed up with fellow KSU researcher Ryan Sharpe to figure out what's going on with all this long-distance bear appreciation.

"Brazil is one of the largest international audiences," Skibins tells me on the phone. "How great is that we can reach an audience and talk about the plight of these bears with folks in Brazil who may never get a chance to see them?"

Forget Brazil—I've been glued to the Alaskan feed from my office in the Lower 48. Letting it play in the background of my monitor at work (sorry, boss!) feels like fair compensation for all the sunny days I spend shackled to my desk (in the service of you fine people of the Internet) instead of running across a real bear in the wild woods of Washington.

And I'm not the only one with a short tether to the web. Roughly three out of every four Americans spend some time online every day, and about a third of those say they are online "almost constantly," according to Pew research. Skibins wants to know if office drones blissing out to pristine

Alaskan ecosystems are having the same kind of emotional experiences that flesh-and-blood visitors to Katmai feel.

"We're trying to understand, after viewing the brown bears online or on-site, what is your emotional response? And what is your connection to those animals?" Skibins says. To that end, he and Sharpe devised a survey that asks viewers to rate how much they agree with statements like "I need to learn everything I can about brown bears" and "I would alter my lifestyle to help protect brown bears."

"That's not necessarily a strictly intellectual response, that's something that's really more heartfelt," Skibins says. That emotional component—as opposed to a purely intellectual interest—can predict whether a person will actually *do* something to help the bears. "We've seen that the stronger a person's emotional response is, the greater the likelihood is that they'll participate in some action to help protect that animal."

If livestreams from a remote corner of Alaska can lead millions of people to form an emotional response to an animal they've never encountered in real life, maybe that means bears have gained millions of new defenders. At least, that's what he wants to find out.

And people say the internet is only good for porn.

Data, Data, Everywhere

Before she started teaching computers to recognize bird calls, Alexis Diana Earl was counting marmots.

At the Rocky Mountain Biological Laboratory, her days were spent conducting surveys for a decades-long study: "It was hiking miles and miles to spend an entire day sitting with your scope, taking notes on what all the marmots are doing."

Don't get it twisted: She had fun. But when it comes to collecting usable data, traditional fieldwork like this is slow and often unreliable. You know that saying: "If a tree falls in the forest and no one hears it, does it make a sound?" Well, for a long time, scientists have needed to be in the right place at the right time to be able to hear what's going on in the forest. But sending field researchers out to count seabirds or listen for frog calls is expensive and limited—a human scientist needs to sleep at some point.

A microphone, on the other hand, needs nothing but a fresh set of batteries and an empty memory card. Scientists are beginning to figure out how to use new durable, affordable cameras and microphones to take bigger, more detailed pictures of the species and ecosystems they study.

But when you start listening to the forest around the clock, you rack up a lot of data in a hurry.

Which is why Earl isn't counting marmots anymore. Now she spends most of her days in a trailer in Santa Cruz, sitting in front of a computer screen and sifting through terabytes of data as an analyst for Conservation Metrics, a three-year-old company that aims to mine and refine environmental data to track elusive and endangered species. Once scientists get a better picture of the animal population they track, managers can make more informed decisions about how to protect them.

Although using audio recordings to track hard-to-spot species isn't new, the amount of information that companies and scientists can collect is unprecedented. Last year, Conservation Metrics' largest project collected 83,000 hours of data. "You can't work with 80,000 hours of data in an Excel file," Earl says. "You can't even open that Excel file."

Instead, the analysts at CMI break all that data down into two-second snippets. They tag a couple of these snippets that sound like what they're looking for—a certain species or a specific kind of call—and feed those examples into an algorithm that finds the similarities between them. Using those shared features, the algorithm builds a template of the sound it's looking for, and precedes to comb through unwieldy piles of data hunting down all of the matches.

In this way, the computers can chew through 83,000 hours of data and count, say, every time a spotted owl calls versus the number of barred owls that called. The results tell scientists and managers a lot that they might not otherwise ever know about the activity of a certain species, the interactions between species, and the health of the overall ecosystem.

In the Channel Islands National Park, for example, Conservation Metrics is monitoring a newly re-established breeding colony of Ashy storm petrels, a migratory seabird that was able to return to Anacapa Island after an extensive campaign to eradicate the invasive rats that had been eating the birds' eggs. Without remote-sensing devices, it would be harder to tell if all that effort to create a safe haven for the petrels had actually worked.

Earl points out that there's another benefit to using recording devices for some of the field work that biologists used to do by hand. "If you're in the field, you're just taking down data around what you're interested in at the time," she says. "But if you put out a remote-sensing device, it's collecting everything—especially if you have a network of sensors, acoustic sensors and camera traps and video. Then you have a full picture of what's going on."

If you find something interesting in the data, you can comb through it again and again, asking a different question every time.

Conservation Metrics is starting to analyze images from camera traps and drone footage, as well—and the parks are figuring out how to deploy these and other technologies. In the future, new devices that can sense minute details of air and water chemistry will help parks subtly monitor environmental changes, and algorithms will help scientists sort through genomes with ease. We will be able to sift DNA from streams and tease out subtle changes in forest ecology from satellite images.

"We're just excited to take on as much data as possible," Earl says.

The surveillance state never looked so good.

Internet Access

Right now, 68 percent of Americans own a smartphone, and 46 percent of them claim they couldn't live without it, according to research from Pew. Bemoan it all you like, we're heading to a world that is increasingly social, virtual, and mobile.

Visitors to the national parks, like so much of the public, are entranced by their smartphones. A 2015 industry survey found that when campers had access to email, they spent an average of three extra days outside. A full 88 percent of respondents took a smartphone camping with them; some brought a laptop or a tablet. Only 7 percent went totally tech-free.

Cellphone coverage and wifi in parks could change more than just the waiting time between taking that Mount Rushmore selfie and letting the "likes" pour in. It could also help lure a wider range of people into the national parks. In a century when America will see the end of its white majority, the National Park Service still looks pretty monochromatic, from its green-hatted staff to its 307 million yearly visitors.

According to a new survey from New America Media, people of color don't feel they have the same access to public lands as white people. Some of that is because of a knowledge gap—half of respondents said that one big obstacle is not knowing that much about public lands. Smartphones could help bridge that gap.

Maybe that's one reason that, in that industry camping survey, African-Americans were the group most likely to favor campgrounds with free wifi. One of the major reported uses of technology on camping trips is to do research on nearby attractions and look up directions. If technology can make this information more accessible to a segment of the American population who might not have parents or friends to induct them into the culture of the outdoors, then it has enormous potential to make parks more democratic.

And that can only strengthen a Park Service hoping to cultivate a new generation of advocates. Overall, younger, non-white people are more likely to say mobile technology enriches their experience of the outdoors, according to a survey by Michael Schuett, a professor of recreation at Texas A&M.

Of course, some people don't want cellphones in the wild, no matter what. "There is, at the core of the parks service, a conservative nature," says Machlis, the Park Service's science advisor; hence all those conservative conservationists complaining about the kids and their Facebooks. The mission statement of the NPS includes a mandate to preserve parks "unimpaired" for future generations, after all. It also includes an inducement to provide "for the enjoyment, education, and inspiration" of the public.

"It's often said that those two are contradictory, but they're not," Machlis says. "They're really organically connected, because it's 'preserve unimpaired' so it can provide a special, distinctive 'enjoyment.' The two fit together."

Timelines

Nothing and no one gets stuck in time, not really—not even sacred cows. In the 21st century, the national parks need to cultivate 21st century fans. Maybe we are all busier, more distracted, and more urban than we were in 1916. We're also more integrated with the social and virtual worlds that technology opens up to us.

"For a long time, the premise has been, national parks thrive on that emotional response people have by being there," says Skibins, the Kansas State professor. "Who isn't awestruck by standing in Yosemite, or Yellowstone, or the Everglades?"

But what if you can get that same awestruck feeling by watching bears swipe up salmon 1,500 miles away, or by that photo your friend posted of the sun rising over over the Grand Canyon, or the lushly saturated pictures the U.S. Department of the Interior's Instagram account posts to its 1.1 million followers every day?

Embracing new technology could help turn casual visitors into passionate conservationists. Virtual reality is emerging as a powerful way to immerse people in exotic settings, and services like Snapchat and Facebook Live give people an opportunity to share experiences with others around the world.

That, it turns out, is an older story than you might think. After all, the parks were established by people who had yet to see them in person.

In 1871, a U.S. Geological Survey made a 40-day expedition through what is now Yellowstone. They were some of the first Western people to marvel at the hot springs and geysers of the central plateau and stand in amazement over the Grand Canyon of the Yellowstone River.

Along with the survey were artist Thomas Moran and photographer William Henry Jackson, who used the technology of their day—paints, canvas, collodion process—to create the first pictures of what is now Yellowstone National Park.

They sent those pictures back to the U.S. Capitol, where they helped convince Congress to establish Yellowstone as the world's first national park in 1872.

"They did it because they had all been there based on virtual experiences," Machlis says. "How is that different than staring at a screen?"

Questions about "If you Think Technology Has no Place in the National Parks, Think Again"

READING AND WRITING TO COMPREHEND

1. **Rhetorically read** and **annotate** "If you Think Technology . . . " and focus on all four rhetorical elements: purpose, audience, claims, and evidence (see Chapter 2 for help with rhetorical reading). Describe Urry's purpose, intended audience, what she is arguing, and the evidence she uses to support this argument.
2. **Notice** how the article "If you Think Technology . . . " is designed and particularly the author's use of different sections such as "Streams, Live;" "Data, Data Everywhere;" and so on. Using the Say/Does approach **reread** and **annotate** the piece. How would you describe the author's use of different sections? How does each function (i.e. what does each section do) on its own and in relation to the other sections?
3. **Develop** a list of the technologies that are described in this piece as having a place in the national parks.

READING AND WRITING TO RESPOND

4. **Write** an intellectual response to the following statement, one of the first quotations author Amelia Urry uses in her piece: "The question is not whether technology is good or bad, or appropriate or inappropriate—it's all those things." (see Chapter 3 for help with intellectual responses). Be sure to address how this quote sets up some of the key issues explored in the article.

READING AND WRITING TO APPLY AND REFLECT

5. **Notice** that the title of this piece is premised on the assumption that technology has no place in national parks. Come up with an example of another space or geographic location where it is assumed that technology has no place and describe why technology either is already present or should be welcome there.

Were Farmers America's First High Tech Information Workers?

By James W. Cortada

This blog post offers a look at the role of technology in farming. Cortada provides an historical perspective on the subject by exploring how farmers have relied on technology for hundreds of years.

Published on the Oxford University Press Blog, November 15, 2016.

Visit http://blog.oup.com/2016/11/farmers-america-tech-information

Settlers in North America during the 1600s and 1700s grew and raised all their own food, with tiny exceptions, such as importing tea. In the nineteenth century, well over 80% of the American public either lived at one time on a farm or made their living farming. Today, just over 1% does that in the United States, even though there is a surge going on in small organic family farming. The majority of American food is still grown or raised in the US, although much is also imported. So, any understanding about the role of information in any century involves farmers, in the beginning because almost everyone was involved, and later because they had figured out how to industrialize its massive production so that farming only required a tiny number of people. Information made that profound switch possible.

Farmers didn't just use machinery that was invented over the past two hundred years, including the tractor in the twentieth century, which massively reduced the number of workers and animals needed to operate a farm. They also utilized data. By the 1870s, the US Government began collecting and disseminating scientific information to farmers. Beginning a decade earlier, Congress passed legislation that funded the creation of state universities for the purpose of doing research on agriculture and sharing the results with farmers. That is how the US acquired massive state universities like the University of Minnesota or the University of Wisconsin.

In 1862, Congress established the US Department of Agriculture and began a continuous program of publishing literature for use by farmers to improve their productivity and to address specific problems, such as curing animal, and crop diseases. By the 1880s, state universities and the Department of Agriculture began hiring agricultural agents stationed in almost every agricultural county in the country to transfer research findings and best practices created at the state universities to individual farmers, one-by-one. They also disseminated information through training programs for future farmers, similar to programs like 4-H today. By the early 1900s female home economists, also funded by the US Department of Agriculture and managed by the state universities, were educating children and women about farming best practices.

Scientific research in the 1920s and 1930s expanded knowledge about plant and animal diseases, development of fertilizers, and hybrid seeds that led to higher yields of such crops as beans, corn, potatoes, and wheat. The US rapidly became one of the world's largest exporters of agricultural products.

Farm by G123E123E123K123. CC BY 2.0 via Flickr.

In the years following World War I, farmers also extended their formal education from roughly the eighth grade through to completion of high school. High schools offered courses in agriculture and home economics. By the end of the 1960s, it was not uncommon for young farmers to have completed a college education with a major in agriculture. During the post-World War II years, the volume of literature on agricultural practices expanded massively and was used by college-educated farmers. They began attending seminars on agricultural practices sponsored by their state universities and county "ag" agents, while manufacturers of fertilizers and other products hosted these too.

Farmers gained access to the Internet in the 1990s, but largely on a wide-scale basis in the 2000s, when they accessed growing amounts of information about all manner of farming issues. They did more than use the Internet. Farmers installed micro weather stations on their properties and subscribed to aerial crop surveillance surveys, including accessing weather reports of their region from satellite-based services. Many communicated data through the Internet.

By the 2010s, wireless communications involving smart phones, laptops, and PCs had enabled farmers to build an extensive information ecosystem in support of their work. Their communications back and forth with agricultural experts, local universities, and vendors became more frequent and increased in volume.

By the 2010s, young farmers had taken to social media. If you subscribe to a CSA (Community Supported Agriculture) providing you with vegetables every week, then you probably also are receiving e-mails from your farmer reporting on the status of this week's crops, also sending along recipes for cooking kohlrabi, and links to other food topics, such as recipes and about the "pros" and "cons" of genetically modified seeds, food, and animals. Go to a food market on a Saturday morning and invariably you will see a few tables with literature about agricultural issues.

The answer to our question is a resounding yes. Farmers used a combination of new tools, science-based information, innovations in fertilizers, seeds, and medicines, and every form of information and its technologies from the 1600s to the present. In each century, they were as "high-tech" and as advanced in the use of information as any other segment of society. And there is no sign that their appetite for big data, use of artificial intelligence, robotics, or digital sensors is going to decline. They continue to use these more than many other professions.

Featured image credit: Farm by Michael Pereckas. CC BY 2.0 via Flickr.

James W. Cortada is a Senior Research Fellow at the Charles Babbage Institute at the University of Minnesota and the author of several dozen books on the history and use of information in business and information technology. His most recent book is *All the Facts: A History of Information in the United States since 1870*.

Questions about "Were Farmers America's First High Tech Information Workers?"

READING AND WRITING TO COMPREHEND

1. **Consider** the importance. According to this article, how has data or information been important to farming?

2. **Analyze** the message. What does this article say we must remember when exploring the role of information in any century?

3. **Reread** this piece using a reading strategy of your choice that allows you to **explain** why it is important to recognize the role that information has played in farming for centuries. In other words, what are the implications of recognizing this? Why, how, and for whom does this matter?

READING AND WRITING TO RESPOND

4. **Multimodal Option.** With the goal of making Cortada's argument that much more persuasive, develop a multimodal project in which you re-present his argument about the relationship between farming and information technology. Then, write a short reflection about the decisions you made in creating this project.

READING AND WRITING TO APPLY AND REFLECT

5. **Research**. This article mentions that in the late 1800s the United States acquired universities that could conduct research on agriculture and share that information with farmers. These universities are often called land grant institutions. Conduct some research on your own and locate the land grant institution closest to your own college or university. Perhaps you even attend a land grant institution. **Read** about the university's history via its website. Then, **write** an intellectual response in which you describe this specific school's contribution to farming and the extent to which you see Cortada's argument about information as relevant to this specific example (see Chapter 3 for help with intellectual responses).

LONG WRITING ASSIGNMENTS BASED ON READINGS IN CHAPTER 10: THE ENVIRONMENT AND TECHNOLOGY

1. **Develop** a synthesis in which you put at least 3 of the selections from this chapter into conversation with each other (see Chapter 3 for help with syntheses). Look back at the annotations you already have on the texts to determine how helpful those are. It is likely that you will need to reread the selections by applying a reading strategy that you think will be most effective for completing this particular assignment.

2. **Develop** an argument. Using your annotations, develop an argument that considers how the selections in this chapter largely avoid the binaries often associated with technology (i.e. technology is good or bad). What kinds of questions seem most central to this approach? Are there moments where the authors fall into binary thinking? How do you account for those? What are the implications of binary and non-binary approaches to questions surrounding technology? Look back at the annotations you already have on the texts to determine how helpful those are. It is likely that you will need to reread the selections by applying a reading strategy that you think will be most effective for completing this particular assignment.

3. **Multimodal Option.** Develop a multimodal advertisement for a national park that takes into account key rhetorical aspects, including purpose, audience, claims, evidence, and appeals (see Chapter 2 for help with these rhetorical components). Then, write a reflection in which you outline your rhetorical choices.

4. **Multimodal Option.** Develop a website that explores an argument about the relationship between technology and the environment. You may quote the selections in this chapter and other sources throughout the website to both support and develop this argument. Then, write a reflection that describes the argument you are making and the decisions you made while developing the website.

REFLECTING ON YOUR READING STRATEGIES AND ANNOTATIONS

Consider the different reading strategies you applied while reading the selections in this chapter. Which were most useful for understanding the text? For figuring out what you think? For responding to the text? Anticipate future uses of these reading strategies in this class, in other classes, and in other contexts. Also, consider previous courses and contexts in which these strategies would have been helpful.

Glossary

Academic Discourse: Specific style of communication used within the academy or other scholarly settings.

Argument: The central idea or claim of an essay that is developed, explored, and supported through evidence.

Annotate: The act of making marks and notes on a text.

Binary Thinking: A system of thought that offers only two options (e.g. right or wrong; black or white; good or bad).

Composition: A field of study that focuses on teaching, researching, and theorizing writing.

Ethos: Within the context of Aristotelian rhetoric, an appeal to character and credibility.

Edit: To correct or modify text.

Genre: A category or kind.

Implications: Effects or consequences.

Intellectual Response: Logical and idea-driven reaction (rather than emotionally driven).

Logos: Within the context of Aristotelian rhetoric, an appeal to logic.

Mindful Reading: Reading that is characterized by awareness and reflectiveness.

Multimodal: Characterized by having many modes. A multimodal composition uses more than one mode to achieve its goals.

Pathos: Within the context of Aristotelian rhetoric, an appeal to emotions.

Position: A stance or arguable viewpoint.

Plagiarism: The act of using another's ideas or words without proper attribution.

Repertoire: A collection, list, or set.

Revise: To re-see or reconsider.

Rhetoric: The art of effective or persuasive communication.

Schema: A concept or framework that supports interpretation.

Summarize: To condense and restate.

Synthesize: To bring together; combine.

Transfer (of learning): The process of using knowledge or learning from one context in another context.

Permissions

Charles Bazerman, "A Relationship between Reading and Writing: The Conversation Model." Copyright © 1980 by the National Council of Teachers of English. Reprinted with permission.

Mike Bunn, "Motivation and Connection: Teaching Reading (and Writing) in the Composition Classroom." Copyright © 2013 by the National Council of Teachers of English. Reprinted with permission.

David A. Jolliffe and Allison Harl, "Studying the 'Reading Transition' from High School to College: What Are Our Students Reading and Why?" Copyright © 2008 by the National Council of Teachers of English. Reprinted with permission.

Anthony Petrosky, "From Story to Essay: From Reading to Writing." Copyright © 1982 by the National Council of Teachers of English. Reprinted with permission.

Mariolina Salvatori, "Reading and Writing a Text: Correlations between Reading and Writing Patterns." Copyright © 1983 by the National Council of Teachers of English. Reprinted with permission.

Robert Scholes, "The Transition to College Reading." Copyright © 2002 by the National Council of Teachers of English. Reprinted with permission.

Robert J. Tierney and David Pearson, "Toward a Composing Model of Reading." Copyright © 1983 by the National Council of Teachers of English. Reprinted with permission.

Stacey Waite, "On the Occasion of Being Mistaken for a Man by Security Personnel at Newark International Airport" from *Butch Geography*, published by Tupelo Press. Copyright 2013 by Stacey Waite. Used with permission.

Sarah Davis, "The 'Blurred Lines' Effect: Popular Music and the Perpetuation of Rape Culture." Copyright 2014 by Sarah Davis. Used with permission.

OUP Blog Entries. Oxford University Press. Used with permission.

Wendell Berry, "Environmentalists Have Given Up too Much by Not Being Radical Enough." Copyright Grist.org. Used with permission.

Amelia Urry, "If you Think Technology Has no Place in the National Parks, Think Again." Copyright Grist.org. Used with permission.

"The Pace of Modern Life." Copyright xkcd.com. Used with permission.

Derrick Jensen, "Forget Shorter Showers." Copyright *Orion Magazine*. Used with permission.